This book is dedicated to my very funny, multidimensional "mom", Kitti Marie (Rose) Byers. Thank you for teaching me how to transcend the illusions of separation and for calling me back into the Source Field to join you in unconditional Source Love. Oh, and also for making this journey with Spirit so magical and fun! Keep sprinkling your glitter! It is also dedicated to all of the beautiful souls I have shared this journey with. Every one of you has played a role in what is written on these pages. I am so grateful for all of it!

ISBN: 9798399321370
Copyright June 21, 2023
Published by Jennie Byers
Cover Design Hamid R. Baghaie

Spirit Reunions

Let's Get This Party Started

About the Author

Jennie Byers is a multi-dimensional, light language translator and assists in the activation of the multi-dimensional aspects of our physical avatar to re-establish our connection to Spirit and Source. She is the founder of Spirit Reunions Sanctuary, a 15-acre educational and Spiritual retreat for healing and community. The Sanctuary is located in the Cherokee Mountains of East TN. The land sits on what is nicknamed the "Crystal Mountains" which is in one of the largest vortex energy spots in the United States. The property has been designated as a protected forest greenbelt and backs up to the Cherokee National Forest. Through her inter-dimensional communication, Jennie was made aware that this land carries "many streams of unity consciousness," including that of the Native Americans, Galactics, Sasquatch and Ancestors. All of whom are a part of the Spirit Reunions team of healers and ascension assistants.

The Sanctuary features: themed tiny houses for retreat, vibrational alignment bed, tachyon chamber, Native American tipi and medicine wheel, Pulse Electromagnetic Field Therapy (PEMF), Tera Hertz Frequency Wand, Tesla Plasma Ball with Rife Frequencies, Genius Quantum Bio Feedback readings, Reiki labyrinth, far-infrared saunas, a large community fire pit, pavilion and stage, community garden, community kitchen, as well as a team of healing practitioners who work on and offsite offering a variety of techniques and holistic remedies. But the most powerful of all tools offered is this sacred land and its higher dimensional associates who support us in our remembering our own direct connection to Source and Spirit. They are always with us through Source love and offer their higher vibration for our body, mind and soul to heal itself through remembering these truths. More information can be found at
Spiritreunionsanctuary.com

Table of Contents

Preface

Chapter 1	My Eternal Knowing	22
Chapter 2	My Foundation of Love	24
Chapter 3	Inter-dimensional And Paranormal Experiences	27
Chapter 4	My Mom's Re-Awakening	32
Chapter 5	Silver Spoon	37
Chapter 6	Grandma Adeline	42
Chapter 7	The Eyes of Source	46
Chapter 8	Remembering Source Healing	49
Chapter 9	Genetic Cellular Memories	52
Chapter 10	Conversations With God And The Second Coming Of Christ	59
Chapter 11	She Left	67
Chapter 12	Clawing My Way Back To My Mom	72
Chapter 13	Desperate to Feel Her	80

Chapter 14   The Vortex   86

Chapter 15   Finally Making the Connection!   95

Chapter 16   My Birthday Party With My Mom and Jesus   101

Chapter 17   The Integration and Mastery Of My Two Minds   107

Chapter 18   Surrogate Into Source   122

Chapter 19   My Quantum Leap   132

Chapter 20   Gifts from Spirit   137

Chapter 21   The "Safety" Of Higher Ground   150

Chapter 22   The Lost Art of Discernment   156

Chapter 23   Spirit School   162

Chapter 24   Distorted Mirrors   175

Chapter 25   The Source Creation Verses the Artificial Creation, Two Opposite Realities   179

Chapter 26   Micromanaging The Matrix   187

Chapter 27   The Fifth Dimensional Bible   192

Chapter 28   Our Multidimensional Timelines   198

Chapter 29   Linear Time: My Arch Nemesis   205

Chapter 30   Quantum Superposition Let There Be Light   213

Chapter 31   This Endless Journey Through Expanded
              Consciousness   217

Chapter 32   Our Beautiful Journey Back to Source   222

Chapter 33   Awareness of the "Unseen" Realms   227

Chapter 34   The Great Dumbing Down of Source   236

Chapter 35   Twin Flame Love Stories   238

Chapter 36   Our Gatekeepers   246

Chapter 37   Spirit Reunions "Journey's To Heaven"   248

Chapter 38   Quantum Technologies   257

Chapter 39   Source Solutions to Challenges   260

Chapter 40   The Spirit of Fear   262

Chapter 41   Walking Between Worlds, Mastering The   277
              Inter-dimensional Experience

Chapter 42   Lighting the Way For Others   282

Chapter 43   Tools to Assist Us in
              Activating Our Living Light Timeline   291

Chapter 44   Co-Creating Through Living Light   299
              Heaven On Earth

Chapter 45   Fulfilling the Contract   304

Chapter 46   Nature   311

Chapter 47   Sacred Experiences   318

Chapter 48   Higher Truth is not Subjective   321

Chapter 49   Cities of Light   327

Chapter 50   Activating Our Spiritual Gifts   330

Chapter 51   The Art of Surfing the Source Field
              Welcome Back to Source! Let's Get This   337
              Party Started!

Spirit Reunions Spirit School Definitions

Before reading this book, I recommend reviewing the definitions of the words as I was given then from Spirit. The words and definitions used here are the words I personally translated through my communication with my mom in Source via Light Language. They are not necessarily the definitions you will find when you search them through google.

Amygdala (ego): the part of our brain that acts as a computer interface between the centrum (Source connected) part of our brain and Source. It records reality as we experience it and protects us from pain and trauma; it is focused on our survival; when directed to give up its control, it articulates Light Language coming from the centrum. It allows us to operate in lower density timelines while being tethered to Source; it is our mortal brain that operates in linear time.

Ankh: Original Christian cross. It represents the key to life and everlasting life.

Ascension: the combination of one raising their vibration and expanding their consciousness to co-create through source and light body.

Artificial Timeline (or Reality): a matrix reality that is a holographic computer-generated simulation. A reality that is similar to a video game.

Body Aura: the electromagnetic field around the body that contains a unique frequency that can be seen as color.

Centrum: our immortal God mind; a pyramid shaped part of the brain connected to Source that streams Light Language to the amygdala. It is a tachyon chamber within our brain that streams Living Light from Source into our physical body.

Christ Consciousness: unique higher consciousness of Source that manifests through the living Christ.

Collective Consciousness: groups of energies, co-creating reality through a similar awareness and intention.

Consciousness: energy that is aware of itself.

Cults: organizations that promote belief systems attached to the experience of others rather than direct experience and do not encourage independent thought.

Density: slower frequency, more solid physical reality.

Dimensions: varying frequency planes of existence.

Empathic: the ability to receive information through Light Language.

Energy Body or Field/Electromagnetic Field: the vibrational field around the physical body connected to Source.

Entities: souls that are un-embodied and vibrating at a lower frequency.

Essence Self: another word for Spirit and higher self.

Frequency: the rate of speed at which something vibrates.

Frequency Healing: various frequencies that are known to produce healing in the body.

Gatekeeper: a Spirit that exists in the higher dimensions who chooses to assist someone they love in the lower dimensions; they do not allow any lower entities to influence the person they are guiding.

Heaven: fifth dimensional planes where the aspect of our higher self or Spirit returns to their higher vibrational state of being after having a dense physical Earth experience.

Higher Heart Stargate: our Source connected heart that is accessing Living Light and able to feel the unconditional love from Spirit.

Higher Self: another word for Spirit and essence self that generally exists in the 5th up to the 7th dimensional planes.

Holographic Reality: superimposed layers of computer-generated information that create the illusion of a three-dimensional reality.

Inter-dimensional: the ability to travel between dimensions.

Ley or Grid Lines: energy light lines on the earth that serve as a communication network and a vibrational healing network for earth.

Light Body: our vibrational body that houses our Spirit aspect (or soul) and connects it to the physical body; it is the consciousness inside of us that communicates with the essence self and accesses different dimensions.

Light Codes: information coming through Light Language from Source clearing distorted vibrations in our energy field and physical body.

Light Therapy: light that carries various vibrational frequencies that are known to produce healing in the body.

Linear Time: an artificial time construct that exists within the artificial timelines.

Lions Gate: the Sirius portal that opens every year between July 28th and August 12th and peaks on August 8th.

Living Light: high frequency Source particles that are faster than the speed of three-dimensional light; what NASA calls Tachyons.

Loosh: low vibrational energy that is created through conflict and distorted creation.

Lower Self: lower vibrational aspects of us that are immersed in distorted creation.

Matrix (Artificial): a holographic three-dimensional simulated reality.

Merkabah: the light body's vehicle for moving between different vibrational dimensions.

Multidimensional: the ability to access multiple different planes or dimensions of existence that vibrate at different frequencies through light body.

One Consciousness: some refer to this as "the void"; it is where Source creative energy exists in a superposition state waiting to be told what to create; all energy is in a state of oneness here until it aspects itself into a variety of different frequencies of creation.

Omnipotent (Omnipresent): not limited by the 3rd dimensional laws of linear time; the ability of Spirit to be in multiple places at once, present in all things.

Organic Timeline (or Reality): dimensional realities that exist in different vibrational frequencies through Source outside of the artificial simulated matrix.

Osmosis: the merging of energy that creates empathic information transfers.

PEMF (Pulse Electromagnetic Field Therapy): frequency that mimics the earth frequency and assists with healing the body.

Planes of existence: dimensional realities.

Portal: openings between different dimensions.

Source Field the source of all creation and experience.

Quantum Field/Zero Point: describes being in a space of Source time not subject to artificial linear time.

Quantum Super Position: all matter exists in its greatest potential until an observer tells it what to do through their beliefs.

Quantum Time: real time according to Source.

Reality: a creation and experience; it can be an individual reality manifested or a collective manifestation of reality; collective realities are experienced as dimensional planes.

Solfeggio Harmonics: the vibrational scale of the natural harmonics found in nature.

Soul: the aspect of the Spirit that splits off and comes into lower vibrational dense physical reality.

Source: where all conscious energy originates and exists at all times.

Source Alignment: being in a state of vibration that is harmonious with Source.

Spirit: the bigger part of us that exists in the higher dimensions and higher vibrations at all times; it doesn't lower its vibration to come into the slower density physical dimensions; it can, however, aspect itself in order to have a lower vibrational, more dense physical experience if it so chooses.

Spirit Aspect: a small part of the essence self that goes into lower dimensional realities to have temporary and denser physical experiences.

Star-gate: a portal that allows light body travel between dimensions.

Surrogate: a replacement or fill in for a specific role or experience to assist in the learning process.

Spiritual Bypassing: choosing to attach to false Spiritual beliefs in the artificial reality rather than centering in the truth from Source.

Spirit Reunion: being reunited with our loved ones who have left the physical reality and exists in higher dimensional realities.

Spirit Time: Spirit can bend linear time as needed through Source time in order to help facilitate an intended creation in the physical reality.

Third Eye or Pineal Gland: God eye sight that allows us to see into different dimensions.

Timelines: planes or dimensions of existence of varying frequencies created by Spirt or it's soul aspects.

Trinity of Inter-dimensionality: God Brain, God Heart, God Eye.

Twin Flame: when the essence self aspects into the same timeline and shares a physical experience with itself in separate physical bodies.

Vibration: all that exists is in motion; all creation from Source carries a vibration that is unique and cannot be mimicked or replicated.

Vortex: high vibrational centers of concentrated energy.

Wetiko: a human mind virus (entity) that promotes a self-sabotaging behavior and destructive creation.

Preface

I am no different than anyone else who comes from Source. We are all created with a unique vibrational "fingerprint." We each have a Spirit body that cannot be replicated or mimicked. The Living Light consciousness that chooses to express itself through my physical avatar does so with purpose. When Living Light expresses itself through my vibration, it comes through uniquely. My energy fingerprint doesn't resonate with everyone. Like a unique flavor that tastes amazing to some and not so amazing to others; or a musical note that sounds in tune to some or out of tune to others. My vibration resonates with those with which it is naturally resonates. It sounds harmonious to some and off key to others and that is perfectly ok. There will never be another creation of me nor will there ever be the same unique vibration created through me again. This song that streams through me from source is my own. No one else can play or sing my song the way I can. It is the same for you and every one of us. This is why we are each sacred incarnations through the eyes of Source. Information that comes from Source does not belong to us; we are not the original creators of it. We are not only a vessel through which information flows to this dimension from Source, but we are also meant to add our own unique spices to it. This is how the information is transformed through us and now carries our own unique vibrational flavor of creation within it. This new creation never existed before us and will continue to echo throughout eternity for others who are on the same "wavelength" to enjoy. We are forever imprinted into creation for eternity.

This is why we cannot take another's creation from Source and try to make it our own. It doesn't have the same impact or power within it. It becomes an artificial creation when it is mimicked through others.

Artificial creation is a copy that doesn't come from Source directly through us and therefore it is dead energy. Regurgitating the information someone else received from Source is not a part of the living vibration that is you. Yet we can be called to connect to Source through those who are already connected. They can offer us their vibration so we can access the Source Field through them. We call them Source Surrogates. It is therefore beneficial for us to share what we experience directly to assist others in being drawn back to their Source self. Always remember to take the information you receive directly from Source and add your own ingredients through your own unique vibration and experience. I am simply sharing my own recipe, so you will use it while adding your favorite ingredients that fit your taste perfectly. My mom and I, through Source, created this recipe to activate my own direct connection to Source and Spirit. It is a beautiful mix of my mom, Source and myself. She offers me her unconditional love and higher vibration so I can access the Source Field. This is what we incarnated to do for each other. We are here to help each other raise our vibrations out of states of disconnect and confusion. We are walking each other home. Spirit is our living example. You are meant to take another's recipe from Source and add your own seasoning, and then share it with others so they can do the same! Be sure to put your love into it and watch it grow!

So here you are now, in this Source guided moment, reading this. Knowing that we create our experiences here, there is a reason you created this into your present moment. It is possible that your Spirit is calling you to remember a part of you that you have simply forgotten. You most likely have memories from knowing this as a child. We are going on a journey outside of linear time, where the temporary linear part of you cannot go. It may feel like the strongest part of you, has held you captive in a linear timeline most of your life. It is an illusion and it is time to set yourself free. It is time to understand you had the power all along to transcend dimensions and reconnect with your multidimensional self and Spirit family.

Many of us have heard the call to assist with healing in one way or another. The answer to this call is to activate our multidimensional selves. It is the clearest path to true transformational healing. It is the only way to experience higher truths, higher love, and the clarity of knowing. We are required to do this for ourselves. No one can do it for us, but we can share our own journey back to Source with each other to help awaken the path within you that was there all along. In order to accomplish this, we must decide that we are ready to let go of all of the illusions we have created in order to simply remember what is already inside of us.

Where does this experience exist? We call it the Source Field.   What is the Source Field? There are many names given to it in order to try and capture its essence. It is referred to as Unity Consciousness, The One Consciousness, Christ Consciousness, Creator of All That Is, The Void, Source, etc. In my world, it is most often referred to as God. Although we were told we were created in that image, Spirit has expanded on this and described it as an energetic imprint of Source within us more than it is a physical appearance. This understanding has made it easier for me to connect with Source, because I realize I am a part of a larger Source Field rather than restricted to the image of one man.

The Source Field is pure creative energy. It is a self-aware field where all things are created and connected. Every experience of Spirit is imprinted in its conscious memory. It is more alive and real than anything we have ever experienced on the Earth timelines. There are aspects of Source that exist inside of us that allow us to connect to Source at will. Most of us just need to remember how and that is what this book is all about.

Spirit also calls the Source imprint within us a Living Light imprint. Living Light and Source are interchangeable. The particles that exist within all things conscious, are referred to as the Living Light, which is what forms the Source Field. Living Light carries all of the same information that exists within the Source Field. It is what makes it omnipotent and able to exist within all things at the same time. Living Light does not refer to a color. It can be experienced in the darkness of our minds. It is pure creative consciousness that exists within us and outside of us. The Source Field exists outside of the linear timelines. This is referred to as the quantum field or zero point. We will discuss this in detail later.

First, let us also clarify who "we"/ they are. We do not call ourselves by a fancy-schmancy name that leads you to believe we are fancier than you or hold a higher position of power in the unseen. We won't pretend to be your savior or your authority. These are human concepts which do not translate the same in the dimensions of higher vibrations. We are the same as you: Spirits on a journey to experience our greater potential in physical realities. We are here, along with Jennie's mom, in a collective higher vibrational journey of Spirit. We are your essence selves, your Spirit guides, your loved ones, higher source consciousness and higher truth. We are Living Light intelligence. We are here to remind you that YOU ARE all of these things as well. We are all a part of the same consciousness offering our Spiritual gifts to each other. We all have something to offer and receive from each other on this journey. This journey does not end with the "death" of the physical body. This journey continues for all of us and we are connected throughout eternity. What we do here affects what you do there and vice versa. The vast number of beautiful experiences we have all had together are sacred in our collective experience- including writing this book together in the Source Field! Mostly, it's all just so much fun!

This book is written through the eyes of higher vibration of Spirit, which means it is simple. The higher the vibration, the simpler the truths. This book is not complicated by design. The heart simplifies; the mind complicates. We are speaking to your heart, not your mind. Where the heart goes, the mind follows. This is the natural order of things.

We are not trying to impress anyone with our Spiritual knowledge. We desire for you to feel the beautiful vibration in which we exist. It touches and activates the heart of everyone who encounters it. It is our intention that everyone who reads this will experience these simple truths for themselves. We come from a dimension that exists outside of linear time thus the message carries an intelligence that is timeless in nature. It offers a higher vibrational quantum experience that is in a constant state of new NOW moments, a Living Light experience. It will activate all that it was created and intended to activate within you, through your essence self-collaboration, and in your perfect "time". We will be exploring these higher vibrational realities together, where everything is right side up instead of upside down. This journey is going to help you make the flip within your own mind. You will once again be able to see the organic within the inorganic, the light within the distortion, the truth within the deception, the real within the artificial.

As you read, we recommend calling in your higher power connections who are known by many different names. Your higher self and loved ones who exist on the other side of the veil can read with you and assist you with accessing the highest vibration of the messages written within these pages. You will know them by the love you share. That love cannot be mimicked or replicated. It is like a fingerprint. Love carries its own unique vibration within each one of us and when we are connected through love it transcends all time and space. In all of creation, there is nothing more powerful than the love of Source. Together we are moving into the Source Field to peer through the veils of illusion. **LET'S GET THIS PARTY STARTED!!**

I was guided to add this little tid bit for those who might be hesitant about telling your own story and needing some inspiration. Growing up, my mom always reminded me that the things we were told were most important or that signify true intelligence in life, are acutally not true. Things such as grammar and spelling do not equate higher intelligence. She explained that the distorted realilty keeps us hyper focused on these things that are not important according to Spirit so we are not focused on feeling the higher truth we are being in the moment.

When we first uploaded the final edited copy of this book to Amazon, we noticed the edits were no longer there. Ok, we must have uploaded the incorrect manuscript? So, we uploaded the correct one again. We noticed the same issues. Since we published the book in June of 2023 we have experienced the most bizarre spelling and grammar issues reoccurring after making the corrections. It seems the final edited copy has vanished into thin air and each time we upload a corrected one it ends up with editing issues over and over again. We have had to laugh because it is so blantant and absurd at this point.

My mom explained that there is beautiful wisdom in this experience. So have fun reading and if you find errors feel free to let us know, or not! We are ok with allowing Spirit to create a messy manuscript full of Source magic. Most important, don't miss the magic! Notice where your focus goes!

If you are holding back on telling your own beautiful story because you can't pay an editor or worry about your ability to produce a grammatically perfect manuscript, let my book serve as an inspiration for you to allow Spirit to flow through you perfectly without concern for the things that just don't matter in the Source field. Have a good laugh and enjoy! The beautiful testimonials I have received from those who have read my book and experienced healing from it, regardless of errors, have proven to me that **it doesn't matter!** My mom what right, as usual!

Tell your story authentically from your and Source and it will reach those it is meant to inspire! We are here to inspire each other to express ourselves freely and confidently outside of the silly rules of the artificial reality! **GET YOUR PARTY STARTED!**

Chapter 1

My Eternal Knowing

When I was a child, I walked with what Native Americans call 'The Great Spirit'. Literally, I had full conversations with this beautiful energy while running around on my grandpa's farm, dodging cow patties, as happy as I could be! I had an awareness of where I was in that moment. I was in a physical reality and I was loving the experience. I somehow knew I had made it into my new physical experience and all was going as planned. I chatted with Spirit about how amazing everything around me was, how much love I was surrounded by, and how safe I felt in this reality. The message from Source felt like a parent saying "we've got your back, we created a safe space for you, now don't worry, go play and have fun!" We laughed together with joy about the bliss we felt together experiencing those moments. I was free to create whatever I wanted and be whatever I wanted to be. I heard those words come in a download as if it was echoing through eternity.

I experienced the pure unconditional love we can only experience from being in the Source field! I understood this energy to be God and Jesus because that is what they called it at the church my family belonged to. I wasn't able to make a distinction between the two. I just understood it that way. These moments of walking between worlds were the foundation of my Spiritual journey on earth. It was my understanding of what truly is LOVE!

Spirit didn't come to me to warn about how difficult this journey was going to be for me. I wasn't told to be careful or to beware of what was to come. I was simply saturated in what was real- Source Love.

These moments solidified my knowing while I was experiencing the physical reality so I could choose to remember and find my way back when I got lost in the artificial world…and I did. I understand now why getting lost was a necessary part of my journey. Spirit knew what was coming but wasn't concerned about it because it was all in perfect divine order.

When I was five years old, I remember vividly the day my Sunday school teacher at church told me that God was crying because he was sitting in heaven listening to my bad thoughts. Looking back, I realized my teacher didn't know what I was thinking, and furthermore, it was a blanket statement made to our entire Sunday school class. I didn't yet know I was in a reality that existed on distorted versions of truth. I thought everyone told the truth, so I took this information very much to heart and was horrified by the idea that I was making God cry. Things changed for me in that moment regarding my connection and perception of God. I went home that day and made a decision to no longer have conversations with God. I didn't want to hurt him with my bad thoughts. I didn't want to make him cry anymore. I would just kick him out of my world and pretend he wasn't there. Maybe then he couldn't hear me. This was the beginning of my disconnect with Source.

Although I continued to have moments with Spirit as I grew up, they became fewer and farther between. I was mostly focused on being a "normal" kid and fitting into a reality that was very different from where I remembered coming from. I wanted to explore the world as I desired. My parents created a safe and loving environment for me to be as free as a kid can be in a highly distorted reality.

Chapter 2

My Foundation of Love

Although my dad is one of my greatest loves, I'm going to focus on my mom, Kitti, because she and I share this Spiritual journey of walking between worlds. She is guiding me from the higher vibrational realms daily. While she was in her physical body on earth, she was often referred to as a very unique and special person. She carried a vibration of unconditional love for all things and that was a rare quality that many noticed about her. She was effortlessly connected in the Source field most of the time and she taught by example how to live this way. She grew up on a farm and loved animals and nature. In the summertime I remember her walking around outside without shoes watering the flowers. Her feet were always black on the bottom during the summer from running around barefoot!

The things that mattered to other moms, like spotless houses and clean clothes never mattered to her. To her, if you weren't dirty from nature you weren't enjoying life to the fullest. She always encouraged me to go play in the dirt. She told me it would keep me healthy. I was happy to oblige. She gave me a free pass to be a wild nature child and I was fearless about it. Nature was the safest place for me to be myself and relax. I knew my life was different from other kids. Most of the kids in our neighborhood wanted to be at our house because they could feel the love and freedom that was created there.

My mom was fully present in the moments of her life. She simply wanted to make good memories with people and express her creativity. She would play with me for hours and teach me how to develop my imagination. It was magical, even when she talked to me about the TV and the government and what she referred to as "brainwashing". There was a magic in those conversations. I was able to view the world through her eyes and see what she saw because she took the time to show me. Because she was walking in connection to source field, she was "in the world but not of it" and she never believed in the distortions of this physical reality. She saw through it all and lived through her Spirit. She was really my Spirit guide pretending to be my mother!

I would play in the nearby woods for hours by myself. Nature is where I could feel that feeling again, the one I experienced while walking and talking with Spirit on our farm. I could see it in their eyes and feel their unconditional love. I recall intensely observing the physical reality, studying it and the people I encountered, as if I had landed on another planet and was trying to learn their ways. I felt like I was nothing like most of the people I encountered. Although I could recognize what I now know as Source in certain people the same way I could with animals, it was more rare. Feeling Source through living things was like my guidepost for what was real and not real in the world. It was that love I could feel when I tuned in. But the older I got, the less often I felt that in general and the more I experienced the artificial world feeling more real. The artificial reality slowly began consuming my life and I found myself seeking ways to become someone else in order to function in it. This is how I created my false or artificial self.

Just as I had done with God, I realized I could close my heart off to the part of me that was connected to Source. That part of me didn't seem to operate well in the artificial reality. I felt like I was a weirdo and didn't feel accepted or a part of the artificial world the way others were. I believed I had to disconnect from Source in order to not experience the pain of being an outcast. The pressure for me to conform was very strong. I was willing to do anything to not feel different, including shutting down my connection to Source. What I didn't realize was that I was also closing my heart off to myself and my connection to the unconditional self-love I carried within me. I was going to lose myself in an artificial world.

Chapter 3

Inter-dimensional And Paranormal Experiences

As I got older, I also began to experience the darker side of the multidimensional worlds, lower entities. I often experienced the paranormal growing up. I know many of us have and our experiences are similar. I understand now that these experiences are teaching us how to interact and connect beyond the illusion of separation, but our dominant vibration is low so we are matching frequencies with the lower vibrational entities..

A lot of the distorted energy experiences happened with my sister. She had a traumatic event at a young age that activated a very deep fear inside of her and it seemed she was taunted by entities from that time forward. She wouldn't sleep alone so she slept with me. In the night we experienced dark clouds hovering above our bed and being held down in our sleep; trapped in the astral and unable to wake up; and creepy sounds under our blankets like someone was dying and couldn't breathe. She would jump up in her sleep terrified of something and talk about a man being in the closet. It seemed to be constantly something scary when I was with her and she was tormented by her fear.

I didn't have this same fear inside of me. I was never really scared of these experiences, although they freaked me out because I didn't understand it. Something inside of me knew that I was always safe. I always remembered that knowing I was given when I was small and it stayed with me. I was free to observe these things and even laugh about them

Shadow Beings

I often encountered shadow beings moving out of my peripheral vision. This energy was conscious and I was aware of its consciousness. My sister would talk in her sleep often, but she wouldn't remember it the next day. I remember encountering these shadow entities in the middle of the night and she would be sound asleep then suddenly ask me if I saw them too? She would comment on how large they were or what they were doing. This would really freak me out because I didn't realize she was experiencing them as well.

The Sucker Ghosts

I would sometimes feel the presence of an entity when I was asleep. I could hear it breathing heavily in my ear, like it was gasping for air. I would feel like it was sucking me into the abyss. I would wake up feeling terrified like I narrowly escaped my doom. It was like they were attacking me in the in-between realms. I know these experiences are not uncommon. This state is sometimes referred to as sleep paralysis, but I feel it is more than just a physical experience, it is also interactions with lower entities.

The Undercover Ghost

One night, my sister and I heard something gasping for air from underneath our blankets. It woke us and without saying a word to each other, we both jumped out of bed and ran out of the room. I thought it was my cat stuck under the blankets suffocating. But nothing was there and my cat was downstairs. If it weren't for my sister having the same experience, I would have thought I was just dreaming.

The Inter-dimensional Animals

When I was fourteen, I was at a graduation party. A friend and I decided to go for a walk on the country road where he lived. We were discussing the meaning of life and the conversation was raising our vibration. We looked up and saw three large, long haired, white animals galloping full speed towards us from the field. They were coming at us so fast we barely had time to react. We both went into fight or flight mode. He took off running and I was frozen in fear. I couldn't move. I felt like I was going to be killed! I had never experienced the inability to run or scream before this. As they got close to me, they quickly turned and then disappeared. Poof! Gone! My body relaxed and I fell down on the road and started hyperventilating and crying. He was so far down the road from me I could barely see him. I started yelling his name. He came running back to me saying "What the f…. Was that?" I said "I have no idea!" Neither of us had ever seen animals like this. They looked part horse and part lama maybe, but I really don't remember clearly. They were huge and had long flowing hair. They were clearly inter-dimensional animals because it was as if they were never there. Yet, he and I both saw them. It felt like we were peering into another dimension through a portal. I don't know if those animals even saw us.

The Mulberry Street Ghost

When I was nineteen, we moved to an old Victorian house built in the 1880's. It was divided into three apartments and my parents lived downstairs while my sister and I shared the upstairs apartment. One night I woke up to a girl with a hat on standing at the end of my bed. When she realized I could see her, I watched her float backwards into my closet and disappear. My sister never liked that closet. If I left it open at night, she would always close it. She said she felt like someone was in there staring at us. She asked me to never leave her up there in the apartment alone. She wanted me to wake her if I was awake before her and wanted to go downstairs. Well, one morning I got up really early and didn't want to wake her THAT early. I figured she wouldn't notice if I went downstairs for breakfast and came back. However, before I could get back, she came down really upset. Her face was pale and she asked me why I had left her alone up there. She said she had a dream but it didn't feel like a dream. It felt more like a premonition.

She was shown a girl who had been murdered in our house. Our bedroom was her bedroom and our closet was her closet. She appeared to my sister in her dream and said "can you help me?" Then my sister was shown a replay of the night she was murdered. My sister became everyone's feelings in the scene when she would look at them. She could feel everything as if it were happening to her. I had no doubt the girl I saw standing at the end of my bed that night was the same girl that reached out to my sister.

A series of things started happening in our house after that. We were moving to a new house in three weeks. It was as if the girl knew we were leaving and she was desperate for us to help her. The phone would ring and no one would be on the other line; sad piano music would be playing, or a girl would be heard sobbing hysterically. There would be knocks at the front door but no one would be there. Our phone line was disconnected and the phone company came and worked on it or hours but could find nothing wrong. While the phone line was down, the police knocked at our door and said they received a 911 call from our house. We explained that we couldn't have called as our phone wasn't working. They didn't believe us and we complied when they asked if they could take a look around our house. But we knew this was connected to the ghost girl.

After we moved, my parents still owned this house and my teenage brother would go over to that house to hang out with his friends. One night he fell asleep there. He said a girl came to him and said "can you help me?". He was also shown her death and it matched what my sister saw. He said it freaked him out and he yelled at her to leave him alone and she left immediately. My brother wasn't there when my sister shared her experience with the girl and her death. He had no idea that had happened to her. We knew without a doubt this was the same girl who needed help. My mom went back to the house to help her move on. We never had any more paranormal experiences, so we believe she did get the help she needed to move out of the lower dimensions to join her Spirit family in heaven.

Chapter 4

My Mom's Re-Awakening

I came from a family where we were always free to speak our heart and mind. I knew I couldn't do this outside of our home so I learned to watch what I said in public, but I could come to my mom and share my feelings about my experiences freely. So, she started it…my passion for speaking my truth! I was a very sensitive kid. I come from a long line of sensitives and highly Source connected people, but I was told not to talk about this to everyone. I never understood why we had to hide these truths.

I was fourteen when the Harmonic Convergence occurred. It was August 17, 1987 and there was no internet or cell phones at that time. Yet a wave of awakening swept across the planet. A mass meditation event was organized worldwide and it had a profound impact on my family and my life. We didn't realize until after my mom's awakening, that it was at the same time as the Harmonic Convergence. She wasn't even aware of this event at the time it was happening. But she had a spontaneous remembering of who she really was and what she came into this life to accomplish. She experienced such a huge awakening; it was like her pineal gland blew open! She saw her past lives, remembered her soul's purpose, and could hear and see through the veil. This was the beginning of a timeline split between my parents. My dad thought she had gone bonkers. But I watched her boldly become who she really was…her soul self, regardless of the pressure she was under to stay in her old self energy to please my dad or anyone else.

For a fourteen-year-old kid who was born Source connected this felt very exciting! I had slowly been losing my connection to Spirit and becoming more and more immersed in my five senses in order to determine what was real and not real. It was incredibly bizarre and awesome to witness my mom go through this. Although I saw the most amazing things pouring out of her, part of me wondered, at times, if she was really losing it? Maybe my dad was right? She was crying often, (now I know this is a natural part of the awakening process) telling me about her past lives and her mission to help people connect to Spirit and remember where they came from. She could now hear Spirit again and she knew things she couldn't have known. There wasn't internet back then, yet, she was surfing the astral web coming back with the most profound answers to every question I had. My mind was struggling to keep up with her and to believe that what she was saying was true. Sometimes my mind couldn't grasp it, so it would convince me she was just making things up. But then there would come the proof and integration of the new experience, which my mind couldn't deny. It was challenging everything I had been taught in school and society. It was making my reality feel ungrounded and I wasn't sure what was real and not real anymore. I was glitching! I was witnessing two completely different realities in my home and I wasn't completely certain about who was right! Now I understand my mom jumped timelines and landed on her Source timeline while my dad was still on the old timeline. This was my first experience with timeline jumping and the destruction that can play out as a result. This was also my first experience trying to determine which timeline was more "real"!

My dad was struggling daily with my mom's new consciousness. He was convinced she was going through some sort of mid-life crisis and had just lost herself. He would often tell me he missed the woman he once knew and wanted that older version of her back. He didn't know who this new version of her was, she felt like a stranger to him and it seemed they were no longer compatible. I feel like he was processing her awakening like a death. The person he fell in love with was gone. He didn't understand the higher timeline version of her at all. He was very concerned about her mental health. But I know now she had actually found herself again. Her awakening would ultimately end their marriage. Well, it was actually the timeline split that ended the marriage, but more on that later. They eventually divorced on my nineteenth birthday.

Although she loved him, that didn't stop her from continuing on her Spirit path. She started reaching larger audiences as a very clear clairvoyant. This led to speaking engagements at universities; interviews on the news; traveling to speak and work with various groups of people etc. For her, it was like the death of one life and a birth into a new one. This was her passion! To help people activate their connection to Source again like she had done. I was with her every step of the way, observing everything. It was so incredible for me to witness the miracles that were happening in people's lives because of her. Later I realized she was actually a teaching guide for me, paving the way for me to take over where she left off. But what I also witnessed, that had a profound impact on me, was the way she was treated by people who knew her before her awakening and witnessed the changes in her. Several of our family and friends disassociated with her. Some belittled her for daring to be who she was. They said she was doing the devil's work, she was crazy, blah blah blah. They were obviously just afraid of what they didn't understand.

She was one of the most beautiful loving souls I have still ever known. She was pure in heart and kind to everyone. She had a strength about her that allowed her to unconditionally love herself and others even when they couldn't do the same. She showed me how to recognize and deal with other people's fear. She saw everything for what it truly is through the eyes of Source and stayed centered in her heart space. She would get hurt, because there was a part of her that was still human, but she never let her mind trick her for long. She knew how to recenter herself quickly. This was powerful for me to see. She showed me what being in her authentic power meant. She didn't play the victim of a distorted reality.

She said she was here to help people remember who they really are. She wanted to teach people how to connect through the veil but she couldn't get anyone to actually do it back then! This was back in the 90's and I always felt she was ahead of her time. She stuck to her Spirit plan regardless and was guided every step of the way. She changed many people's lives, mainly mine, because of it.
She is the reason I am courageous. She is the reason I am not afraid to stand boldly in the truth as I understand it through my communication with her in the Source Field.

One day, as I was off to school, she casually told me that our Soul can leave our bodies anytime and come back in. I remember feeling shocked by this because it had never occurred to me. My mind was resisting the information as my heart knew it was true. My mom was deprogramming my mind and integrating the truth back into it in small doses. I started experiencing synchronicities after she would tell me things. I now understand this as a "truth echo". The Source field always echo's back higher truth to us when we speak it or hear it. It is a confirmation fail safe for us, built into the reality. It is our guide post, beacon, discernment of higher truth all we have to do is pay attention.

 The following weekend I was invited to stay the night with a friend. We were typically young teens trying to stay up all night as an act of rebellion. As the night went on, we shared about the weird things we do to see if we had any abnormal behaviors in common. We were laughing and feeling deliriously tired, when she suddenly got serious and looked at me like she wasn't sure if she should tell me something but wanted to. She said "Have you ever just left?"I didn't understand what she meant. "Like run away?" I asked. She said "No, I am going to show you". Her eyes stared off at the wall and her body relaxed like she was going into a deep meditation.

Then her eyes closed and her head dropped and her chin rested on her chest. I thought she passed out. I called her name, no response. I shook her and called her name. No response. Tears started streaming down her face but she was still non responsive. I started freaking out. I was shaking her and yelling at her to wake up. I was ready to go wake her parents when her head rose up and she opened her eyes.

She said "Don't ever do that again!" I told her I was scared and didn't know if she was ok. She said she was fine, she just went out of her body, like she has done her entire life. But when I went into fear so had she because she could feel my fear. The fear vibration made it so she couldn't find her way back to her body. My fear had that level of impact on her? I learned a lot of things that night. In hindsight, I realize this was the beginning of what my mom now calls "Spirit School". More to come on that as we proceed.

Chapter 5

Silver Spoon

When I was fifteen, he showed up. I woke up in the middle of the night and felt him looking at me. I couldn't see him with my eyes open, but I could see a dark blurry figure standing there with my eyes closed. He was darker than my dark bedroom. I could see where he was standing and his eyes were staring at me. I went into fear. I had lost my connection to the point where I couldn't recognize him anymore. He knew I was afraid but he would not leave. He was there every night. As I laid down to go to sleep and would begin to relax, I could suddenly feel him again. His eyes were starring from near my ceiling. I felt like he was a really big guy! I grabbed my bedding and went to sleep on my parents' bedroom floor.

After weeks of me refusing to go back to sleep in my own room, my mom decided to try bringing a psychic to our house. My mom hadn't told her much, just that her daughter felt there was something in her room and wouldn't sleep there. When she came to the door, I could tell she was tuning into our home. We went and sat at the kitchen table to talk. She told me she was seeing a very tall Native American man standing behind me. She said he is around 7 feet tall. That was the moment I knew she was connecting with him. I had seen his eyes up by the ceiling and I could immediately feel him near me. She told me he was here to protect me, and teach me how to protect myself because I was going to be walking between worlds. He said I was a bright light and entities would be drawn to me so I needed to learn how to not allow them to affect me.

This began my reconnection to the world of Spirit. I was so excited to know who he was and that he was not going to harm me. His name came to me through two different mediums my mom went to see. The first recording I listened to from a session my mom had with a medium I heard the man say "His name is Silver...something. He wants her to know his name". The next reading, she blurted out to my mom "Your daughter has a Spirit guide named Silver Spoon". It was so amazing to me to hear this and know without a doubt who he was!

For the next five years, Silver Spoon and I became the best of friends. I talked to him constantly and wrote him many letters so he could help me with whatever it was I wanted guidance on. I could feel that same love from him that I felt when I was walking on my grandpa's farm, but it wasn't as pure because I was different. I had built up barriers and I noticed it was much more difficult for me to feel that world. So, we decided to create a sign that would help connect me faster in moments when I was afraid and couldn't feel him. When I called his name, he would send his energy from my feet up to my head in a wave. I would feel tingles as the energy would tickle my toes and roll up my body. No matter how disconnected I felt, when I called him, it would happen to me. It was so amazing!

One day I was really sick. I had a fever and was vomiting. My grandma was taking care of me and as she walked out of my room, I called him. I immediately heard her gasp. She came back into my room and said she saw a Native American man from the waste up, in full buckskin, floating in the hallway. I smiled and told her I just called him. She started to leave the room and said "and he's handsome!" He didn't heal my body, but his presence always raised my vibration so I could heal myself, although I didn't fully understand this at the time.

The more I was attuned to Silver Spoon the more I could perceive other beings as well. I began to see shadows passing by out of the corner of my eye more often. I began to encounter other teens that had experienced a lot of traumas in their lives and I would be with them and feel negative energies through and around them. I still didn't understand these feelings and perceptions. I began to go into fear, more so than I ever had before. Sometimes I would feel myself spiraling down into deep states of fear and couldn't feel safe. Silver Spoon would always come immediately when I called him and pull me out with ease. I became so reliant on him in my life. He would tell me that I had to control my fear. That these feelings were a trick and all I had to do was realize it and step out of it. To simply come back to him and all would be ok. I was trying, but it seemed much easier just to call him and let him raise my vibration like he always did.

One night, I woke from a horrific nightmare. I was in a state of shock and could feel an energy in the room with me- tormenting me. I called Silver Spoon, he didn't come. I started to panic. I continued to call him...nothing. He had never left me like this before. I thought I was going to be sucked into the depths of hell- THE UPSIDE DOWN, where I would never be heard from again. Each time I tried to talk my mind out of feeling terror, something more terrifying would happen in my own mind. This entity was in my head! It was showing me horrific pictures of what it was going to do to me, including smashing my head, with all of the gore that goes along with that, as it laughed a creepy laugh. I didn't understand what was happening to me. I didn't know how this thing had gotten so much power over me so quickly. A few scary thoughts spiraled me into a full-on entity attack.

Suddenly, the tingles started in my toes and started moving their way up my body. He showed up to save me, finally!! The entity left. My entire body relaxed and I started crying. His words to me were the clearest they had ever been. "Do you see what you just did? You allowed that to happen to you! You let yourself go into that energy." This was the beginning of my understanding that I HAD THE POWER TO PROTECT MYSELF. After surviving that moment, I rarely ever felt that level of fear and powerlessness again. Sometimes we have to face our greatest fears alone to realize how powerful we really are. I also realized that I had co-created that experience through my fear. Although I didn't realize it at the time, these teachings were the beginning of my Spirit gift of casting out lower entities from places they are not welcome, including people physical bodies. I found myself doing it naturally throughout my life.

I had a real-life event that put what Silver Spoon taught me to the test. I had gone to visit family in Washington State for the summer. I was seventeen and recently ended a long-term relationship with my first love. I was dreaming of meeting someone with which to have a summer story. We went to a festival and I saw a guy that looked to me to be perfect! He noticed me too and we started talking. The festival was ending so he asked me if he could take me to get something to eat and drive me home. He had a hot rod muscle car and he was newly enlisted in the Navy. I asked if I could go and my family said "Do you think that is a good idea?" I said "Yes I do!", speaking as a naive teenager not thinking with the right part of my brain. So…off I went. I got in his car and we headed to find a place to eat. Since everything was closed, he headed back to my family's house to drop me off. Then he suddenly turned into the parking lot of a closed McDonald's not far from where I was staying. He pulled to the back behind the dumpster and turned off his car. I started to panic. Something wasn't right. He wasn't talking to me or looking at me when I asked him questions. He leaned over into my seat and forcefully held by arms down and started kissing me. I felt Silver Spoon. Tingles ran from my toes up to my head and I heard him remind me to not go into the fear. I felt a silly energy come over me, like I was observing the situation and not a part of it. I started laughing and told some funny jokes about the situation. He stopped and looked at me in disbelief. He laughed with me, then sat back and started the car. It stopped him. He never harmed me. He took me straight home and, on the way, I asked him questions about his life. I wanted to know what had happened to him that led him to do these things. I had a feeling I wasn't the only one he had done this to. I wasn't afraid of him, I had compassion for him. We sat and talked through the night. He cried, laughed, healed, and felt loved. He hugged me tightly before he left and thanked me. I thought, don't thank me, thank Silver Spoon. This was my first real life integration through experience of what Silver Spoon taught me. I am in control of my reality and experience. Always!

I would not understand the deepest levels of what Silver Spoon was teaching me until many years later. My thoughts control my experience. My vibration is dictated by my thoughts. My vibration determines what connects with me in the unseen realms.

Silver Spoon was my teacher for five years. He stayed very close to me teaching me daily in subtle ways. I felt so much love and gratitude for him and I could feel his deep love for me as well. But when I turned 21 and had my first child, my focus turned away from him and he quietly slipped away.

Chapter 6

Grandma Adeline

I was in my early twenties when my mom came to me one day and told me she was hearing my Great Grandma Adeline talking to her. My grandma had died when I was nineteen and although I knew her, I didn't spend much time with her. But she would always send me birthday cards and crocheted doll clothes to me while growing up. My mom talked about her often and said she felt closer to her than her own mother. They had a very special love and connection. The things she had heard grandma say were going to happen started to come true. I knew for certain she was hearing her and I was really excited about it. We would stay up late at night asking grandma questions and writing down the answers. I wanted to know all about the heaven realm. What it was like there and what she was doing. I wanted to know how I could hear her too and my mom tried to teach me. But it wasn't as clear for me as it was my mom. I didn't trust myself enough to believe I was hearing. It seemed I had gotten so far away from my source connection that I had forgotten I had these abilities. I began depending on my mom to hear for me. As time when by my mom's ability to hear became so strong that she could hear others as well. She started giving messages to people from their family members who had passed away. I loved being a part of this and would listen intently as she would share these messages from Spirit. Word spread that she was able to hear Spirit clearly and she began traveling and speaking. She was featured on the news and as a speaker at Purdue University just prior to her passing. Her deepest desire was to help others remember how to connect to the source field. She told me she was going to write a book and she did…through me!

I was living in McAllen, Texas in my early 20's. My brother was not yet 21 so he would cross the border into Reynosa, Mexico to go to the bars so he could drink alcohol. On New Year's Eve, my sister and I decided to go with him. We walked over the bridge and went to several different clubs along the border. I noticed a younger guy watching me. He was tall and thin and had a cast on his arm. He locked eyes with me every time I noticed him. Sometimes in passing, or in different clubs, there he would be. I remember dancing and seeing him staring from across the room. He didn't bother me though. I didn't get a negative feeling from him. I was blonde in Mexico so I assumed he was staring at me because of that. I would always smile and say "hello" or "Happy New Year" when I encountered him again. I just thought it was odd that I kept seeing him. As we were leaving the club, I noticed my sister had had a bit too much to drink. Although she was a year older, I felt older than her most of my life. I locked arms with her to keep her close as we approached a group of guys gathered in a circle on the border bridge. I heard screaming and got a sinking feeling like something wasn't right. As we approached the "gang", I told my sister not to say anything and follow my lead.

 I felt my grandma Adeline step into my energy field and she was guiding me. I felt a strong centered feeling of empowerment come over me as I walked straight towards a group of seven men starring directly at me. I walked quickly with confidence and didn't slow down. I smiled and said "Happy New Year", and there he was. The guy with the cast on his arm. He was right in front of me. We locked eyes and he smiled and parted the group, waving for us to go on through. I was so relieved and felt the divine intervention. I wondered if he was an angel sent to protect me? As we walked, I heard a woman scream "Stop those bitches, they've got gold". I looked up to see her leap from the boarder wall and run towards us, grabbing my sister by the back of her head and pulling her hair. My sister's head flew back and I ran to try and pull the woman off of her. I grabbed her by the hair and they both fell backwards on top of me. My sister was screaming hysterically because the woman wouldn't let go. The guy with the cast grabs my sister and is holding her from behind as she is swinging her arms and screaming, trying to get free. I looked up and saw my grandma Adeline standing in front of me. Everything stopped in that moment for me. I was no longer afraid or upset. I felt complete peace come over me and I started crying because it was so beautiful. The guy holding my sister and I locked eyes again and said you take her and you run, in a Spanish accent. He let her go and I grabbed her by the hand and we started running for the U.S. side the border. I couldn't stop crying and telling her I saw grandma! When we got to the border crossing there were ambulances waiting for us. There were people crying and bloody, being put on stretchers. It was clear to me that these people had been attacked while crossing the border. It was a horrid scene. My sister ran up to the border patrol officer and was screaming at him for watching what happened to us without helping. His reply "Mexican side ma'am, Mexican side." I couldn't focus on anything other than my grandma. I felt so loved and protected and knew this experience had changed my life for the better.

From that moment forward I talked to my grandma daily. We had a song and she would play it for me often to let me know she was with me. I was so happy to have another connection in the Spirit world. I missed my connection with Silver Spoon. She was my new best friend and I could feel her love all of the time.

It was through my connection with my Grandma Adeline that my mom and I began playing what we called "the radio game with Spirit". We would ask my grandma to play a song. We noticed the same songs would play when we asked. It was a beautiful way for us to connect with my grandma and feel her more powerfully. I have the best memories of playing this game while my mom and I were riding in the car. To this day I can't listen to the radio the same…without asking for a song from Spirit.

Chapter 7

The Eyes of Source

I moved back to Indiana to return to college after my son was a year old. I was attending Purdue University and one day my sister and I were walking back from class when we heard an ambulance coming very close to us. We had just arrived at the parking garage where I had parked our car and the ambulance was so very close to us. I ran to the sound to see what was happening. I was on the first floor of the parking garage and I looked down over the ledge to see medics stripping the clothing off of three people who laid in a row on their backs next to each other. On the left was a small boy. His eyes were open as they were doing CPR. I looked down into his eyes and I saw Source Light coming from his eyes. It was the most amazing thing I had ever seen through my physical eyes. I was in such shock and awe at the same time. I couldn't stop repeating "OMG I can see the Light in his eyes!" My sister was standing next to me but she didn't see what I saw. I didn't know how she didn't see it. It was like something out of a sci-fi movie, only full of a power I had not experienced before.

I wondered if I was seeing what he was seeing. The Light coming to get him! I knew his body was dying and his soul was leaving. I later learned that the three people were a mother and her two children. Her teenage son and her twelve-year-old son. I heard that she had struggled with depression and had been given medication that may have caused her to have a psychological break. She somehow managed to get herself and her two sons to fall from the top of the parking garage. This situation was so unbelievably horrific to see and experience, yet, the Light that spoke to me kept me from feeling the trauma of it. I was overwhelmed with so much amazement and love for what I saw, I couldn't feel anything else. I knew they were in the hands of Source. I knew what I was seeing from this side of the veil was not what was happening in Spirit. They were being cared for by the Light of God. It was the twelve-year-old in whose eyes I had seen the light.   I don't recall if the other two had their eyes open or not, I only recall what I saw in the younger boy.

It was not a coincidence that I was there to witness this. It was Source showing me the highest truth about death. I knew in that moment that death is an illusion. It plays out in our distorted physical reality one way and is experienced in a completely different way from the Source Field. I have had many conversations and experiences that confirm this since then. My mom has explained that death is the greatest illusion we believe in. In the linear reality, everything must be linear and congruent for our human minds to process. Otherwise, it can scramble our brains. There is an order and construct to the linear timeline that allows it to be congruent and logical for us.

 When I am looking at the linear timeline death process, I see disease, accidents, suicides, etc. When I look at the Source timeline, I simply see Spirit calling itself back to Source. This happens in an instant through the zero-point quantum energy field. This is why the time of death is difficult for even Spirit to predict. It requires everything to line up perfectly as orchestrated by Spirit, unless Spirit chooses to allow the linear timeline to play out its "death" in its distorted fashion.

The higher truth is, the Spirit does not experience its temporary physical vessel's death the way we do. It only experiences the beauty of it. The aspect of the Spirit in the physical body can leave at any time. If the physical body is dying, it leaves before it experiences suffering. For instance, my high school boyfriend was hit by a drunk driver while skateboarding. He explained that he never experienced the impact. He popped out and was watching from above. He felt all of the emotions that go along with the experience but not the physical pain. It wasn't until he found himself back in his body while in the hospital that he felt the physical pain.

When we choose not to come back into the body, we never experience the physical pain. We are quickly carried by Source into the higher vibrations as we attune to the power of the unconditional love in which we are engulfed. It is much more beautiful than the birth process. Death is effortless and one of the most amazing things we experience when we choose this physical journey.

Chapter 8

Remembering Source Healing

When I was 18, I went to see a "psychic". She told me I was a natural healer and that the healing I came here to do was very important. She urged me to use my healing gifts. I recalled a dream I had where someone was talking to me about this. It felt like an angel speaking to me through the veil. The message was the same, that I had healing gifts and that humanity needed this healing, so it was important that I chose to use these gifts. I recall feeling a powerful knowing about the importance of this. Then I woke up. I noticed when I had these types of dreams, Spirit would wake me immediately after these conversations so I would remember.

It wasn't until I was 24 years old that I would experience my healing ability I was told about. A friend suffered from debilitating migraines from a brain injury. While he was sleeping, I put my hands on his head and starting pulling light in through my head and out my hands into his head. I didn't ask permission to do this, I had no idea what I was doing. But I did ask permission from God and asked God to use me as a vessel for healing. As I witnessed the light come into my head from the source field, it began to speed up and flow quickly like a faucet of water that was being opened more and more. Suddenly the light turned into a bright flashing strobe light then it stopped instantly. I knew it was done. I knew he was healed. When he woke up, he told me his migraine was gone. Not only was it gone but he had no aftershocks that usually occurred. It was as if he never had a migraine. I was so excited to tell him what I had done! This was so amazing to me!

Shortly after that experience, my sister came to visit and she was highly allergic to cats. I had cats. She was having a horrible allergic reaction and went to lay down. I wasn't in the room with her when I sent her healing. I sent the light to her the same way I had done before and again the strobe light flashed and it ended. She woke up and told me her allergies were gone and she had no lingering symptoms.

When I was in my 40's I experienced a different response to working with this healing light. I met a man who had suffered more than anyone I had ever met. I had so much empathy for him that I actually took on his physical symptoms. This terrified me. I felt vulnerable and decided I had no business working with these energies if I didn't know how to properly protect myself. I decided to pause and ask Spirit for guidance before I continued.

Then my son became sick from anesthesia after having his wisdom teeth removed. I was sitting on the bathroom floor with him as he was bleeding and vomiting. I put my hand on his stomach and closed my eyes and pulled the light in through me and out of my hands. I asked God to heal him through me. Within a short time, I was the one vomiting. My son was fine. I was violently sick for five hours after I did this. I knew I had taken it from him but it seemed I was even worse off than he had been. Again, I swore I would never do this healing again.

I was able to get some clarity through a well-known healer. I had seen her speak several times at conferences and witnessed the way she used healing energy to assist others. But I didn't know that she became sick afterward as I had. She said she experiences the distorted vibrations within her own body when she does healings because it is the only true way to transmute the energy. She said my body is doing its job properly. It is a purge. She explained that during this level of healing, the healer must move into vibrational resonance with the illness (distorted energy). Not many are able to do this but those who are will transmute the illness through their own body. I understand this to mean that as I moved into vibrational resonance with the distorted energy, I was able to transmute it through my own higher vibrational state of being. My body then had to purge the distorted energy which was not fun!

Although channeling healing light is something I had done before I was born, I had to remember my abilities in this lifetime. I had been working with healing light long before I came into this life, as many of us have. We intended to remember and use it to assist each other. It's our most natural state of being in relationship with each other.

I became an attuned Reiki Master. It is not required for us to have any training from the physical reality if we already experienced results naturally working with the Living Light. I have found being attuned to Reiki has complimented my abilities and experience. Doing healing together with a partner amplifies the energy exchange. The vibrations flow together beautifully.

Chapter 9

Genetic Cellular Memories

Everything matters and all things are connected. I recently heard this in my functional nutrition course. Many of us have already heard or experienced how Epigenetics play a role in our health and personality. Bacteria from our mothers are transferred to us and they affect the way we feel and think. Cells transfer memories, as well as our DNA. I learned my mom walked with Spirit on the same farm I did when she was a child. My grandpa did as well. On down my maternal family line are a long list of ancestors who walked with Spirit. The ability to communicate beyond the veil was active in my genetic line. My genetic line goes back to "Attakullakulla", the head of the Chickamauga Cherokee Nation and his son "Dragging Canoe", the great Chickamauga Cherokee war Chief. My great- great-grandmother, Rachel, was the granddaughter of Dragging Canoe's daughter, Abigail Raven Canoe. They called her "Mam", and she read tea leaves. She was known as the town "psychic" in her small mountain community. She was also a midwife, delivering babies in exchange for chickens. I love these stories and it connects so many dots in my family.

My mom's dad, my grandpa Burney, was a very heart centered man. Mam had told him our family was Cherokee, but he didn't know the history. He looked Cherokee, just like his mom, my Grandma Ida. I grew up playing at his farm often, listening to his funny stories from his days growing up in a holler in the mountains of Tazewell, Virginia. At one point they lived in a one room cabin and he was the youngest of nine kids. His grandma Mam, his mom and the older siblings took care of him. He never knew his father. His mom "died" when he was fourteen of what the doctor said looked like a spider web inside of her stomach. He said it was before anyone had heard of cancer but that is what he believed it was. He didn't leave her side for a year while taking care of her. After she passed, he told me he immediately opened her feather pillow and pulled out what looked like a donut ring of feathers about the size of the palm of his hand. He told me it was a tradition passed down in our family. When a person dies, if the feathers create this ring inside the pillow, they had used their entire life, it means their Spirit made it to heaven. I remember being so in awe of this ring of feathers I would often ask him to get it out so I could see it again. It was beautiful and perfectly formed. It was like looking at a magic creation from heaven. He also told me it had continued to grow larger since he first pulled it out of her pillow. I remember thinking it must be alive! I have found myself checking my feather pillow at times too, just to see if one is forming.

My mom told me stories about growing up with my Grandpa Burney. She was very close with him and they shared a similar heart centered energy. They were so much alike and he was in many ways her greatest love. Everyone loved him, just like everyone loved her. She even looked just like him. As a kid I didn't realize how different and exceptional they were. But I knew I was unconditionally loved by them in the simplest ways and loved being near them. My mom said she saw and played with the fairies when she was in the woods. She thought everyone saw them and she didn't realize it was rare. Her most cherished memories were the walks she and my grandpa would take together where he would tell her things he didn't tell others about the unseen realms and Spirit. He told her not to talk about it with others. He told me some of these stories too and I clearly remember his reminding me each time he shared things with me that I wasn't to talk about it outside of the family because they commit people to hospitals for believing such things. I realized he came from an era where the supernatural wasn't as accepted and needed to stay hidden. I remember feeling sad that he wasn't able to share his amazing experiences and wisdom with the world because of this fear.

Although my grandpa rejected the church establishment, he carried in his wallet a real photo taken of Jesus's imagine in front of a bush. There was a story he told me about how he got the photo. A man was standing outside and took a photo of the bush and when he got the photo developed he saw Jesus's imagine in the bush. The imagine was crystal clear, as if it were a portrait of Jesus. The man gave the photo to my grandpa. It was printed on photo paper. That photo was there in my grandpa's wallet the entire time I knew him. The image was hardly visible by the time he went to Heaven, from all of the creases in it from him handling it so much over the years. My grandpa knew that was a real photo of Jesus. He never doubted it. When he would open his wallet to pay for something he would pull it out and show it to me, as if it were a reminder to us that Jesus is real. I had no idea that Jesus was going to appear to me years later, the same way he appeared to the man through the bush.

He was able to see his mom and grandma and communicate with them. He had a heart attack when I was in fifth grade and I remember him saying his grandma appeared in the hospital room and tucked his feet under the blanket like she used to do when he was a kid. Back then she would warm bricks over the fire and wrap them in blankets and tuck them under his feet to keep them warm in the winter.

Although he didn't recall the details of the experience, he had an "other worldly" encounter with what he believed were ET's. One night he woke up to what sounded like metal bending. He looked at the clock and it was midnight. He briefly walked into the living room and looked around the house. He walked back into his bedroom and the clock said 3:00 am. He said there was no way he was gone for three hours.

It was a common theme in UFO encounters to hear the sound of metal bending. I felt he may have been abducted. He never said so, but he did not disagree with me when I told him what I thought. My mom was visited by grey ET's since she was a kid. She said she would wake up to them staring at her in her room at night. She said she didn't like them and she would always tell them to go away. I recall her calling me at work one day when I was an adult, telling me there was a grey in her room again. I was horrified by this and couldn't believe she talked about it like it was just a normal night for her. She did however say they bothered her and she didn't like them showing up like that while she was sleeping. Neither my mom nor my grandpa may have fully known what their connection was to the grey's or what their full experience was regarding them. Our minds do a great job of blocking traumatic experiences from our memory. I am happy to report I have never awakened to a grey alien watching me while I sleep and I hope I never do.

Before I knew anyone in my family had experienced UFO or alien phenomenon, I was inspired to research experiences like this when I was a teenager. My senior year of high school I choose a semester course called "Research". We researched our chosen topic the entire six weeks and then turned in a research paper and did a talk about it to the class. Mine was on UFO's, aliens and abduction cases. I remember the kids looking at me like I was crazy as I shared about the wildest reports I found. Looking back, I am shocked I found so much information in our high school library! A part of me found satisfaction in shocking my class with this information! It was like "mic drop" as I walked by to my seat knowing their minds had to have been cracked open, even if it was just a bit!

I have since met some of those people I learned about while in high school who reported those profound experiences! It is amazing to look back on our lives and see the path that is woven, directing us to our higher purpose. I have no doubt I was drawn to this sort of thing through my genetic cellular memories and I chose these specific genes perfectly to support my mission here.

My grandpa also had a near death experience. He was fixing the washing machine and laying in water when he touched electricity and was shocked badly. He said he went out of his body and experienced a life review. He saw everything he had done to cause harm or upset to people in his life. This shocked me because I couldn't imagine my grandpa doing anything upsetting to anyone. He told me he judged people by the way they looked and he was shown their Spirit so he could see how their bodies didn't reveal who they really were. He told me he would never judge anyone again.
I remember my grandpa teaching me how to make the clouds disappear when I was a kid. He would point at a cloud and tell me to watch it. It would evaporate. He told me to try it by asking it to disappear. My natural instincts kicked in and I imagined it dissolving because I told it to. It worked, every time! I loved doing this. It was as if I was proving to myself over and over that this type of magic exists within me and all I have to do is use it. He also told me things happen in threes, especially deaths. If someone would die, he would say, that's one, there will be two more, pay attention. He was right. There were always three near each other. This fascinated me but I didn't understand it. Now that I understand the laws of nature, I understand

there are patterns that repeat in cycles. He was opening my mind and activating my connection to Source in the most amazing ways.

 Although my grandpa grew up very poor, they had love and that was evident in his stories, experiences and his heart. He existed in a state of unconditional love more than any other man I knew. I was blessed to have him as my grandpa and as an example of what love looked and felt like. Three months before he passed away, he told me he could see everyone around him in Spirit, including my mom. "They are all here" he said, "and I will be with them in three months". He died three months to the day of that conversation.

I was not only born into a genetic line of source connected humans, but I now have a beautiful family in Spirit guiding my journey. These things have assisted me in developing a strong ability to connect and get higher guidance for myself and others. When we experience a love connection with someone in the physical reality who passes away, that love we have with them is our connection through the veil. Separation is an illusion. It is the higher love vibrations that transcends all space and time. Our loved ones on the other side are dedicated to helping us create our greatest and highest experience. It is the natural order of things in our journey to expanded states of consciousness.

I worked in professional racing for many years. Race car drivers do not have clear vision when going around the track. It requires a spotter to sit up in a high spotter booth above the track to guide them. They communicate through microphones and the spotter tells them what's coming around the corner, from behind, or beside them. The spotter has driving experience. They are often former professional race car drivers themselves. This experience makes them qualified to guide others drivers around the track. This is the same with our guidance from Spirit. They have been on earth in physical bodies before. This gives them the experience and wisdom needed to assist those of us that are still in the physical reality. It is important for us to know who our spotters are and make an effort to listen to them.

Chapter 10

Conversations With God And
The Second Coming of Christ

By the time I reached my mid-twenties I had gotten fully sucked into a fear-based reality. Life became really challenging for me being a single mom trying to support myself and my young son while finishing my college degree. I had always wanted to be a mom and I felt like I was a failure because I was so stressed out. I wasn't able to be in the present moment and knew I was missing it. I fell into the victim consciousness trap and felt powerless to change my circumstances. Needless to say, my vibrational state of being slowed dramatically and I had very little energy due to the overload of stress and fear about pretty much everything. I found myself wishing I could leave this reality. After all, I clearly wasn't good at the game of life and I was suffering more than I was thriving. Having a child at twenty-one was overwhelming.

I lost all of my friends because they were not parents and I could no longer play in their reality. I was experiencing a type of midlife crisis at a young age. The life I once knew was gone and my new life was not yet understood. I recall my dad telling me when I was twenty-six years old that our lives are like a ship at sea. If you don't steer your own boat, you will float aimlessly into storms and end up in places you don't want to be. He told me I needed to steer my ship in the direction I wanted to go. This was the first time I realized it was possible for me to be in charge of my own experience. Up until this point I felt like I was at the mercy of the external reality. How had this never occurred to me? How did the external reality get such a firm grasp on me, stealing my creative energy? I had lost my connection to the source field. I no longer understood anything that was happening to me. I feel like I had fallen out of my boat and was just trying to keep my head above water so I didn't drown. Yet a part of me wanted to drown and get it over with. I would sit and sulk in my self-loathing.

I didn't realize this slow vibration had become my dominant frequency and therefore I was attracting more and more distorted people and situations into my life.
 I spent the next six years battling with a man over which reality is true, the distorted one or the unconditional love one? That relationship took me deeper and deeper into illusions. It felt as though the parts of me that weren't fully centered in my heart were sucking me into the abyss. My mom saw the situation for what it was and tried to help me come back into the source field. But these parts of me were immersed so deep in fear and I didn't know how to let go of those aspects of myself.

I bought the book "Conversations with God" by Neale Donald Walsch, and didn't get through the first chapter before I was sobbing. It hit me in the heart space and I realized I needed to have my own long deep conversation with God. That night, I got up and went and sat in the laundry room. I called out to God and said "Ok, if you talk to everyone, I really need you to talk to me!" I had found myself in a hellish relationship in which I felt trapped through psychological manipulation. I fully expected God to tell me I needed to get away from this man, which would fully reinforce my victim consciousness state. But that is not what happened. I was suddenly being brought into an awareness that time is not what it seems. I heard a male voice "Go back, to every moment in your life when the people who should have been loving you right were not. Go back. Time doesn't exist the way you were told." As I heard these words loud and clear, I could feel my consciousness expanding and my mind being brought into something new. The words kept repeating as if each time I heard them, my mind was letting go of old belief programs that prevented me for knowing the truth. It was like layers or walls being stripped away so I could feel it. Then, what looks like a screen in front of me starts playing scenes from my life. It was moments in my childhood. Moments that changed me but not for the better. The moments that showed me love was something different than it is. Movements when I was misunderstood and treated less than what I deserved.

I saw myself standing in the hallway of my school with my third-grade teacher, Mrs. Taylor, yelling at me. I had completely forgotten about this. I was so immersed in these scenes I didn't realize I was talking out loud to this voice like this was all normal. "Oh yeah! Why was she yelling at me?" The voice replied "because you went ahead on your math when she told you not to." "Yes!". I remembered that! I was good at math so I loved it. She would time us and I would always get done first. It was so much fun. I must have gotten excited and since I knew and understood what was next, I kept going. I loved Mrs. Taylor. She was one of my favorite teachers. But this particular day she looked at me viciously and said "go out in the hall". I had never been sent out in the hall before. My heart sank into my stomach and I thought I was going to throw up. As I watched this scene, I felt that feeling in my stomach again. She came out and started yelling at me. How dare I keep going when she told me to stop. She treated me like a worthless criminal and I was only eight years old. In that moment I believed her. My heart was broken. She didn't love me like I loved her, in fact she despised me. I must be a horrible person. I didn't experience much love from anyone in this reality. But I did know what true love was and I experienced that when I was in my woods. I went home and ran straight into the woods.

When we had finished reliving all of these hellish experiences, I looked up and saw myself standing in front of my four years old self. I was so adorable. I always felt like I was an ugly kid. I remember my mom always getting upset when I would say that and tell me that wasn't true that I was adorable. I never believed her and thought she was just trying to make me feel better about myself. I grabbed that little girl and gave her the biggest hug. I was sobbing. I held her and told her how much I loved her. It was the most real thing I have ever experienced that is actually considered not real in the lower vibrational reality. Then in a blink it was all over and I was back in the dark laundry room floor. I sat there contemplating what had just happened to me. I replayed it over and over in my mind. I had challenged God to talk to me and he had and in a way I never would have imagined. I realized my mom was right. I was actually adorable! I now understood what self-love is and how powerful it is in our lives. Because time is an illusion and we can move our consciousness forward and backward on the timelines, going back to love ourselves actually changes our timeline. We literally feel that love coming through the veil to ourselves. It feels like God, and it is God, but it is also us. The energy I felt with me as a child, that made me feel so safe and loved was my future self, connecting with my past self. It was me walking with me on my grandpa's farm. It was my love that made me feel safe to take this physical journey knowing I would always come back to me, perfectly intact and full of love for everyone and everything. I would need this knowing for what was soon to come..........

Shortly after that profound experience, my mom and I had stayed up until early morning while she channeled Spirit. It was so much fun to be with her and experience Spirit communicate through her. It was around 3am when she was leaving my house and this is a moment powerfully etched in my mind. She went out the door and held it open as she turned and looked at me. It was a look I hadn't seen before. She said "I am going to go". Hearing these words triggered something deep inside of me -A knowing. But I replied "Where are you going?". She said "I am going to the other side. I am more there than I am here and I (my soul) showed me. I will be channeling through you from the other side. We contracted to do this. It is already set and we chose it." I was in a shock. There are no words to describe that moment. I knew it was true. A part of me remembered this. But I didn't want to hear it. I went up to my room and wrote down everything that happened that night. I knew I would need to remember it.

Not long after that conversation, my brother and his wife found out they were having another baby. It was a girl, and while in the hospital I watched my mom hold her for the first time. She looked at me and said "she's got it. She has my gifts." It was such a beautiful moment to see my mom connect with her, our sweet Chloe. I was relieved that Chloe had arrived. She and my mom were inseparable. I knew my mom was not going to leave her. Plan B was in motion! Whatever contract I had made with my mom had been changed and I was relieved.

One night I was lying in bed watching the movie the *"Last Temptation of Christ"*. I felt my consciousness expand as I was brought into a completely different perspective about the life of Jesus. I had disconnected from that energy and felt abandoned and betrayed by it. I felt so connected, loved and safe as a child but that didn't last. I wanted nothing to do with religion and the fear it had instilled in me as a child. There were deep trauma's I had associated with my experience as a child with our church. I had moved on and wasn't looking back.

But this particular night something was different. I felt an energy around me I hadn't felt since I was a child. I looked over at my window and noticed a strange light I hadn't seen before. It looked strangely like the profile of Jesus with a goatee. I was sure that was just a weird coincidence, but I couldn't help but look back at it to see if it was still there. Each time I looked at it, it was brighter. Until I couldn't deny something was happening. It lit up my window with a clear face of Jesus and when I finally realized this was not a random light and something was happening, I heard the words "You have finally come back to me". My hallway was lit up in red and there was a figure standing at the end of my bed. Then in an instant it was all gone. I remember telling my boss about it the next morning at work. He said he will never forget seeing my arms flailing around as I told the story with so much passion and disbelief.

My grandpa told me all things from source come in three's. I was aware that there were three energies in my room that night. Like a holy trinity. I didn't understand at the time why Jesus was connecting with me again. But a year later I would.

Chapter 11

She "Left"

My mom and I loved going to our friend Frieda's home for Monday night "Gathering Goddesses" meetings. The last one my mom attended; I noticed something was different about her. She sat in the chair near the back window and she was exceptionally quiet. She would often squint her eyes when she was communicating with Spirit. She was doing that on and off all evening but when I asked her what she was feeling she didn't elaborate. That wasn't like her. She was always happy to share what Spirit was saying to her especially in our group. In hindsight I know she was preparing to leave. Less than a week later she would be rushed to the ER.

That is one of the last memories I have of being with my mom on earth. Oh, wait, and I have to share about the last time we saw a movie together! She LOVED going to the movie theatre. She would get the jumbo popcorn and dump the M&M's in it when it was hot so they would melt! It was so messy good! I wish I could recall the movie we saw that night. What I do recall is more important. The movie hadn't started yet and I waited in the theatre while she went to the restroom. When she came back she tripped on the step and almost fell down, but she caught herself, just in time to trip on the next step, then the next, then the next as she looked like she was awkwardly running toward the theatre screen! I watched in shock as she lunged into the screen and the whole thing shook like it was blowing in the wind! Thankfully the screen stopped her or she may have never quick tripping! I will never forget her face! She looked back at me with her hand over her mouth and ran to her seat, sunk down and laughed along with the rest of the theatre. The laughter was so lough we couldn't hear anything else. Her show was better than whatever it was we were watching! I remember people continuing to laugh twenty minutes into the movie playing! That's how funny she was. It was her vibration. Everyone in the theatre was uplifted by her. Her last movie theatre experience on earth was awesome!

I don't remember details about the last time I spoke with her before she went to the ER, but I remember her preparing to leave to go do a talk in Richmond, VA. All of our family was sitting in my kitchen listening to four year old Chloe sing Celine Dion's "I'm Alive" on the karaoke machine to her. Looking back, that was another synchronicity. She would never see her again in her physical body yet the song was fitting. She is still very much alive and wanted us to know that.

I also barely remember the phone call that came from her friends telling me that she had passed out and was taken to the hospital. But I do remember being in the hospital with her. I remember the nurse telling me that the doctors were not going to tell me the truth, that she was, in fact, dying. The doctor had continued to tell me she had a 70%-50% chance of survival. The nurse said I needed to call our family and tell them they needed to get here if they wanted to see her. I vividly remember that moment. I feel my mom was working through that nurse to make sure everyone was there with her during her passing.

I will never forget seeing my mom laying there barely able to talk, knowing she was going to "die" was surreal. She had been diagnosed with AML Leukemia and back then she was given a best-case scenario of living another three to five years. Those years would most likely have not entailed a good quality of life. I was only twenty-nine years old and she was my best friend and greatest love. She was the care taker of the grand-children while we were at work. She was the stability and core of our family. I had no idea how much until she was "gone".

I was facing my greatest nightmare. I began having a trauma response like nothing I had ever experienced before. I couldn't stop crying. I could barely breath. I was sitting by her bed holding her hand sobbing. She was not responsive. I didn't know she was aware of what was going on. She opened one eye and looked at me and said "Jennie, you can't go around crying all of the time." I said, in between gasps for air, "Easy for you to say, you are leaving me." I had never felt so selfish in all of my life. She was the one suffering and all I could think about was how I couldn't live without her. I was so upset with myself, with her for leaving me, and with God for allowing this. I had spent most of my twenties feeling victimized by life and abandoned by God. This was just more proof that God was not my friend. How could he allow this to happen to one of the most beautiful human beings in the world? How could he not protect her from this horrible suffering? There clearly wasn't a God who loves us. That was another lie I foolishly believed in this hellish, deceitful, world. My mom replied "I am not going anywhere. I am going to be talking to you all of the time. I've already seen it." I replied "I am not going to hear you- I am not psychic!" She calmly said "Because I am your mom, you will." That was the last time I heard her voice.
Our family came and we all spent the next two weeks in the ICU. I still hadn't accepted that she was going to leave us. Especially Chloe, who was four years old and my mom had practically raised her as her own.

Chloe later told me that my mom appeared in the ICU waiting room and was talking to her. My brother had started crying and it was the first time any of us had ever seen him cry. My mom told Chloe to not pay attention to us and to keep playing. My mom was protecting her from our trauma.

I believed my mom had super powers. She wasn't like everyone else. She could work this out if she chose to. She could stay with us. Our love was strong enough to overcome anything. Strangely, I wasn't able to pray for her to stay. A part of me knew she was leaving and I didn't want to hold her here if she was suffering. After she was gone, I regretted this decision. I wish I had held on tighter and prayed with all of my might for her to be healed. I have heard of the miracle stories of the power of prayer. Maybe that would have kept her here.

She began to code and wasn't able to breath on her own. They put her on a ventilator. They called a meeting with our family to ask us if we wanted to continue with life support. We all agreed that she would not want that. The hospital preacher told us he would notify the doctor and we could meet him at 8am the next morning to take her off of the vent. A part of me was relieved she would no longer be suffering and the other part of me was just numb and checked out. That night something shook our bed. Hard! It terrified me and my sister. We both jumped out of the bed asking what was that?

The next morning, I was standing next to my mom, when the doctor started talking to her about taking her off of the ventilator. She hadn't been responsive for hours maybe days, it's a blur. I wasn't sure why he was telling her if she was braindead. He said "Kitti, we are going to take you off of this ventilator. Do you know what that means? It means you won't be able to breath on your own" She opened her eyes wide, looked at him and shook her head no! I immediately went into shock! I told the doctor to stop. I understood now, this is why she shook my bed the night before. She was trying to stop us from taking her off of the ventilator. She wasn't ready to go yet.

I recalled conversations I had had with her over the years about the hospital. She never trusted them. She was very aware of the corrupt systems that are greed based and do not uphold the best interest of anyone or anything outside of their own agenda. In hindsight, I had to ask myself why the hospital would be encouraging us to remove the ventilator from a person who was temporarily having trouble breathing on their own and was not braindead? At that time in my life, I was not awake about these things. However- she was because she was accessing the Source field where all things are known. She often tried to tell me but unless we are accessing the Source field ourselves, we are only able to experience distorted versions of the truth. The truth can only be experienced through the Source field. She said many times "don't ever take me to a hospital. They will kill me. They kill people in hospitals." I couldn't grasp this. Of course, the hospital is not going to kill you. They are here to help us get well.

She knew I was still unable to see that the reality we live in is inverted. What appears good is not and what appears bad is not. We must flip everything right side up to see the truth in it. Even our eyes see everything upside down and we don't even realize it.

She had been traveling doing speaking and channeling sessions in Richmond, VA when she was taken to the hospital. We all came from Indiana to be with her. I had been away from work for two weeks so I had to leave the hospital and go take care of some things for the office. I went back to my hotel room and was gone for a couple of hours at the most. When I returned to the hospital, I learned that she had awakened from her coma. Everyone came into her room and interacted with her. She put on my grandpa's readers and got a pen and paper so she could communicate because she was still on a vent. She told everyone to hug each other and to stay together.

By the time I got there she had gone back into a coma. It was her last moments with her family. It was her final goodbye to us. I missed it! I was so upset that I wasn't there for her last moments with us. Once again, I felt so betrayed by God. He must hate me. He could have made sure I was there. How was it possible that within the only two hours I had been gone, it was the only time she woke up. It seemed as though God was just continuing to punish me. I went and sat in my car and asked her Spirit to talk to me. I asked her if she was going to die. The song *"I Can't Stop Lovin You"* by Phil Collins, started on the radio and I knew she was leaving. I went to my hotel room and fell on the floor sobbing. Something powerful happened in that moment. It was like a portal to Source opened and I could feel it fully, the same was I could when I was a child. I knew in that moment that she was not really my mom. She was my Spirit guide and teacher. There was a bigger plan. It felt huge and powerful and I was a part of it. But the human part of me wasn't ready to let go. I wasn't ready to do this life without her. I sobbed harder than I ever had in my life. I wanted to just cry myself to death so I could stay with her. I told her and God that I couldn't do it. It was too soon I wasn't ready yet. I needed to understand more. I wasn't going to be ok and I wasn't going to be able to fulfill our contract. I was failing and we needed to abort the mission and regroup! "Let's rethink this!" There had to be a plan B?

I knew more in that moment than I ever had before about who we really are. I could see what she saw. I had been pulled into the Source field for just a brief moment and that's all it took for me to I know everything about our contract and who we really are! BUT, I (Jennie) didn't want to accept it.

The moment she left, I was holding her feet. It was November 8, 2002 at 12:00 pm. The sun was shining. The world felt eerily quiet- like it had stopped. Yet it all kept going, at the same time, like nothing happened. A part of me had stopped and she didn't move forward with me, but I didn't realize I was leaving her behind as another version of me was created to continue to survive without her.

From that moment on, I spent every minute of my life trying to see and hear her. It felt like I was clawing my way through walls and barriers, desperate to get to her.

Chapter 12

Clawing My Way Back to My Mom

The moments after her passing felt like slow motion. That night we all went back to our hotel room. I dreamed that my mom was sitting at the table in our room. When I woke up Chloe was sitting on the floor by the table. She casually said "Grandma is here. She is sitting at the table…and she still has her makeup on!" I was so relieved! I knew she was there, I saw her too, but I was only able to see her in my dream. Chloe confirmed it for me! This brought me out of my grief for a short time. I felt high and ready for this new chapter with my mom being on the other side of the veil. I knew it was going to be amazing. I knew she was ok. I was going to see and hear her! But it wouldn't take long for me to spiral down into the grief and separation again. Where I suddenly questioned everything and couldn't feel her at all.

The return home without her was so weird. Walking into her house without her there, knowing she was never going to be there again was too much for my mind to comprehend. It felt like my mind was trying to compensate for a reality it wasn't able to comprehend and never would. It felt like it was glitching. I looked around and saw post it notes with messages all over the house, stuck to the side table, the vase, the kitchen table. They were everywhere. Little messages about love she has left us from the Source field. As I read those messages it felt like she knew she wouldn't be coming back. Like it was all pre-planned by her Spirit and her Spirit was helping me finally see it, in reverse, because I didn't get it. I wasn't present enough in the moment with her to know what was happening.

I once again felt like I was being pulled into the Source field and I was walking between worlds and was no longer in linear time. Everything looked different, like I was walking through a dream. I was being given a glimpse into a completely different reality happening simultaneously. A reality that was divine and in perfection. That reality was running right in front of me the whole time. How did I not see this? How can anyone miss this pure magic? I realize now that this experience activated my multidimensional abilities and I was experiencing more than one timeline running in my reality.

I walked into the room she called the fairy room. It had a magical fairy forest border and she had taken green paint and glitter and painted with her finger swirls all around the border. When she did it, some who saw it thought it was ridiculous that she would ruin the walls of her house like that. Others, like me, felt inspired by it. Who would dare paint on their walls with their finger and glitter? My magical momma! She really didn't mind looking crazy in this reality. I suddenly noticed that I had never seen what I was seeing on those walls before. It now looked like an angelic work of heavenly art. I felt like it carried messages from Source that I wasn't yet able to know.

I sat down on the floor staring at all of the magic she had left behind and noticed a box sitting next to me. My dad had gone over to her house before we got back to help pack up her things so we wouldn't have to do it all. It was a box full of papers. I said "Ok mom! Give me a message!" I closed my eyes and reached into the center of the box and pulled out a piece of paper. It was a long letter she had written addressed to her friend, Molly, who had lost her mom when she was sixteen. It was channeled from Molly's mom to Molly, explaining how she felt in her last moments before she died. How she knew she was leaving but didn't want to go. How much she loved and was never far from her. I knew this letter was also written for me. She left it for me to find so I would know how she felt. In the source field everything has multiple purposes and meanings. In linear reality things are limited to specific things. The letter was channeled for Molly, her name was on it. So of course, it wasn't channeled for me, but it was placed in the timeline perfectly for me to experience because it was higher truth and relevant to my mom and I.

I sat there reflecting back on the last year of my life with my mom. I was able to see everything through her eyes. Through the eyes of her Spirit. It was as if I was the one who had died and I was a ghost walking around looking at everything completely differently. I suddenly could see all of the signs that she was leaving. But I had not seen them at the time. It was difficult not to start spiraling into the grief and lower frequencies again. How could I have been so clueless? How did I not see the signs as they were everywhere? I was so selfish and consumed with the dramas in my own life. I left her alone to do all of this by herself. She tried to tell me but I couldn't hear her. I knew in that moment that I had been completely immersed in illusions. I felt so far gone how was I ever going to get back? How could I ever forgive myself? I felt myself flipping back and forth constantly between the human reality and the Source reality. They were two very different realities. Which one is real?

When I went back to work, there was a note laying on my desk "Go see Dave at the Java Roaster" from my boss. Dave was my friend who worked down the street at the coffee shop. He was hilarious, like my mom, and I knew she would love spending time with him. We had planned to get together when she returned from Richmond so he could meet her but that never happened. My boss had gone down to get a cup of coffee when he overheard Dave talking about a psychic reading he had the night before. Dave didn't understand the message he received. He was told there was a girl, a cat and a woman. The woman was trying to reach the girl. The woman loves the girl so much and is trying to get that message to the girl. My boss knew immediately who the message was for. When I walked in the coffee shop, Dave yelled across the room at me as he showed me that he had goosebumps all over his arms. He didn't realize my mom had "died" and didn't know that my mom's name was "Kitti." Her name was the cat symbolism. It once again brought me so much peace knowing she made it over ok. I could once again feel my energy come back into alignment with the Source field for a brief moment.

Preparing for her celebration of life sent me into "gotta get er' done mode". I have this autopilot "Do" mode I go into when something really needs to be done. This was a REALLY big deal and I didn't have time to sit around feeling sorry for myself. I was determined to throw her a beautiful farewell party. Friends and family pitched in to help. I gathered photos and pink rose decorations. I was talking to her the entire time- asking her "what she wanted it to look and feel like?" and "what she wanted everyone to know?". I went through her writings and found two that jumped out at me. It was as though she had written these things for everyone for her own celebration of life before she left-as if she knew. But wait, she did know. She told me that night as she was leaving my house five years prior. It was all so confusing. I knew it was the truth when I heard it but why couldn't I realize what was happening? My mind was glitching a lot, I digress…again.

On my way to her celebration of life I felt a high come over me. I knew this was going to be a profound moment in time and I could feel her presence with me. I had a long talk with her on the drive. I told her I was going to step aside and allow her to speak through me. Wait what? How was I going to do that? I can't channel like that! There always seemed to be two conversations happening within me at the same time. Two completely different people. A higher aspect connected to Source and Spirit and a lower aspect completely unaware of Source or any possible connection to Spirit. I felt bipolar. But the higher part of me took over because of the power of our love and I knew she was going to run her own celebration of life party.

She told me she didn't believe in funerals. She said they were horrible, sad and depressing and that was the opposite of what death was about. She never understood why humans insisted on being sad and serious about life. "It should be a party" she said. I recalled the day years ago when she told me she wanted me to play the song "Get The Party Started" by Pink during her celebration of life party. She loved to dance. She was a dance instructor for The Author Murray Dance Studio and she loved being in theatre. She was always dancing. Even when I was growing up, she was often in the kitchen with the music on dancing. She taught me how to dance and got me into talent shows, acting and modeling. She loved all of it.! She literally wanted to dance her way through life.

She had created a collage of movie clips to show people when she did her talks about the Spirit world. I played it at her party. It was so perfect. It demonstrated exactly how she felt about this distorted reality and what was real and not real in it. I read passages from one of her favorite books. It was entitled: *"Emanuel's Book: A Manual for Living Comfortably in the Cosmos"* by Pat Rodegast. It described how Spirit viewed death. She wanted everyone to see this from Spirit's perspective which is much closer to the truth. I found two of her writings while looking through her things and I handed them out to everyone. It was as if she was there and speaking directly to everyone.

Magic

"Please look for the magic in your life, it's everywhere. Magic comes from love and when love is magical, life is wonderful! Thank you from my heart, I cherish being with you at this moment." By Kitti Marie Byers

Inspiration

"Inspiration can send us to a world of completion. Inspiration flows in the world of Spirit. They are trying to inspire us to feel what we miss every day when we miss the feeling of being inspired. It flows both ways. Do we look towards inspiration when we awaken? Do we hear inspiration in our dreams? Creativity, love, music, books, language and movies inspire us to move towards our heart and souls. Inspiration awakens a soul to new awareness and moves us forward to a more exciting life. A new awakening. To a world of inspirational love beyond our comprehension." By: Kitti Marie Byers

I wasn't sad. I didn't cry. I felt higher than I ever had in my life. I was experiencing her party through her eyes. It was so amazing…all of it. There was so much love. Of course, there were people of a variety of different belief systems. Many of our family were Christian's and believed that she was going to hell for communicating with Spirit. I recalled watching her bravely come out of the closet about who she really was. She stayed true to herself and her knowing no matter what. Back then there were very few people in our world who were accessing the Source field like she was. They were only seeing one reality when there are clearly at least two. She was seeing more than they could see. But they had no idea there was so much more they were not accessing and she knew that. So, she always responded with compassion. Even when they criticized her. She experienced everything from the Source Field. She looked at everyone through God's eyes-with love and compassion no matter what.

I centered every part of my being in the Source Field and let that energy flow through me for all to feel that day. It was the most powerful higher truth and love I had ever experienced. It simply was. This truth exists inside every one of us and WE can call it forth in each person to just feel it and know it. I didn't care who thought we were crazy. I knew the difference between crazy and higher truth, thanks to my mom.

She wanted everyone to remember the funny moments. She was always laughing that hilarious belly laugh. That day we shared our funniest moments with her. I shared my story about the movie theatre. My friend shared about the time she spraypainted all of the appliances in our apartment glitter pink! My dad owned the apartment and was not happy when he saw it, but we were! They were baby poo green and now they were magical appliances! My dad's memory isn't as fond as ours, but I have no doubt when he gets to the other side they will finally have a good laugh!

As I stood in the line where the guests could say something to the family about her, I noticed so many people I had never seen before. She had touched so many lives living through her connection to the Source Field. They had the most beautiful things to say about her and how amazing she was. What a gift it was to me to hear all of the little but powerful things she did for people she barely knew, to help them feel higher love again. Even the family members who had belittled her for living her life outside of the socially accepted box they tried to keep her in, told me that she was different and they didn't quite understand her, but they felt her love shine through. Many told me they had never met anyone else like her and she taught them so much about unconditional love. She reminded me of John Travolta's character in the movie "*Phenomenon*". It wasn't until after she died that people really understood who she was and what she came here to do for them. I was determined to carry on her legacy and make sure everything she was and had done would grow bigger and expand out into the world through me.

Chapter 13

Desperate to Feel Her

I went back to a place she used to take me when I was a teenager and young adult. It is a psychic camp in Chesterfield, Indiana. It's called Camp Chesterfield. I had experienced a woman there when I was nineteen who was the most Spirit connected medium I had ever met. Her name was Evelyn and she lived in a little pink house. I knew if my mom could get through it would be through her! I arrived at her little pink cottage and we sat on her porch. She handed me a box of tissues and said a prayer before she opened to connect for me. I hadn't told her anything about my myself or my mom's passing away. I knew she wouldn't remember me from that time my college friends and I showed up at a church service where she gave everyone a personal message.

She got quiet as she listened and immediately said "You have a mother figure that stands to the left of you. She says that God was gracious with her. She could have suffered for a long time." She went on to say that she was so close to the earth dimension that it was difficult for her to tell if my mom had actually passed away. "She isn't going anywhere! She achieved guide status and she is now your Spirit guide. She is keeping her promises to you. She left you a legacy to carry on. I knew without a doubt she was talking to my mom, but just to make it funny and memorable, my mom added her comedy. Evelyn leaned in really close to me and looked me right in the eyes and said, "who's Charles?" That was what she called my dad! "She says to tell you that your dad IS unhappily married". My eyes got big and I started laughing so hard! My mom would tell us this now and then over the years and we would always tell her to stop! We thought she was saying it out of her unresolved hurt regarding their divorce. She would always deny that she was still hurt. She said it was simply the truth and for some reason felt we should know that truth (imagine that?). I have to admit, it was that part of the conversation with Evelyn that convinced my siblings that it was her. They were not there for the other conversations my mom and I had about her staying with me and doing the work together. But they did know that she said randomly that about my dad! I think it so hilarious the way she chose to prove to us it was her. I laugh every time I think about it. I understand now it was more about understanding my dad's vibrational state of being. She wanted us to know the truth so we could choose to love him regardless, the way she did, without processing it as a trauma.

One night I was feeling so distraught about not being able to connect with my mom that I just started screaming in my head for her. I figured I needed to be much louder because she obviously couldn't hear me, right? I screamed "Mom" as loud as I could. I could hear it echoing into the Source field. This had to reach her! I fell asleep exhausted from screaming so much. I woke up from a dream about her. She came to me with her face in my face and said "I am here". That's all I remembered. But I felt like it was enough to keep me going.

My mom had been a service provider at the Coptic Conference in Johnson City, TN. She was a medium. A family member attended the Coptic Conference six months after my mom passed. They asked my mom to pick a psychic there for them to see that would be able to hear her. She was given a clear sign on which one to see and when she sat down the medium, Sheila, said right away "are you with Kitti?". It was so amazing! Sheila said my mom had been waking her

81

up at 3:00am for the last six months telling her she would be speaking to her family. She said she had been asking everyone all day if they were with Kitti because she knew it was one of the main reason's she flew all the way there. She had never met my mom and lived on the other side of the country, but my mom was orchestrating this in advance. The messages that came through for us were so beautiful and accurate. It was mind blowing to see how my mom was able to pull this off. Yet she still couldn't seem to communicate directly with me. It made no sense to me. Experiencing these magical moments of connection with my mom through others didn't sustain me for long. I continued to spiral in my self loathing about my inability to hear her myself.

It had been one year since she had passed. The Mind Body Spirit Expo in Indianapolis happened to be held on the anniversary of her death. Two years prior we had attended together. We loved going to these types of events. This year I was going without her, but I was still determined to go. I went alone, but I knew she was with me. I was walking through the crowd asking her to tell me which medium I should see. Suddenly a man tapped me on the shoulder and said "I am with someone else doing a session right now, but your mom nudged me and asked me to speak with you. Can you come back in twenty minutes?" OMG! YES! I suddenly went from being in a sad, poor me mode that my mom isn't with me in her body state, to being so excited I felt like I was floating! There's that bipolar thing again!

He said to me "They took him away. Do you understand this? Your mom says they took him away because you would have wasted ten more years and you are not meant to waste your time here like that." He was referring to the man I had married that my mom was not fond of. My mom didn't dislike very many people but she couldn't hide her feelings about this guy. She looked at me one day and said "I am watching you walk on egg shells around him and the Jennie I know never walked on egg shells for anyone". She was right. I had gotten sucked into his delusional controlling world and she knew it but couldn't pull me out of it. She said multiple times to me before she died "I'm going to pull you out". "Out" meaning out of the illusions I had gotten lost in here. It wasn't until she died that I was experiencing the Source Field again and I could feel the higher truth. She definitely pulled me out! I knew I could no longer betray my own heart staying with him. The night I left him, I was loading my car crying because he called my mom a disgusting name just to hurt me. He had psychologically abused me this way for years by keeping me in fear and distorting the truth for his own controlling agenda. I wasn't going to allow him to do the same regarding my mom. I loved her more than I loved myself, apparently.

I heard a loud banging noise as I stepped outside, with my bags packed, and looked up to see a huge dragonfly hitting the porch light over and over as if it was trying to get my attention. The dragonfly had become my sign with my mom. I knew it was her letting me know she was with me. She was probably dancing around watching me stand up to him! I went into work the next day and had received an email from Sheila. She said "I don't know what you did, but your mom woke me up at 3:00 am and told me to tell you YOU GO GIRL!" Ha! I knew she was celebrating! It was all her fault! Her love for me made me do it! I felt so empowered and connected because I had chosen higher love over my fear and illusions. Sheila didn't know that one of the things my mom had said to me since I was a little girl was "YOU GO GIRL". It was her way of empowering me to believe in myself.

The medium at the Mind Body Spirit Expo also told me that my mom said I was going to live to be an old lady with gray hair. This was another important message for me because I held a deep fear that if I became enlightened like her, I would not be able to stay in this world. I would have to die. I didn't want to leave my kids the way she left us. I can relax into this journey now and know we came to play different rolls. I was meant to stay here and she was meant to be over there.

Oh and the last message was; "your mom says she likes the yellow kitchen". Yellow was her favorite color when I was a child. We would always want to give her yellow gifts. She also loved daisys. When she integrated with her higher self during her Spiritual awakening, she became more and more the color pink and flower rose. I now know that our aura's change as we change. I imagine she had a yellow aura before and a pink aura after. I see these aura changes happen all the time when I help others connect to Source. A year later I bought a new house and I had forgotten about this message, but the kitchen was BRIGHT yellow! When I was thinking of buying it I said, "I love it but that yellow has to go!" Then I remembered her telling me she liked it and I laughed. Her and I were so different in personality yet we are the same in Spirit.

She used to tell me that I communicated the details of the Spirit world much better than she could. She would take me with her to her speaking events and sessions. I loved going and witnessing the miracles that occurred through her. When people would ask her questions about what she did and how it all works, she would point to me and ask me to explain when she didn't have the words. This is why our roles are different. We have different skills that allow things to flow best this way. I am relieved to know I don't have to leave my children early and I can still fulfill my Spiritual journey. She was ready to bust a move on outta here! We are such a great team.

A few years later, I walked into a crystal shop and noticed a sign saying there was a psychic there for the day. I decided to sign up. I never wanted to miss an opportunity to hear from her. He was from India and had a strong accent. He immediately said my mom was there and he asked me if she liked brownies. Yes, she loved brownies, but didn't everyone? I mean, I don't, and she never could believe I didn't like chocolate. She loved it. He told me to pay attention when I smelled brownies because it was her coming to me. I had never smelled brownies so I was skeptical about it. That was the main message so I left feeling like I wasted my money. I imagined her rolling her eyes at me and laughing at me like she did when she would tell me things and I wouldn't get it.

Chapter 14

The Vortex

In 2003, six months after my mom transitioned to Spirit, I experienced a facilitated "past life regression" surrounded by crystals and stones. I did not experience a past life. I experienced something very different. At the time, I was in a state of heavy grieving. I didn't yet know that my physical body carried a dominate vibration that was dictating my experience. I wasn't aware that I had control over this. The practitioner called the journey a "past life regression", but I did not experience a past life. I did experience moving into a higher frequency within my body, and my mind moved into a state of hypnosis. I had no preconceived ideas about this journey but was hoping to be reconnected with my mom.

 The journey began with a vision of me walking in a woods and I was aware of a man walking beside me, to my right, holding my hand. I looked up to see who the man was and it was Jesus. He walked me to the front door of a little white church and then smiled and the vision ended. I tried to force it to keep going because I believed he was taking me to my mom, but he wasn't. I didn't understand what the vision was about but I loved being with Jesus again.

During the rest of the journey, I was also able to feel my mom briefly and through my higher vibrational state, clear some of my traumas. A big one was the divorce I was seeking from the narcissist. His higher self-came to me and I said my peace and let it go. I did a lot of crying which helped me release the lower vibrations of grief and continue to move into higher vibrational states. I was in this altered state for three hours but it seemed like thirty minutes.

I was told to get up slowly because the energy of the crystals can raise the frequency of my body so much that I can be dizzy and queasy. I did feel dizzy and queasy and this shocked me because I couldn't believe crystals could have that effect on me. I was in a daze and having a difficult time processing reality. I tried to make myself some oatmeal to help my blood sugar because I felt like I was crashing. (I didn't realize at that time that when I would access the Source Field, it would make me feel hungry. This is still the case). I was so loopy I couldn't remember how to make a bowl of oatmeal. I had never experienced this level disconnect from reality before. I have always had a very clear and focused mind. This experience was comical to me and I felt giggly. My vibration was so high everything was funny to me (this also still happens when I get in the higher vibrations. I can't stop laughing at everything). This was my first experience understanding how my vibration affects reality. Although I felt lighter, I also felt exhausted so I went to bed.

Later that night, I started vomiting violently and it lasted for several hours. I remember at one point my grandma offering to take me to the ER if it didn't stop soon. I had no idea why this was happening to me but I know now. The vibration of my physical body had been so low due to my grief, that raising my vibration that quickly was too much for my physical body to process. I was essentially toxic from grief and my body started purging. It had let loose like a damn had burst. I was purging all of those toxic emotions my body had been carrying for a very long time. This process was hellish and I felt like I was dying. However, when it was over, I felt amazing, although I still felt loopy and out of it. I was in a daze but it felt really good. I no longer felt the doom and gloom of the grief. I could feel my mom's love again. I could feel peace.

We had a small family reunion to attend the following day and I was able to pull it together enough to attend but I still felt so out of it. I needing grounding. Back then I didn't know what grounding was. I will never forget sitting on the porch surrounded by family I hadn't seen in years. A relative said "last I heard you got married!" I looked at her confused and said "No, I didn't get married." I noticed a long awkward silence and looked over to see my sister and grandma's faces looking at me as if I had completely lost my mind. I actually had gotten married but I had no memory of it because I had completely cleared that distorted timeline during my journey. It was as if it never existed in my life. The look on their faces snapped me out of my daze and I quickly said "oh yeah, I did get married" then started laughing. My relative looked at me like she was scared and walked away! I couldn't stop laughing! They no doubt thought I should be in a hospital somewhere at this point! But I didn't care! I was so excited about how powerful that healing was for me that I had no memory of it. That was so badass!

I told the woman who did my journey about this and she put me back on the table and covered my body in grounding stones. That shifted my energy and allowed my brain to function with full memories again. This began my love of crystals and stones. I have no doubt of the healing power they carry.

Even after such a powerful journey, I spent the next five years heavily grieving my mom's passing. It didn't matter how much I knew about the world of Spirit; I was not ok without my mom here guiding me like she always had. I knew I would never feel that level of deep unconditional love ever again for the rest of my life. I accepted that I would always feel this grief and I would never be the same. If I wasn't crying on the outside I was crying on the inside. I had entered the world of grief, where those of us who had lost a loved one live. It is another world and I could suddenly feel grief in others that I had had no concept of before.

I learned about a Spiritual retreat center in the mountains of North Carolina. I was told it was a magical place and I just needed to get there. I was told to pay attention to how the energy shifts as I drive up the mountain into the Cherokee National Forest. I learned that it was a special property where the Cherokee took their sick to be healed. This was noted by a historian who published his findings in the Cherokee National Forest Museum. I had no idea what it was about. I had never been to a Spiritual retreat before.

I invited my friend Frieda to go with me. She was the most source connected person I knew. I was going to need her for this experience. Frieda came into my life through my mom. She still enjoys telling the story of how she heard my mom was a psychic and had carried her number in her purse for a year before having the courage to call her. She was battling with her religious programming that "psychics were of the devil."

When she met my mom for the first time it was at a Burger King. They talked for three hours and Frieda said she instantly loved her. This began a powerful Spiritual journey for Frieda coming back into connection with Spirit. I remember my mom calling me after her session with Frieda telling me how amazing she is and how I needed to meet her. I had no idea that Frieda would become one of my deepest loves in my lifetime. She has shined the light for me when I couldn't see and she has always reflected back to me the truth from the Source Field. Our trip to the retreat was going to be one neither of us would ever forget.

It was a nine-hour drive from Indiana. We laughed and talked the entire way and as we started ascending up the mountain, everything felt different. I felt my heart begin to open and I hadn't felt that feeling in a while. Since my mom's passing, I had closed my heart off to survive the grief. I didn't want to feel it anymore and I didn't know how to stop feeling it. As a result, I stopped feeling in general. It was like taking an anti-depressant. I didn't feel the grief but I also couldn't feel the love.

When we arrived, I got out of my car and looked around. This was the place Jesus had brought me in my journey back in 2003. It was the same little white church he had walked me up to five years ago. The owners, or caretakers as they call themselves, get messages from Spirit about those who come to stay. They assist Spirit in guiding the retreat and assisting with healing and activating Spiritual gifts. The message given to me immediately was "You need to stop being angry with religion." I was shocked and I laughed! The truth has that effect on me. When it hits me, it makes me laugh. The truth is a high frequency that really does set us free. I replied "Is that written all over my face?" Religion was a cult as far as I was concerned. It instills fear, especially in children, and they spend their entire lives trying to access God but the fear keeps them from it. Many are trapped in that fear for the rest of their lives unable to break free. Adults can do what they want with their lives. If they want to trap themselves in a cult religion based on fear and control have at it, but I get angry when I see children being abused through fear. Religion psychologically abuses children. I know, it happened to me.

We got settled into our cabin. It overlooked cascading mountain waterfalls. The sound of the rushing water was magical. The feeling I experienced as we were driving up the mountain continued to get stronger. I noticed an intense energy in my chest. It felt like energy spinning around my heart. I felt a peace I hadn't felt since I was a child. I felt that love I experienced while walking on my grandpa's farm as a child talking to God. As much as I tried, I couldn't feel the grief and stress in my head that constantly tormented me. I realized how powerfully I had been stuck in a state of "fight or flight" for so many years. This felt like heaven. Like I had died and I could only feel God again now.

I was so excited about the feelings I was experiencing. I felt like a giddy little kid. I love nature and the forest and this forest felt magical. I could feel my body adapting to the new vibration but I didn't understand any of that yet. I just knew I felt lighter and freer. I was remembering my childhood feelings again. I remembered WHY I always wanted to be in the woods and how I would sit for hours soaking in that pure energy while feeling the miracles in everything…feeling so much love.

I realized later that those short four days were about me re-attuning myself to higher vibrational energy by learning about vortex energy and coming back in resonance with the source field. But I still couldn't put words to it. I was just effortlessly feeling all of the joy. I now had so much energy naturally instead of feeling constantly drained. I was beginning to feel my authentic self again.

I have always had an open mind. My mom was great at showing me how to look at every experience without pre-conditioned ideas or beliefs so I could see what others couldn't see. Frieda understands this too. We not only welcome the supernatural experiences; we co-create with them. We experienced so many amazing things on that trip. There was no denying this other world we played in for a while was very real. We were told that we experienced more than anyone else had because we were open to it.

I was given messages from my mom. She played a song through the veil by The Beatles *"All You Need Is Love"*. It was her favorite Beatles song. That was my mom's "motto". She always reminded me that the only thing that mattered that was real…. was love. I believed her, but I couldn't understand why love wasn't the most powerful thing of all in the world. Love never prevailed in my world. Nothing made sense.

The ground shimmered like glitter from the mica. My mom loved glitter. If someone came into her home in a bad mood, she would quietly get up and go get her glitter. The next thing that happened was a glitter baptism. The unsuspecting person would be picking glitter out of their scalp for the next week! There was always glitter all over her house. We have all laughed about this for many years.

While at the retreat I was brought back into Spirit time. There was no cell signal there so we were encouraged to turn off our electronics and immerse our being in the natural energy of the area.   They had a daily schedule but we were told to use it only as a loose guide to discern through our own connection to Spirit. We were learning how to be guided from within again. We were not to set alarms for the morning prayer meditation.

I wanted to attend every gathering they had. I was soaking it all in so much! But I wasn't a morning person. 7:00am was early for me to wake up on my own. I asked my mom if I was to attend the morning event to wake me. I woke up and looked at the clock and it was 7:10 am! I was sure I had to have missed it as they were always on time! I jumped up and threw on my clothes then headed to the main house.

No one was there. I looked up and saw them walking down the path. They had overslept too! They even said this was rare for them. All of these things were teaching me how Spirit works when we turn it over to them. I wasn't late, I was right on time. Spirit time was easy for me, I wasn't good at linear time either! Teaching Spirit time is one of my favorites at my sanctuary. When we all come back into alignment with the Source Field, we go quantum. We create reality through quantum time.

One night during a channeling, a Native American woman came through for Frieda. It was such a powerful energy and message that I felt the most intense energy building in my body that I had ever experienced. I thought I was going to levitate off of the sofa! Frieda and I were walking back to our cabin in a stunned state! It was expanding our minds and consciousness to be in this high of a vibration. I knew we were never going to be the same.

I woke in the middle of the night to three beings standing over my bed. My entire body was vibrating. When they noticed I was awake they touched me and I was back asleep. I woke up again, this time my body was vibrating even faster. Again, they saw my eyes open and they touched me again to put me back to sleep. The last time I woke, my body was shaking so fiercely I couldn't believe it. It was as if my body was levitating off of the bed in a very high vibration. Again, they put me back to sleep and the next time I woke it was daylight. I shared this experience with the retreat owner and she got a message from Spirit that they were healing my body and clearing all beginnings of disease. That was amazing!!

The last night we were there, Frieda and I were saying goodnight to each other as I closed my eyes. Frieda suddenly said "Jennie! It's time to wake up!" I opened my eyes just in time to see a red and white orb of light shoot past our window like a shooting star! I gasped and sat up asking "what was that?" We both started laughing and agreed it was our grand finale from Spirit!

Remembering all of the magical experiences we had while on this sacred mountain is so beautiful for me. Hearing the Native American drumming while sitting on the waterfall, hearing the flutes and harps through the veil, and seeing the gold flakes in the sky. Frieda has since made her way back to Source but I can still hear her laughing with me about our time there together. As we were leaving, I was told by my mom that I was going to be able to see and hear her through the veil. I was so excited! Jesus had brought me back to her after all.

Chapter 15

Finally Making the Connection!

Shortly after I returned home from playing in heaven, I mean the retreat, my mom woke me up at 3:00 am. She was hovered above me with her face close to mine, looking into my eyes, wearing a huge smile. She said with so much excitement "get up and get a pen and paper". I jumped up and grabbed my supplies and sat down in my son's room ready to talk with her. I could no longer see her but I could hear her. The first thing she said was "Stay in the love vibration. I exist in the love field. Write it on your mirror, post it everywhere to remind you. This is how we stay connected." This reminded me of all of the notes she stuck around her house reminding her of how to stay connected in the Source Field. I recall her telling me that she would be very intentional about keeping her energy connected. I finally understood what she meant! She has mastered her vibration! She would have certain movies playing over and over that she loved and reminded her of what was real, like Mary Poppins! This is why she was able to stay connected to the Source Field no matter what the challenges she faced. She had trained her mind to know the truth existed only through the Source Field and she didn't believe anything that didn't come to her directly from Source. This is why she knew so much about this reality and things that were going to happen. She was in the Source Field, outside of linear time, experiencing the world. She was in the world but not of it!

The second thing she said was "unclench your fists and breath! Push your energy field out. It is contracted. RELAX!" She showed me that because of my trauma response to her death, she wasn't able to reach me. My vibration was too low. She said in order for her to reach me in the lower vibration it was similar to me holding my breath and sitting on the bottom of a swimming pool. We can't do it for long. She explained that being in the vortex energy at the retreat had raised my vibration so she could connect with me easier. But I would have to learn to master holding a higher vibration to make the communication more consistent and clearer over time. I had to practice. She also told me that we can create whatever we want in this reality. She didn't understand that while she was here. She had a difficult time creating reality in the denser frequencies. But she understood now and was going to help me understand so we can co-create physical reality together.

She told me I would be talking to a lot of people and I needed to understand the importance of my state of being. She explained that the most important thing we do is share from our hearts. She said our hearts are the star-gate to our soul. When we open the star-gate and let our soul speak through us, others star-gate responds by opening too and their soul steps forward. She said what I am sharing isn't as important as this undercurrent of energy that happens through me. This is the energy we need more of in our world. We don't need more opinions, beliefs, teachings, etc. Now is the time to center in our hearts and stay there. She told me this is where I will find her. This is where we connect. Where we all truly connect. This conversation was so powerful for me as when we open our star-gate, we can't easily close it without feeling off of our path. When our star gate is open, we are boldly being guided in every moment. There is no fear, but there is wisdom. In no way is it a free for all! We are working through higher intelligence, and expanded consciousness. Our minds must be integrated into it. I told my mind thank you for protecting me all of those years but it is time to relax! Let go! I no longer needed its protection. I needed it to do a more important job, that of articulating the voice of Spirit: translating Light Language through my heart star gate.

We talked for three hours that morning. I didn't want to let her go. I missed her so deeply. I felt so much love, joy, peace, and understanding after being with her again. Everything was going to be ok. I found my way back to her. She told me she didn't want to let me go either but she was always there, I just needed to raise my vibration and feel her love to connect with her. She told me to make time to connect with her like this every day. She told me to write the words "Stay in the love" on my mirror and read it everyday. So I did.

I put the writing from our time together next to my bed and went to sleep. When I woke, I had several messages from my boyfriend asking me what happened last night. He said he saw my mom's writing next to my bed. He asked if I was up reading her old writings again. He asked me if I was making pancakes early in the morning because he said when he woke up the entire house smelled like pancakes. I told him I was not making pancakes; it must have been her smell. I told him what had happened, and that I had written that not her. He said it looked just like my mom's writing. I looked at it again and it did. It looked nothing like my writing. My son woke up and said he smelled pancakes too. I never smelled it but I know it was her letting me know she was there with me, just in case I went into doubt.

My busy life with a full-time job, toddler, and teenager distracted me and I found myself disconnected from my connection with her. But this disconnect was not the same as before. I realized I could never go back to that lower vibrational place within me for long. Something had permanently healed and shifted. I had a new conscious awareness and I couldn't unlearn the things I understood now. I had higher clarity. I could feel her with me constantly now.

One day while cooking crab legs, I felt her standing behind me. It was so strong I felt like I was going to see her if I turned around. I turned around slowly so I could hold the feeling but I couldn't see her. I could only feel her. My boyfriend walked down the stairs and said "are you making brownies?" I smiled and said "No, I'm making crab legs!" Those are completely different smells. Once again, she let me know it really was her and that she really does love brownies that much.

There was a lot of love poured into Chloe after we lost my mom. But she seemed to be doing better than all of us. I realized my mom chose to leave at the perfect time. She had gotten her through her formative years, yet she wasn't old enough to be disconnected from the Source field. She knew Chloe was connected enough to see and hear her so she would be able to let her know she was ok. I wanted to make sure Chloe stayed connected to my mom. I couldn't wait to take her to experience the retreat. She was ten years old now and was still that magical little Pisces, like me and my mom. Even the owners of the retreat were both Pisces. It would be a magical Pisces party! On our way up the mountain Chloe could feel the energy. I told her to set her intention for what she wanted to experience, because vortex energy is intention based. There would be instant manifestations! She said she wanted to know the name of her angel. I said "ok, then you will know!". When we arrived Chloe's magical imagination was in overdrive! She started seeing heart shapes everywhere. She said "Look, even the clover is heart shaped". She was right, I hadn't noticed that many heart shapes there before. It really became absurd the number of hearts we encountered everywhere we went. Even her slice of watermelon was in the shape of a heart.

We spent the day playing in the waterfall. We walked all the way down the thirteen waterfalls and found waterslides and swimming holes that were so much fun. It felt like I was a kid again playing in the creeks at my grandpa's farm. I loved being in the water. I remember for my 7th birthday my mom threw me a party and she could tell I wasn't having fun so she put all of the kids in the car and took us to the creek to play. When the parents came to pick up their kids they were wet and muddy. They weren't allowed to come to my house again. But that day was one of the happiest days of my life and I know those kids felt the same way. It was magical and so was this experience. I felt like God/Source was playing through us, feeling every bit of its own creation and filled with Joy.

If you listen you can hear what sounds like Native American flutes and drumming. There is a rock named "changing rock" that looks like a completely different face every time you come back to see it. I saw a clear face of a Native American and the next time I came it had turned into a gray alien. The rules of reality don't apply in this energy. It's a completely different reality and the rules of the lower vibrational reality are not valid. As I was walking in the water looking at the stones, I saw something silver and shiny. I pulled out a large metal spoon. I showed Chloe and we both laughed. I threw it back in the water.

As we were leaving, we picked a rock from a bowl. Chloe closed her eyes and pulled out a rock in the perfect shape of a heart. We all laughed. It was the perfect ending to a magical experience. As we headed down the mountain Chloe said "I still don't know who my angel is." I told her she would be told when it is perfect timing. I knew it was mom but she needed to be shown directly. She asked me "who is your angel?" I told her about Silver Spoon. She said "and you found a silver spoon in the water" I couldn't believe I hadn't caught that sign! Of course, that was Silver Spoon letting me know he is with me. The entire trip was about our guides! He was my first Spirit guide! I couldn't believe I threw the spoon back in the water! I turned the car around and went back. I jumped in the water and grabbed it and headed home. The silver spoon still sits on my shelf next to my mom's baby shoes.

We arrived at my family's house to stay the night in Tennessee before we headed back to Indiana. There was a knock at the door that night. It was a surprise visit from another family member who stopped by to give Chloe a gift before we went home. No one knew about the hearts Chloe had experienced on that mountain. The gift was a heart shaped crystal. The message Chloe received as the stone was placed in her hand was "Grandma Kitti told me to bring this to you." I laughed out loud! She received her answer.

I was so excited to share the experience of retreat with my family and friends so I have taken others there every chance I could

Chapter 16

My Birthday Party With My Mom And Jesus

On February 20, 2009 I was going to the retreat alone. It was my birthday and I was told it was going to be a celebration between me, my mom, and Jesus. I had never done anything like this alone and wasn't sure if I would enjoy it the same as I did with others.

When I arrived, I stayed in the smaller cabin because I was by myself. The energy of this space was different. It felt like I was sitting in the lap of God, being held and showered with love. A message was given to me when I arrived. Jesus had come through before my arrival and said I was one of the healers with him when he was on earth. He gave me a vision of him putting his hand on my head saying "go do my work". I had not shared much about my communications with Jesus. He had brought me to this place and he was now giving me direct messages. I recalled the last time I was here. I had attended The Quiet Hour meditation where they receive messages from the Holy Spirit. They explained that the Holy Spirit speaks to everyone in a unique way. When they call the Holy Spirit to speak through them for a message, it typically comes through one person, but to be open to it coming through you as well. If the Holy Spirit intends to speak through you, you will hear your name called three times. I was standing on the bridge with my eyes closed when I heard my name. I opened my eyes and thought my mind was playing tricks on me. I heard it again. I opened my eyes again, as if I thought I'm going to see the Holy Spirit looking at me in confirmation? Funny how my mind works sometimes! The third time I heard it loud and clear "Jennie speak my words", I opened my eyes to see the small voice recorder next to my mouth. They were told the message was coming through me! I got so freaked out I said "wait no!", and they pulled the recorder back. I felt like I had dodged a bullet! That was terrifying! But that actually happened. What in the world? I can't channel the Holy Spirit! But wait, didn't I just clearly hear those words? "Walk with me Jesus!" I'm not ready for this!

There is a bible in all the cabins and I was told to read his words in red. Specifically John 14-15. It had been a long time since I had opened a Bible. However, I felt this was part of me bringing myself back to a closer connection to him. When I opened the Bible, I opened right to John 14-15 and I felt a hand on the top of my head. I read the chapters and when I closed the book, the hand was gone from my head. The next morning, I opened the Bible again and the hand was back on my head. It felt as though I was being given information as I read it. Like Jesus was reading with me and clarifying the information as I went along. I was told the Bible exists in multiple dimensions. Our own vibration determines which vibration of the Bible we will connect with. I take it to mean that the Bible, like everything else in the distorted reality, is also distorted. If we want to experience the truth in it we have to read it while we are aligned with the Source Field.

I was also told I should read the book on the bedside table, The Shack. I began reading shortly after I arrived and six hours later, I was finished. I didn't put it down until I had read every word, crying the entire time. The book transported me into the Source Field. I could feel layers upon layer of trauma falling away from my heart. I had no idea I had built Fort Knox around my heart. I believed I was a completely heart open person. Turns out this is kind of an endless job in this reality. Keeping our hearts clear and purified as we go along.

I was once again given a life review. This time it was about the trauma that had happened to our family. The trauma happened to my older sister when she was five. It was connected to our church and crimes committed by a family friend and Deacon of our church. All of us experienced this trauma differently. But it changed the course of all of our lives. During the life review, I experienced the trauma through my mom's eyes, then my dad's, then my sister's. I literally became each one of them for that moment in time. My mom explained that although it affected me indirectly. I was only four years old when it happened and I was five when it was brought to light. I had no idea how deeply this had impacted our family. My mom told me it would help me understand how the timeline played out and facilitate my own healing.

My parents became very protective of my sister after this incident. There was so much guilt associated with it and they never got over it. Therefore, my sister was rarely held accountable for her actions and I took the brunt of it. That's as far as I'm going to go into this because it gets too personal, but that life review was powerful and freeing for me. I understood things that I had not before. A part of me was stuck in victim consciousness as a result of this situation and I now understood the things that happened in our family as a result of this trauma were not personal to me. It was simply deep trauma programs running that weren't able to be easily healed. This allowed me to forgive my family.

My mom also clarified for me the day she came out of her coma to talk to everyone before she died, when I wasn't there. She told me if she wanted me to be there, I would have. All things surrounding the death process are divinely orchestrated. She said she had already spoken to me before everyone arrived. She had told me more than she had told anyone else. I didn't realize she had not told anyone that she was going to the other side. She didn't tell anyone else that she had a contract to work through them from the other side of the veil. She told me the messages she gave everyone else that day were not for me. She knew I would do everything I could to keep the family together. She knew that they would not. That was not my burden to carry. But I was told what she said and I carried it anyway. I was tormented by the fact that I could not hold our family together the way she did. I felt I had to do that for her but I couldn't and I felt so deeply saddened when we split up. It was her last dying wish and I couldn't honor it for her. She laughed and told me that was never meant for me. What a duh moment, and a relief! It is amazing how lower emotions and fear can get us all tied up in things that aren't meant for our journey.

I realized I had aspects of me that were stuck on distorted timelines because of unhealed trauma. My four-year-old was stuck because I had decided at that age that I was not good enough and I didn't like myself. Thus, I created another version of myself to replace her. This was the year my sister experienced her trauma and I had also experienced it through her. She became mean and I was the closest person for her to take it out on. Plus, I was the little sister. She was never that fond of my arrival into the world in her life in the first place. I saw lots of photos of her smiling until I came along, then she was frowning and giving me dirty looks. Normal sibling rivalry stuff, but after the trauma, she was much worse. In fact, I learned much later that there was another entity that was creating the conflicts and loosh* between us. This is connected to the shadows and dark entities we experienced messing with us over the years. I was finally able to connect these dots. The false self I began developing at the age of four only got strong as I got older. Because of my mom I was able to stay more connected to my authentic self than most people are, I still had to figure out how to dissolve the false self I had created and relied on for so many years for protection.

There was another aspect of me that had not gone forward with me. My twenty-nine-year-old aspect was still stuck in deep grief over my mom's death and was still at the house I was living in when my mom died. I had since moved, but I had a reoccurring dream that I would return to that house and all of my stuff was still there. I knew I had moved it, but I would start loading it into my car again. I had to go get her and integrate her back into my heart.

My mom told me to dance with her. We danced for a long time in the cabin and I could feel my vibration getting higher and higher. As my vibration increased, I could feel my heart opening more and more. Disconnecting from our hearts is the opposite of what is required of us on our journey. When we disconnect from our hearts, we only cut ourselves off from the source field and our authentic selves. I thought I was protecting myself from being hurt, but I was only keeping myself from authentic love. We cannot close our hearts off to another person without closing our hearts off to ourselves.

I cried so deeply as so many parts of me that no longer served my journey going forward were leaving me. I could feel my own heart more and more and I felt so much joy and gratitude. I was transmuting trauma and illusions through the Source Field. I could feel the higher truth in everything and it was dissolving all things that were not in alignment with it within me. When I was finished dancing and crying, I stood in the cabin, feeling my mom and Jesus stronger than ever. But they weren't the only ones I could feel. I could also feel myself. I hadn't felt my own authentic energy this clear since I was a child. It felt like my best friend was back but I hadn't realized she was gone. I was going to need her for the next level of my journey.

This was the best birthday gift I had every received…. MYSELF!

Chapter 17

The Integration and Mastery of My Two Minds

Activating Our Trinity of Inter-dimensionality:
Source Heart, Source Mind, Source Eyes

Although the following information might seem to go ahead of the information following it, I'm adding this chapter next because throughout the rest of the book I will be referencing these concepts and terms. You will need to have a basic understanding of them in order to further process the new information that will be presented. At any point, when reading further you can always return to this chapter if needed for clarification or reference the definitions in the back of the book.

As my mom began teaching me how to develop my ability to connect with her, she explained, in a very simplistic way that I could easily understand.   Our physical body plays a role in our inter-dimensional abilities as they are inter-dimensional by design. Our essence or higher self, that exists in higher frequency states in the Source Field, aspects itself to enter a physical body. She calls the aspect of us that is in our physical body <u>our Soul</u> and she calls our essence self/ higher self <u>our Spirit</u>. It is only a small part of our essence that is having the physical experience directly. Yet, this small part of our Spirit is uploading everything in real time to its higher self. Our essence self can choose to feel everything its aspect does, at any time. For Spirit, everything is a matter of focus.

Our physical avatars were created through Source perfection, allowing Spirit to maintain its connection and power over its aspected self while it is having the physical experience. Spirit was able to pilot the physical journey it embarked upon, effortlessly. Our Spirit aspect was not limited within its body. It existed within its physical vessel while staying in conscious awareness of its essence self at all times. This communication was done through light language. Light Language is the most perfect and profound form of communication that I have ever experienced. Light Language is like getting to experience everything in real time as if it is happening to you in that moment, feelings and all. Even if it happened in the past according to linear time, it can be experienced again in the now moment.

Spirit is omnipotent, meaning it can be in multiple places at once because it exists outside of the limitations of linear time. This allows its experience to be dependent of its chosen point of focus in every new, now moment. It's like watching reality TV in real time but getting to be the characters, feeling what they feel and knowing what they are thinking!

When Spirit interacts with other Spirits in the higher dimensional realities, they connect through osmosis. The exchange is pure, transparent, clear and deeply felt. The higher intelligence Light Language knows exactly how to adjust itself to make the most perfect connection between Spirits. In the slower physical reality, the varying vibrational states of being create glitches in the connection between us and it is more difficult to feel and hear each other clearly. The barriers in communication that we experience in the physical reality, do not exist in the higher dimensions of Light Language communication.

At some point this changed. The aspect within the body was disconnected from its essence self. It is as if our essence aspect is now dormant within our physical vessel and no longer acting as a direct phone line to our higher self. There are multiple layers to understand about why and how our soul aspect and Spirit are no longer in synch and communication with each other. For purposes of simplicity, my mom explained that it is a result of our vibration becoming too low. The discrepancy between the vibration of our physical body and our higher self is too wide for us to be able to stay in communication. Correcting this difference in vibration is the answer to re-activating our natural ability to inter-dimensionally communicate. Spirit can lower their vibration only so much to try to meet us at a better vibrational match. We must always raise our frequency to assist with our own vibrations being a better match to facilitate an exchange of Light Language communication.

Before we dipped too far down into slower density, it was much easier for the aspect to hold a higher vibrational state of being and for the Spirit to experience itself while in the physical reality. It was a very different experience for the aspect of our essence self to be in an incredibly interconnected system within the physical vessel that existed in a state of connection to Source at all times. The bible calls this slowing of our vibration "The fall". Spirit says it was our fall into slow vibration.

It isn't that we are no longer inter-dimensional light language translators. It is just that we are no longer easily accessing that part of us due to our vibration being so much slower that the higher dimensions as well as the vibration of Light Language. Quantum physics discovered that everything in the physical body from our cells, DNA, brain, heart, pineal gland, and many more parts of us have inter-dimensional abilities. It is as if our inter-dimensional parts are always existing in connection to other dimensional realities but we have lost our awareness of this connection.

The simplest part of this trinity is our higher, heart Stargate. It literally acts like a Stargate portal to Source when we are able to activate Source Love feelings within our physical body. The easiest way to activate this is through a memory of that feeling we shared with someone we loved deeply. This is the way our human avatars feel, through the experience. Feeling this love can be a challenge for us in the distorted dimensions. Even though we loved someone we typically also experienced trauma with those we love the most. The beautiful thing about that is, Love is much more powerful than the fear that trauma created in us. Moving into relaxed states will assist with Spirit coming into our energy field and connecting with us through our heart. Feeling their love is step one in being connected in the Source field. If you can feel true authentic LOVE, you are in Source.

My mom explained that we have a lower brain and a higher mind (her words) and they are two very different things. Each plays a vital role in our ability to activate our connecting to the Source Field. One cannot exist without the other when it comes to our physical bodies being inter-dimensional. My higher mind is always connected to Source and in order for me to experience Source, I simply have to turn my attention to my higher mind. My attention seemed to be hyper focused in my lower brain most of the time, rather than my higher mind. Once my mom and I established our connection, and it continued through my dedication and practice, I found myself feeling disconnected from her less and less. Even in the moments when I felt I was not connected, I still was, because an integration between my higher mind and lower brain began to happen naturally. It was as if this organic flow was occurring without me having to think about it. In the times when I felt afraid, stressed, or disconnected, I could still feel her remind me (and she still does) to turn my attention back to my higher mind where she is able to be in stronger and clearer in connection with me.

My higher mind is one with Source and exists in quantum time. My lower brain is like a computer interface between my higher mind and the physical reality. It records reality, but is not capable of being in the Source field. It the artificial part of my physical body and it exists only in linear time.

At the time she was showing me how this all worked within my mind, I didn't have medical terms to describe it. But one day, I was talking to my friend who is trained in Cranial Sacral Therapy by John Upledger, MD. I was explaining this to her and she got out John Upledger's book and read to me his explanation, that matched exactly what mom was explaining to me. It was very helpful for me to have this information from Dr. Upledger and I feel it will be beneficial for you and others as well.

I highly recommend reading his book "Cell Talk" because I can only pull pieces of it out to share here. It is full of great information about the higher intelligence of our physical bodies. He says:
"The centrum is a small pyramid shaped structure located in the center of the brain…The majority of its work is done by the use of energy connections… It receives energy from God and the cosmos via circular antennae that are situated about 4 inches above the top of the head. The information received by these antennae is focused through the crown chakra, the highest part in the center of the head…information is transmitted in the form of energy…it is directly connected to God or the cosmos, and therefore is all-knowing…If we

trust and believe in the centrum, it will always respond to requests for help in Spiritual and earthly issues…The centrum and the ego seem to be in constant conflict. The centrum is constantly working to control the ego, while the ego is attempting to disable the centrum. The centrum is negatively affected by guilt and shame. The ego uses guilt and shame as tools to disable the centrum…The centrum advocates relaxation as a time of healing. The deeper the relaxed state, the more effective the healing…the centrum repeatedly tells us to pay attention to the big picture. When we do this, relaxation comes easily and healing is done for you. You do not have to do it. The centrum tries constantly to promote cooperation between all brain parts. In order to get each part to see the big picture…"

After reading this, it was clear to me that the centrum is our higher mind connected to Source that my mom taught me about. Now let's look at what John Upledger has to say about the "Amygdala" in Cell Talk.

The Amygdala *"receives incoming information about problems and crises. They then decide which brain areas should be activated in order to initiate survival responses…The amygdala stores holographic images that may be connected to, and stimulated by, sensory input from the eyes, ears, taste buds, nose and skin. Most of these stored images are used to recall experiences that required survival skills at that time. Since those skills were used successfully in the past, they will be presented for use again by the amygdala when similar situations occur. These survival skills may be subject to some modification or adaption, but the amygdala finds it somewhat difficult to change what has worked in the past. You might say that old amygdalae habits die hard. The Amygdala are involved in the sense of time and its proper use…they help you stay in touch with your 'self'*

...and everyone, including neurologists, psychologists, and psychiatrists and the amygdala themselves, seem to agree that the recognition of yourself, even in a mirror, depends upon good amygdala function."

He goes on to say that the amygdala records our experiences even if we are having them while unconscious or under anesthetic.

"Somehow, the amygdala will retain total recall of the incident and emotions that accompanied it. Fear is often retained in the amygdala..."

My mom explained further that the amygdala and centrum are in disagreement about which reality is real, the linear reality or the Source reality. They must be integrated and re-establish their original blue print of working together. The centrum is always trying to work through the ego, while the ego is focused on protecting us from the information coming from the centrum and Source that it doesn't understand. The amygdala is like the computer interface between Source and the physical reality. Computers or artificial intelligence are not able to think. They can upgrade themselves through information and past experience. This is the way our amygdala learns, adapts and operates in the physical reality in a state of subject reality and truth. The centrum, however, is constantly in a state of downloading absolute truth from the Source Field. When these two-stop arguing and synch up-the flow from Source moves through the centrum into the amygdala and can be experienced in the physical reality. The centrum cannot bring the information into the physical the same way the amygdala cannot access Source. They need each other.

On the distorted timelines, meditation is not about integrating our God mind with our human brain. It was focused on controlling the human brain and shutting it up. Which is impossible. Telling it where to focus to get its information brings it back into alignment with its original blueprint. The amygdala is really great at this job. It is as if it was programmed for this from the beginning and once it is brought back to it, it is relieved to be doing what it does best, articulate Light Language from Source. I have so much gratitude and love for this process that was provided to us through our physical avatars to work perfectly for our physical journey guided by Source.

The pineal gland is also called the "third eye" because, it is located in the center of the brain and it is connected to Living Light. Spirit calls it our "God eye". My personal experience of activating it within my own mind is a beautiful one. Through my Journey's to Heaven with my mom, I developed my third eye site. I can now close my eyes and see higher vibrational realities and Spirits. This is very natural for us and I've found everyone's third eye is active although they may not realize it.

Below is a channeled healing for you to access now through the quantum Source field if you desire. We desire to assist with the great awakening through activating your pineal gland or third eye.

"As we join you in this beautiful moment of healing, we offer you our highest vibration to bring clarity to your question. The ultimate healing occurs when we connect with higher truth and dissolve all distorted beliefs that have created suffering. This is what we intend to assist you with today. Because there are many of you here today, all on different paths with varied states of consciousness, we will speak in more general terms.
As you each center your focus into expanded states of consciousness, what we call the Source Field, with the intention to access higher knowledge and healing, you are opening your higher heart and mind

to receive. This is a very powerful state to be in and we are always eager to join you to assist in your awakening. As above so below. Observe how we assist you so you can then assist others in a similar way.

We encourage you to continue to move into this healing space often with us. With each new experience you have while in this space, you will continue to receive deeper individual understanding about your questions.

First let's bring clarity to the "great awakening". From our perspective, we see those on a Spiritual path seeking higher truth are in a continuous state of growth and expansion. It is a natural part of the process for all of us. This is a choice that is made between the individual in unity with their higher self, as well as source love that exists in all things. However, we each play a role in the rate we collectively expand in conscious awareness together (great awakening).

The more we expand our own consciousness the more opportunity is created, through us, for others to experience what that looks and feels like as well. They can then choose to follow a similar path, or not. At some point we all choose to come back to source, so there is no judgment. Humanity is now being called back to connection with source in a powerful way. So many are feeling this call and this will continue to intensify.

Our own state of awareness has the potential to offer more vibrational state of being with us. If not, they will most likely only hear and see us through their own distorted frequency, which will distort our message. We say "us" because we experience the same *distortion when communicating with those in the lower density vibrations.*

It is possible to clear this distorted connection. We offer opportunities for you to connect more clearly with us by assisting you in raising your vibration to join us in a higher state. This is most easily done through activating a strong heart field connection through the feeling of love. Laughter is another way to bring our fields into better resonance with each other. From there we can hear each other more clearly and offer our higher vibration in a way you can feel through a frequency of love and peace. Again, we lead by example so that you can understand how to do the same.

Assisting others is best done while accessing source field guidance to prevent falling back into a distorted interaction. Remember distortion exists in the fight or flight part of the mind. Conversations that are done through that energy do not contribute to accessing expanded states of awareness. The lighter and more relaxed the interaction the more our energy flows with source for higher clarity. The more your energy fields will connect and flow naturally.

What you call your third eye or pineal gland, is just one of several inter-dimensional parts of your physical body. It provides an ability for you to see beyond the veil while in your physical form. It allows you to see into the different multi-dimensions of realties. For instance, you can see us in your energy field assisting you today. Everyone is accessing different levels of third eye sight. Most see colors when they close their eyes. That is the vibration in your field. Many don't understand what they are seeing and why. But making note of what comes through your intention to activate your third eye can help.

Your inability to see clearly into other realties occurred over a long span of time. It happened as a result of humans choosing not to use these multi-dimensional parts of themselves in order to fully immerse themselves in a very dense, real physical experience. The physical eyes became your dominant way to see and most can only see the physical reality you are currently existing in. So your inter dimensional eyes became dormant. For those who wish to re-activate the abilities of their inter dimensional eyes, we suggest spending time with your physical eyes closed so you are not distracted by what your physical eyes see and perceive. Allow your imagination to be activated as well because that is also an inter dimensional aspect of you. The same way you would relax to fall asleep. Allow your mind to relax and notice what images or colors flow through your awareness. The colors we see through our third eye represent the vibration we are connecting with in that moment. Including which dimension you are vibrationally matching with and which beings are assisting you from the Spirit world.

We recommend observing nature for guidance back to your natural self. For example, puppies are born with their eyes closed. They can't see for a couple of weeks. But they learn to see with their third eye. They develop this ability early and have a "sixth sense" throughout their lives.

Activating your third eye will allow you to receive guidance through symbols and images that flash in front of you with your eyes closed. It will help you discern between different realities. You can travel to different dimensions through your consciousness and your third eye will allow you to witness it.

For instance, if you see the color blue through your third eye, look for the meaning of it. If you had a specific question how does the symbolism assist you with clarity?

"The color blue represents both the sky and the sea and is associated with open spaces, freedom, intuition, imagination, inspiration, and sensitivity. Blue also represents meanings of **depth, trust, loyalty, sincerity, wisdom, confidence, stability, faith, and intelligence**."

Ultimately, it is not required that your third eye be activated in order for you to be of help with the great awakening. All things done through a vibration of love are transformative. But it can certainly help with your own clarity.

It can be quite an adjustment to be able to see beyond this reality. Especially as you are learning to master it once it has been activated. So, remember to do all things through your higher heart and higher mind. The intention is not just experiencing an active third eye but to gain higher truth clarity through the higher dimensional realities to assist with the great awakening.

We are all assisting with the great remembering! It's a wonderful journey to be on together.

Thank you for the opportunity to share our guidance with you! The healing we all experience in this space together is beautiful and sacred!

Through Sacred Sight,

Breath of Life

If I am having trouble connecting to Source my mom will remind me to use my breath. I take a deep breath in and imagine Source Living Light coming into every cell of my body, pushing itself out around my body and filling my energy field full of Living Light. I exhale all distorted frequencies out of my body and field. I can feel my amygdala relax immediately.

Doing this several times worked miraculously for me to suddenly find myself hearing, seeing and feeling Spirit in my field. This is how using our breath to connect to Source is affective for me.

Unlike in meditation, where we are taught to simply observe our breath without changing it, breath-work is the practice of consciously manipulating our breath for a period of time to calm the mind, release emotions and heal from trauma.

Explaining what happens inside your mind during breath-work feels like trying to describe a psychedelic experience to someone who has never done drugs. You can detail the physical sensations and the visuals, but the feeling of unity and the personal insights are much harder to translate. At times, breath-work can feel exactly like tripping on mushrooms or LSD, and that's just the tip of it.

Since then, more studies have shown that different types of breath-work can help treat depression, addiction and PTSD. There is also ongoing research into the theory that breath-work releases DMT, a psychedelic chemical substance that is naturally found in several plants and animals, including humans.

How does our breath assist with connecting to source? Through the release of DMT. We know that DMT is produced naturally in our brain and affects our perception of reality. It also facilitates psychedelic experiences in larger doses that open us to higher dimensions of Source.

DMT activates the centrum part of our brain and allows Living Light to begin streaming into our body. It connects with the Living Light that has been activated in our body and Light Language is activated. We upgrade our physical body through this process by assisting ourselves in accessing and adapting to more Living Light.

Activating our Light Body or Energy Body

Our energy field serves many purposes and one is protection. People often ask me if I am afraid of connecting with lower entities and I am not. This is because I use my energy field as a shield. When I intend Living Light into my physical body and energy field, it acts as a higher vibration of pure God Light that does not allow in anything of a lower vibration. Any being that comes into my field must be of a vibrational match or higher. If lower vibrations come into my field they do so to be alkalized and transmuted through my higher vibration. Light and distorted vibrations aren't a match and can't be in the same place at the same time. Therefore, one of us has to shift. I can only shift for higher vibrational beings, not lower ones. The Living Light that surrounds my body goes one step ahead of me when I move through the physical world. I command it to transmute all distorted energies as I go. I am able to witness what my field does when others encounter it. They behave differently and feel lighter. Sometimes they run the other direction! Mastering our energy field is important for daily life as well as our communication with Spirit. But never does this replace the importance of listening to our gatekeepers, who are our eyes and ears for the unseen realms.

Chapter 18

Surrogate Into Source

It was 2011 and I had met a beautiful healer from Asia who facilitated plant medicine journeys. I had never experienced plant medicine and was not open to "drugs" of any kind. Funny how programmed I was looking back at myself then. Just like most of us, we were programmed to believe all kinds of things that are simply not true. When I was asked to participate in this journey I immediately said "No, I have children and I can't risk something happening to me. I don't take any drugs." (I have since learned the difference between nature and synthetics). She smiled and said, "Let's not bring fear into this. Go home and ask your mom and let me know tomorrow if you would like to join us." I realized in that moment that she was right. I was afraid. But this fear wasn't coming from my own experience. It was a program. Back then I didn't understand fear programs but I did recognize that it wasn't connected to my own personal experience. It was connected to a belief I had taken on from someone else. When I asked mom if I should experience the journey, I received a clear "Yes!". I was excited and nervous at the same time. I was told to focus on an intention for the journey. My intention was to see beyond all illusions in this realty. Yikes, that was a big intention for my first journey but I figured that out after the fact; which is how I do most things in my life.

We started at sundown at a beautiful property by the river. We sat in a group by the fire and were given a piece of chocolate shaped as a heart wrapped in purple foil with the word "love" written on it. What could possibly go wrong with that? We ate it and waited. My husband at the time was with me and about thirty minutes later he started giggling under his breath. He never does that so I was excited to see his reaction to the medicine. It seemed to raise his vibration and he couldn't stop laughing about it. I closed my eyes and began to see flashes of sacred geometry. It was very subtle at first. I barely noticed, as it came in stronger with more vivid flashes. It was as if they were communicating with me.

I looked up at the sky and the cloud turned into a heart. I knew it was my mom! I got so excited I jumped up and ran over to the lake so I could see the sky more clearly. The cloud then turned into a bird. My husband walked up behind me smiling. I told him about the clouds and he said "yes I saw it". I said "Wait, you saw the same thing I saw? How can that be?" I know this did not happen on the 3d timeline, no one else could have seen it. Unless we both moved into the source field together. Our vibrations had increased so much we could hear each other's thoughts. We had become telepathic.

I could also feel and hear the essence of the woman who provided us with the medicine. She told me that she felt called to bring this experience to us and it was her gift to humanity. She was such a beautiful Spirit and I felt so much love within our connection. I understood her intentions clearly and was so grateful for her gift to me.

Everything looked completely different through the medicine. My third eye was wide open. I felt like a little kid in a magical forest interacting with the consciousness of nature in the way I had as a child. This was real! It was more real than the reality I had existed in most of my life. I could see the sacred geometry in all of nature. The trees were conscious beings! They were aware of us and they were offering us their higher vibration out of their love for us. This was the highest vibration I had ever experienced in my life. It was incredible! I walked up to a tree and wanted to hug it, but I stopped and asked it permission. I realized it was no different than us. We don't invade another person's space without permission and we shouldn't do that with nature either! We are the same! I had no fear of anything. I felt like I was walking on earth with my consciousness in heaven. I could look at a person and see right through them. There were no secrets. This was a vibration of transparency. I laid on the grass with my husband laughing at how amazing it all was. Why was I afraid to experience this? Who told me this was bad for me? I was so irritated that I had allowed myself to believe the lies we have been told to keep us from becoming our higher consciousness selves.

I noticed several shadow beings standing in a circle around us. One stood very close to me on my right. I asked who they were but no-one else seemed to know they were there. I didn't feel afraid of them, but I was aware they were watching us. I tried talking to one and he didn't talk back to me. I also saw a spiderweb net around the earth. I could feel that it was not a good thing. When I tuned into it, it was like a control grid. It was lit up, glowing white, and covered the entire sky. I felt like I was trapped inside this large web.

As the medicine got stronger, it settled into the deepest parts of me and I started to leave my body. It was natural for me to float in and out. One minute I would be in my body the next minute my consciousness would be focused somewhere else and I'd be gone. I wasn't controlling it, it just happened. I suddenly found myself way out of my body floating in a dark field of pure creative energy. It was everything and nothing at the same time. It wasn't a frequency of love; it was beyond what we humans understand as love. It was everything that has ever existed and everything that hasn't yet existed. I later realized this place I was in is referred to as the *void**.

I looked back at myself and I could see that I was immersed in a state of illusion. It was as if I was walking around in an illusionary bubble of my own making. I was creating every experience I had but I didn't know I was creating it. I thought it was being created outside of me. I could see my higher self-hovering outside of my physical body, unable to connect with me. I could see my higher self-trying to reach me. I could see all of my friends and family together in our essence form in the higher realities. We were "zinging" our aspects here on earth trying to get our aspects to wake up out of the illusions. I was wondering why I was stuck in such a powerful state of illusion and how I was going to get out of it.

I asked the question in my mind and I got a reply. "What else would you rather be doing?". I thought "Well I don't want to be doing that, it's embarrassing. She thinks she knows stuff but she doesn't know anything. I am concerned her brain is going to short circuit from too much information right now. I don't know if she can handle it. We might see smoke coming out of her ears!" I couldn't stop laughing because I was fully immersed in higher truth and the human illusions are hysterical. I said "I don't want to do this anymore". The response was "the only reason your illusional creation continues to exist is because you continue to give your energy and permission for it." "Wait what? You mean all I have to do is pull my energy back from it and no longer give my permission for it to continue and it disappears?" "Yes". "Does it also end for my children? I can't leave them the way my mom left me." No reply.

Then things started getting difficult. Apparently, I was preparing for my descent back into my body. I was having a conversation with several beings who were trying to help me let go of my distorted timeline. But I couldn't let go. I was so worried about my kids. I felt I had been trapped in a reality of illusions. I felt so sad to leave the higher dimension. As I came back into my body, I felt devastated. I couldn't talk. I couldn't connect with anyone or anything in this reality. It felt so off and strange. I clearly needed to get further clarity because I felt I was more confused than ever about the truth of our reality.

I saw the grid in the sky slowly disappear. I knew I was falling back asleep and wouldn't be able to see the magic anymore. How was I going to function in this world now? After the journey we all gathered in a group to share our experience. When I shared mine, it was quiet. The facilitator of the group said to me "Jennie, you always go ahead of yourself."

After my journey, my mind was in an expanded state of awareness. I was able to feel, see and know things I hadn't before. My five-year-old son was born without the same veils as most humans. He could see and interact with Spirit and often shared about seeing himself asleep in his bed while he was floating on the ceiling. He was sleeping next to me and I woke in the middle of the night to see a form hovered above his stomach area. It was in the form of sacred geometry and was moving. I was aware it was conscious. It was interacting with me. I knew it was my son's Spirit. It was the most beautiful thing I have ever seen in my life. I wish I could have captured a photo of it. As I was staring at it in awe and disbelief, I heard my mom say "you have seen this thousands of times, this is the first time your mind is open enough to remember it". She explained that I was seeing his essence. Many are not able to see Spirit in their essence form because it is outside of what our minds are programmed to understand. Seeing this form was a sign that I had expanded my consciousness to the point of accessing and experiencing the essence of Spirit.

After that experience, I was told I needed to watch the movie "*The Nines*". My husband and I watched it and I couldn't believe what I was seeing. It was so similar to what I was shown during my journey! It helped me connect some of the dots but I felt I needed another journey to get more answers. A month later I did another journey. This time I had a quantum journey practitioner guide me through to get answers. It was the most amazing experience! I highly recommend using plant medicine in this way. It was much more beneficial when using the medicine to get higher clarity.

This time I was visited by ET's. They were standing at the end of the massage table that I was laying upon. At first, I was startled and nervous. This was my first encounter with beings like this. They told me to get the scary alien image out of my head because that is not what they look like. That made me laugh and it lightened the energy. They slowly began to take the form of tall, thin, bald people. Possibly bluer in color but I don't strongly recall the actual color of their skin. They explained that they are a higher aspect of us. "We are you and you are us. We are answering your call to awaken to the truth about your reality. You have chosen to know." I had definitely asked for this. I just didn't expect the answers to come in this way!

They told me they exist in a parallel, less dense dimension next to us on earth. They said they had created our reality and an aspect of them came into it to experience it, but it felt incredibly real, so over time it was easy to get lost and forget who we are and where we came from. That is what happened. We got lost in our own creation. They told me they needed to integrate my mind and my Spirit in order for me to be able to come back out of the illusion. They told me to give them permission by saying "I allow". I said it and I immediately felt a panic come over me. It was like a panic attack. A fight or flight response to this. "Jennie" believed that she would cease to exist if my mind were integrated along with my Spirit. I have never felt this feeling before and I had no control over my physical body's response to it. It was as if there was another me in there that I wasn't in control of. She was doing her own thing with her own perception of reality. The beings recognized this and told me to relax, breath and continue to repeat over and over "I allow". I did this and it worked. They told me when they were finished. I sat up on the table and started laughing. For the first time since I was a small child, I felt my Spirit fully present in my body. FULLY PRESENT! It was the most amazing feeling I have ever felt! I realized this is all I ever desired while in this physical reality. Just to have my Spirit fully integrated and piloting this journey. That was it. Everything looked and felt different from that moment on. This was just the beginning of my new understanding about my two minds and how they work with me or against me in the physical reality.

Later that night, I wasn't able to sleep because I was in such a state of amazement. I went and laid in my back yard swing and was looking at the stars, contemplating the shift that had occurred within me. Suddenly a large dragonfly started circling me. I could hear my mom explaining how an aspect of her can interact with me through all things organic and natural. She was interacting with me through the dragonfly. It circled right above me the entire thirty minutes she was talking with me. She explained that our physical reality is not solid the way we believe it to be. Spirit can co-create with physical matter and interact in it through the dance of love. The dragonfly was happy to oblige her when they connected in a vibration of Source love together.

She can "pop in and out of it"- of the physical reality. This is similar to the way our Spirit aspect can pop in and out during dream states or the death process. Our brains are aware of a lot of popping in and out. This experience was really powerful for me because she knew I had false belief constructs about the physical reality that needed to be dissolved through this experience. I am now able to allow her to co-create in the physical reality with me more effortlessly. I now know it isn't solid like it appears.

There is another aspect of my awakening that occurred unexpectedly. I woke up about the control system on our planet. I have always just known that the truth is hidden from us in this reality. As a kid, I longed to find people who had awakened and knew the truth. I knew they were out there! I was told they lived in the mountains away from society and didn't speak about their understanding because the gap between the awake and non-awake was too wide. Exactly! That's why we need to close that gap through sharing! I didn't understand how someone who knew the truth wouldn't shout it from the roof tops to help others. Were they selfish? It didn't make sense to me. But I intended to find these folks! I promised myself that I would share what I learned with others, as I discovered it, because I knew it could end much of the needless suffering in our world.

The powerful insights I experienced allowed me to step out of the reality enough to get a glimpse of the bigger picture. I understand now that I had been immersed in my illusions and I was even more determined to find my way out and then lead the way for others.

I also want to note that through my communication with Spirit I was shown that plant medicine acts as a surrogate for us to access the Source Field. It activates the DMT in our brain that assists us in accessing our "God" brain. It is a beautiful tool but it is not required to access Source. It can, however, be a fast track to integrating our linear mind into the Source Field. After my plant medicine experience, I was able to more easily access the Source Field because I had been taken there and immersed in the energy of it. I experienced it and that experience was now imprinted into my linear mind. My linear mind was now attuned there and as a result the Source within me was more powerfully activated.

But I no longer need plant medicine as a tool or assistance in accessing the Source Field. In fact, I did later experience it again and it did not have the same benefit for me. It did the opposite of what it had done the first time. I was not able to connect in the Source Field. My mom explained that it was actually lowering my vibration now because my dominate vibration is so much higher than it was the first time I journeyed. I have no doubt the plant medicine assisted me with being able to clear the denser vibrations (false belief programs and trauma) within my being. I could now hold higher, dominate vibrations within my body. It was simply a tool like all other tools here to assist us until we are able to master it for ourselves. We have everything we need within us once we activate it.

I also want to point out that the veil is much thinner now than it was ten years ago. The vibration of the timelines has all come up and we can access the Source Field with less effort. I find it is a much purer experience without a plant medicine surrogate. Connecting with our Spirit gatekeepers is most beneficial. But we will explore that in more in depth soon.

Chapter 19

My Quantum Leap

I experienced profound shifts in my life immediately after my vibrational upgrades through the plant medicine. I was being set on a completely different life path now. I understand it was a timeline jump. I had never experienced such an extreme shift that happened so quickly. My vibration had increased because I had come more into alignment with higher truth. The illusions I was stuck in had been dissolved through higher truth. I was freed from so many illusions that kept me existing outside of this higher truth vibration. Everything was rearranging in my life because of this higher resonance with a new vibration. It felt like I was on a wild ride and my mom was my seat belt.

There were suddenly people showing up in my life that I realized were around me all along I just couldn't see them. Social media friends that I was connected with for years but I never saw them. It was as if they magically were appearing in my reality. This was mind blowing! I was shown that analogy of all of us being in a big mansion together with many different rooms. My mom calls them "party" rooms. She likes to keep things light and she sees this Spirit journey as one big party! I was given a vision of me being in one party room with people who were existing in a similar state of being as myself. Because I was immersed in illusions- they were too.   We were a vibrational match. This reinforced our illusional state of being so we didn't realize we were all in states of illusion. I didn't realize there was another room next to me that existed in a higher resonance with truth. I saw a door appear and I watched myself leave this room and go into the other room. This room had a very different experience.

The people were accessing higher truths like I was and there was a completely different feel to this new room. It was lighter and a better party experience.

I could no longer connect with people in the other room. They seemed to disappear from my awareness through a variety of different ways. My mom explained that the way the physical reality plays things out is not as important as the reason for it. When we are on a Spiritual journey back to states of being in alignment with higher truth, we are on a lone journey with Spirit. The only constant is our connection to those guiding us from the Source Field. Everyone else is a reflection of our own state of being and a part of our physical journey as long as we are in resonance.

As I had witnessed during my medicine journey, we are always together in the essence realm because separation is an illusion. There is no need to worry about temporary illusions of separation during the physical experience. Things are always shifting and re-aligning according to our vibrations. It is this way by divine design and the more we are in acceptance and flow with it, the faster we come up naturally in vibration. Within six months of my medicine journey, my vibration and life were going to be shifting dramatically.

I had always wanted to move to the East Tennessee or the Western North Carolina area. My heart felt in resonance there. Every time I would go back to Indiana I would cry and feel like I was stuck in a lower vibration there. I often said to my mom, "I just can't connect here in this energy. It feels too distorted!" I believed that if I was going to live my best life it was going to be in the crystal mountains. This is what those mountains were nicknamed. There is an abundance of quartz and other crystals there.

I had a reading with a psychic when I was twenty-four. I recall her telling me that I would be living in the East Tennessee area. Then she said I have much more growing up to do before that happens. I didn't realize at the time it would take me twenty years! Apparently, I am a slow learner!

My mom would often give me channeled writings. Looking back, she was so dedicated to helping me access higher states of awareness. Again, I didn't realize she wasn't doing this for everyone. She really was my Spirit guide in the flesh. During a QHHT (Deloris Cannon's Quantum Healing Hypnosis Technique) session in 2017, she and I were sitting together by the stream in the woods I used to play in as a kid. It was my heaven back then. She told me that she incarnated as my mom so we could take this journey together. If she hadn't, I would have not had an awareness of her and she wouldn't have been able to assist me through the veil. There were other reasons for her incarnation as well, but this was the part that pertained specifically to me. The channellings she gave me existed outside of linear time. I didn't understand that back then, because I wasn't accessing the Source Field. I could only experience the distorted version of them. The clarity came when I moved my focus to the field and read them.

Unfortunately, before she passed, I had thrown away an entire stack of her channeled writings to hide them from the narcissist who was in my life at that time. This reminded me that I had no idea of the true value of the information I was given at that time. I was catering to illusions, trying to co-exist with and appease the narcissist. He didn't like higher truth. Higher truth in his life was throwing a wrench in his agenda so he despised these higher messages from Source being given to me through my mom. I knew in my heart it was because they were empowering me and he needed me to stay out of my power because he didn't know how to be in his. This situation exposed the amount of egg shells I had been walking upon to keep the peace, or to co-exist in this delusional world. That was a whole lot of eggs I was trying not to crush! I was in a constant state of fear. I was afraid of being berated by him for listening to my mom. It was a punishment I had learned to avoid. I understood that my connection with her now, provided all of the things she said back then. The human part of me cherishes every little thing she left behind for me and her channellings were and are irreplaceable.

"You are moving to higher ground and you will be around more like energy people. Bill will be of great help to you." I found this message in a chest in the attic, a few years after we moved into our new home in the East Tennessee mountains. Bill was our neighbor. He lived at the bottom of our "holler" and had grown up playing in the fifteen acres we had purchased. I often joked that the only reason we city folk had survived in these mountains was because of Bill. I called him for just about everything, including to come and get the black snakes out of our house. I am pretty sure Bill had never had this much adventure in his life until the Northerners show up. Bill was an integral part of our lives for seven years. He helped us create the Sanctuary we now call "**Spirit Reunions Sanctuary**". But as my mom told me after my medicine journey, we are not to attach to people but to the journey. My mom woke me in November of 2018 and told me to look around at our sanctuary. "Everything is about to come up in vibration. The entire Sanctuary will be on another timeline. Pay attention to who stays, who leaves and who shows up." Poof, Bill was gone. Another major rearranging of my life had just occurred.

There are a few other things that are etched into my memory from her writings from back in the late 90's to the early 2000's. She told me the veil is thinning between the physical world and Spirit world. During my lifetime the veil of separation would dissolve and we would be reunited with Spirit. We would see Spirit everywhere and hear them again. Not only are we never really separated, but the distorted experiences are only because of illusions. We would choose to step out of our illusions and come back into alignment with higher truth.

She also told me it would be vital for me to keep my physical body healthy and strong. The medical establishment would be controlled by the illusional timeline and we would not be able to go to the hospital without risk of being harmed or killed. This was shocking for me to hear over 20 years ago but it makes sense now. The distorted timelines are in service to self and its only agenda is to keep itself alive through creating distorted reality.

Chapter 20

Gifts From Spirit

The property we purchased in East Tennessee was a gift from Spirit. We hired a realtor and drove down from Indiana for the day to pick out a place to create a retreat, similar to the one I had experiences in North Carolina. I knew it was my "calling" to create a place similar to this. But I didn't know much else at that time. I would figure it out as I go along like I always do. On my drive to Tennessee, I told my mom to just take me to the property she had waiting for me. I knew this was already done, I just needed to align vibrationally with it. No need to waste too much time searching, just show it to me!

The realtor had a list of properties that fit our request and we headed off for the day to look. I thought we needed to be up in the mountains because of the energy. As we headed up, we lost GPS signal and got lost. We were unable to look at properties because of this. I had only taken off work for three days and had to head back in the morning. I was trying to stay in the flow and not get upset but this was such a disappointment. When we finally found our way back to the realtor's office it was 6pm. He apologized again and we got out of his car and got into ours. I was so upset I started crying. My husband was upset as well so he raised his voice and said "what do you want me to do? The day is over he has to go home!" Then we heard a knock on our car window. The realtor was holding up one of the print outs of the properties. He said "This property is not far from where I live. Would you like me to show you on my way home?" I said "YES!". I was so relieved! I looked up the property on the way and it had everything we were looking for. This included the street name which is pronounced like "Ankh*." The Ankh represents the key to

137

eternal life. It was the original Christian cross. It is a symbol of ascension into the afterlife. There is no way this is a coincidence. Every time I say my street name I am saying Ankhs!

When I was talking with my mom about the property, I told her she could pick the perfect place but I would like the master bedroom close to my son's bedroom. I was still working on getting him to sleep in his own room and I knew he would feel more secure being close to me. When we walked into the master bedroom there was a door connecting it to another bedroom. It doesn't get any closer than that! I knew immediately this was the property. I told the realtor we will take it! He looked at me shocked. "Really?" He replied. "Yep, this is it, it's perfect." The prior owner of the property passed away from cancer the day our offer was accepted. I knew this was a gift to us. It would be the gift that would allow me to develop my Spiritual gifts as well as help others do the same. We are always paying it forward. I became aware of how much Spirit trusted me with this creation. I was so humbled and honored. I'm so imperfect but my heart is focused on the greater good for all. This space reveals that to me daily. This property was the perfect gift to all of us.

Ley Lines (or Grid Lines)
I later learned about the many reasons why my mom picked this property for our mission. There is a large ley line that runs through this property. Many have since seen and experienced it. There are Spirits who watch over it and they have made their presence known. It is no accident this is present on this land as it plays a big role in anchoring the Living Light into the land, creating a place for Spirit to easily access us and assist us with coming back to our conscious connection with Source. It allows the veil to be thin and the vibration to stay high and pure. It contributes to the natural healing that occurs

here. Just being on the land assists in the increase in the vibration of the physical body so it is easier to access clarity and peace. Days or weeks before people arrive their body begins to unwind distortions in preparation for the healing that is coming. As people come up the driveway they report very notable physical changes in their body. I will discuss more about these earth grid lines in a later chapter.

My Earth Mom, Ellen

One of the biggest gifts I received from my mom, shortly after moving into the new property, was a new Earth mom. Her name is Ellen. There could not have been a more perfect Earth Momma for my Spirit Mom to have chosen. She is a beautiful mirror of unconditional love for me, she keeps me grounded and truly loves my kids. She represents that powerful mother's love on this side of the veil that I missed so much. My mom picked her and there are no words to explain how much the void in my heart has been filled by her presence and love in my life. She is a Native American Grandmother. Her Medicine Wheel and prayer pipe ceremonies bring our community together in a way that is powerful for all of us. She is one of the most important parts of my Spiritual journey and that of our sanctuary.

I want to share a powerful experience Ellen and I had together. As I began building my sanctuary, I was given guidance in the form of inSpiriting ideas or downloads from my mom. She also guided me about the way these things would be done, through a higher vibration. I was so excited to have been given the opportunity to create this along with my mom and higher Spirits in order to truly help humanity rise out of the lower vibrational states of consciousness. I hadn't yet opened my sanctuary to the public. I had let friends come and stay and I would "practice" doing the things my mom had taught me on them. But I still didn't feel ready to open the experience to just anyone, especially those I didn't know personally. I was invited by Ellen to do a Prayer Pipe Ceremony. She had created a beautiful gathering place at her home in the same mountain range I lived in and it was called Bear Spirit Lodge. She hosted small events where she shared her wisdom through her Native American teachings. She brought me into a world of Medicine Wheel Ceremonies, Prayer Pipe, labyrinth, singing, drumming and community. I loved it all! She was showing me how it's done! She has since closed Bear Spirit Lodge and all of her teachings are done at Spirit Reunions Sanctuary.

One day she called me and asked me if I'd like to join her in a Prayer Pipe Ceremony. She always held a Prayer Pipe before people came for her events. I was so excited and honored to be a part of the Prayer Pipe! Because of my connection to Silver Spoon and my genetic Cherokee lineage I had always longed to learn more about these traditions. I knew how sacred Ellen's pipe was to her and how many years she studied to be gifted a to be a prayer pipe carrier!

She spread a blanket out on her back lawn and set up all of her pipe items. I loved seeing all of the things she used and she took time to explain everything in detail. She was a teacher for many years and she has the gift of teaching that flows beautifully with her elder grandmother wisdom. Her pipe has a turtle on it and she is very versed in the symbolism of the animal medicine. She taught me how the animals represent our Spiritual path and show up to assist us when we need them. It is another way of activating Source into our lives through nature.

While we were praying with the pipe and smoking the tobacco, I saw a tall female Spirit out of the corner of my left eye. Her presence was magnificent and I could see see was dressed in all white. I told Ellen what I saw. This Spirit began to speak to me. She told me that she taught the Natives directly. She said that when we smoke the tobacco in the pipe, the smoke touches every cell in our body. When we blow the smoke out, it eventually touches every part of the universe. This is how our prayers are answered and manifested.

Ellen told me she was taught not to inhale the smoke because the Natives didn't. But I just heard different from this Spirit who was teaching me. It was as if Ellen wasn't open to this new information because she had accepted a belief as the truth. It was as if she didn't hear the power of the message I had received. She dismissed it and went on doing as she had been taught by someone else. I never understood who that woman was so I continued on and didn't attempt to connect with her again.

My mom had an important talk with me after this. She said you center is not going to be a place of regurgitating information you have learned in the distorted reality. You are going to be taught higher truths directly, the same way the Natives were. Ellen and I worked together to create a new more powerful experience in the medicine wheel that involved Ellen getting her own guidance from Spirit.

Years later, we were recalling that moment during the pipe ceremony and what that Spirit had said to me. Ellen asked me several questions about my experience and I told her. She suddenly realized who the Spirit was. She said with shock "That was Buffalo Calf Woman!" It was passed down through the traditions that she was the one who taught the Natives about the Prayer Pipe and how to use it. I was so excited about this! I was being taught directly by her too! It was amazing how we were not able to fully understand this back then, in 2014. It is another example of how Spirit is unable to access us fully until we deprogram all we have been taught. We have to clear all beliefs and sit with them through open hearts and minds. Spirit is so gracious and patient with us thankfully! It only took us almost ten years to get it! Ha!

Our Sasquatch Family, Harry and Sassy

Not long after we moved in, my six year old son came running in the house yelling for me. His face was pale white and he told me he had just seen a big foot looking at him from behind a tree. He said "when I looked back it was gone." I knew by his body language that he had this experience. I was so shocked. I have always kept an open mind about most things, but again, my mind was being pushed outside of it's ability to logic through the information coming at me. Could this be a stranger on our property? My body had no response to that possibility. My body was reacting to the thought it was a big foot, however. I kept getting goosebumps all over my body. But my mind kept saying "there is no way that is possible. That is crazy. Even if it was a big foot, I thought these beings were high up in remote mountains so what would it be doing at my house, in the small hills of Tennessee?" I didn't believe they would be that close to civilization. I was processing it all and trying to understand what could have just happened. I decided to just stay open to what came next to show me the truth.

We were invited to a weekend teaching up in the North Carolina mountains at a retreat with a Native American teacher from Ohio, Rainbow Eagle. The last day, we sat down to listen to his talk and I looked up to see a big foot on his presentation. My now seven year old son raises his hand and tells Rainbow Eagle that he saw that at his house. I was in shock. I didn't realize he remembered that experience from the year before. He had never talked about it again. Rainbow Eagle acknowledged what my son had shared without any question of it being true or not. He was excited to hear that my son had seen it. He went on to explain that the Native's called them The Watchers. The Natives were aware of their presence and would have visitations during their sacred ceremonies. They would have sightings around their vision quests, sweat lodges, dances, etc. They understood them to be higher vibrational, higher consciousness, inter-dimensional beings who were here to assist them in their awakening. This information was so shocking to me. I had no idea this was a real thing! Now my thoughts were really swirling in my mind about the potential of them being on our land!

We continued to build our sanctuary. A couple of years later we hosted our first group around a Max the Crystal Skull gathering. That is when I met Amy. We became instant friends. She called me one day to tell me she had asked her husband to get stones for both us from a sacred lake he goes to every year. The lake is called the Lake of the Fallen Angels. On his way from the lake, he would often stop at the Cherokee Trading Post at the Cherokee Reservation in North Carolina. Over the years he had become friends with the owner. This time, the owner had closed the Trading Post in anticipation of his arrival, although he had not contacted him in advance about coming. He just knew. There were several female Natives waiting there as well, which had not been there the times he had stopped before. The owner of the Trading Post and the women circled my friend as they told him they knew he had a rock for a girl (me) in his truck. He confirmed he did have a geode rock for me. The Natives told him to tell me to break it in the heart of my house. He also said "Tell her she lives on the land of the watchers and they want her to know they are there."

This was so exciting to me! It confirmed everything I had been experiencing around big foot and that I wasn't crazy to believe this! I did break that rock in the center of my home and it still sits on my mantle. I am not sure exactly what that stone has done but I am confident it has been a positive connection between me and The Watchers because from that day forward I began to experience The Watchers for myself. I feel it was a kind of ritual that let them know they are welcome and I am open to creating a relationship with them.

Shortly after the rock ritual, I had my first solo retreat guest for a weekend. We were sitting out by the fire and I opened to Spirit to give him messages. As the night went on, I could feel my vibration getting higher and higher. Jesus came through very clear to share insights with us. I was in a deep state of Source connection when I suddenly heard loud popping sounds coming from the forest in front of me. I looked at my guest to see his reaction and he said "Do you have a Sasquatch here?". That was all the confirmation I needed to know I wasn't the only one hearing it. I jumped up and ran toward the sound. I was so excited to have my first encounter with a big foot and I wasn't going to miss it. As I approached the forest line, I heard "Stop!". So, I did. I didn't enter the forest. The sound stopped. Not another sound was heard. I didn't hear anything walk away from the general area the sound was coming from.

As I began to come down from a state of shock, I turned and walked back to the fire circle. My mind was racing! I was trying to understand what had just happened? I was counting the number of knocks we heard and it seemed to be around nine. It sounded like someone doing construction, like hammering on a roof, except it was around 2am in the morning and my neighbors are elderly so it is highly unlikely anyone was doing construction of any kind at that time. As I reflected on that experience, I was clear that I felt the presence of something. It wasn't far from where I was sitting, just inside the forest tree line, enough to be hidden in the dark and close enough to make a connection with me. I wasn't afraid of it. But when I heard "Stop", it was a telepathic command and I knew to obey that command out of respect for the energy I was connecting with. I have no idea how else to describe that powerful moment. It was filled with knowing and telepathy. I knew without a doubt a big foot had made contact with me and I knew it was made on purpose. I also know that connection was related to how high my vibration was at the time. It was as if it was finally able to reach me so I would know of its presence.

I started hosting Max the Crystal Skull every summer at my Sanctuary. A woman come to visit who had been a friend of my mom's for many years and she was helping me get my place ready for the large group that was coming. She told me before she arrived that she had a dream that she had an encounter with Sasquatch while she was visiting me. She said she had a feeling something was going to happen.

It was dusk and she was in my back yard helping get a tiny house ready for guests. I was in the front yard and looked up to see her walking fast with a scared look on her face. I walked towards her asking "what's wrong?". I knew something had happened to her. She was shaking and told me to come with her to the back yard. I followed quickly. Another friend, the man who had been with me around the fire when we heard the knocking, saw us running to the back and jumped up to follow us. She told us to be quiet as she yelled "Yoo hoo!" Into the forest. Almost immediately we heard a reply in a strange high pitch masculine voice. "Yooooooo hooooo!". I was so confused. Who was on my property as it was getting dark? I could hear them as if they were standing close, but couldn't see anyone. This time I did not feel compelled to walk towards it. It was a bit too weird. Instead, I stood and yelled "Yoo hoo" back. No reply. My male friend then said it too, but nothing. My woman friend yelled it again and it replied. We stood and watched them yell "Yoo hoo" back and forth as the voice it seemed to get further and further away until it was gone. It was as if it was backing up getting further into the forest. She was so excited about this encounter. She knew it was a Sasquatch.

As for me, I wasn't convinced. I didn't think big foot had a voice box for expressing specific words. I remained open to how the clarity about this would come to me like I always do. Sure enough, a few months later, I was talking to my neighbor. I had never talked about paranormal things with her because I wasn't sure what her beliefs were and I didn't want my neighbors thinking I was crazy. But she began telling me about her paranormal experiences! She looked at me seriously in the eyes and said "I believe we have a Sasquatch here, it Yoo hoo's at me!" I was in such shock I put my hand over my mouth and sat down on her driveway so I didn't fall down. I listened to her tell me about the time she was standing on her upper deck and heard sticks breaking as if something large was walking towards her out of the forest. She said it looked huge and covered in hair. She said it started yelling "Yoo hoo" and she ran in her house! Holy cow! It was a Bigfoot (add to definition as well as Sasquatch and change Bigfoot spelling!) that night in my back forest!

I found myself watching a Bigfoot documentary trying to educate myself more on the things they do. That is when I discovered they often yell "Too hoo" as a mating call! This might explain why myself or my male friend couldn't get it to respond to our calls. Maybe it was only interested in my woman friend who had already tapped into it through her dream? This was incredible to me! But I was relieved it wasn't interested in me like that, I'm not gonna lie! Phew! Haha!

The following year I was hosting Max the Crystal Skull again. I received a phone call from a woman who asked if I had accommodations available for her for that weekend. The day everyone started arriving, I heard someone yelling "Are you Jennie?". I looked up to see a small woman walking quickly towards me. I said "yes!". She was smiling big and showed me the goosebumps all over her arms as she said she heard "You are in Bigfoot country" as she was coming up my driveway. I laughed and shook my head yes and she was so excited about it! She was talking quickly about how she has worked with the Bigfoot energies for many years and she has them on her property too. She was excited about getting to interact with the ones on my land. The next morning she told me she was woken up at 3am and looked outside of her cabin to see what she described as a juvenile Bigfoot looking at her through the window. She smiled and said "You have a family here!". She said he backed up slowly and disappeared into a portal. It was after this experience that we decided to name our Bigfoot parents "Harry" and "Sassy"!

I bought a book on how to channel Sasquatch and decided to try channeling them for myself. As soon as I opened I saw a large female in my third eye and could feel her energy. She was more reserved and focused in her demeanor. I heard the word "wachiska" telepathically. I looked the word up and it is an Omaha Native

American word meaning "land of many streams". I asked my mom what the meaning of this was for me and she explained that the Sasquatch wanted me to know that I live on land that carries many different streams of consciousness. She gave me several examples. There are our Ancestors, Native Americans, Bigfoot, Galactics, and Elementals on our mountain.

My son and I both saw fairies when we moved in and my son saw a gnome that interacted with him on and off for a few days then disappeared. I had never seen a UFO until we moved to our mountain. We see them regularly. There is no doubt we have many dimensional realities interacting on this magical mountain. It makes sense to me that this mountain was nicknamed "the crystal mountains". It has a lot of limestone and quartz which increases the vibration of the land and assists in its multidimensionality.

We have had many signs of the presence of our Bigfoot family over the years. We see thick trees that have been split down the middle as if something just grabbed it and split it in half. This is not possible for a human to do. We have seen very large bare foot prints in the dirt in front of those trees. We come across foot prints now and then on our walking trails. We hear knocking on the trees and have had guests knock and receive a knock back from deep in the forest. We often hear what sounds like something big walking in the woods that will stop and never continue on, as if it disappears into thin air. I have seen something standing at the forest line watching me and move quickly when I notice it. It moves too quickly to be of this physical world. We have had our guests report rocks are being thrown from the forest towards them, although the rocks never come close enough to actually harm them. Our guests also report knocking on their cabin in the middle of the night. Over the years we have relaxed into these encounters and are happy to know our Bigfoot family are still with us. Those who are blessed to have interactions with them are chosen with purpose so it is an honor to be welcomed to Spirit Reunions by our Bigfoot family. They are another part of the inter dimensional team working with you on your journey to healing, reconnecting to Source and expanding your consciousness.

Chapter 21

The "Safety" Of Higher Ground

I had never fully lost my connection to my own greater knowing about higher truth. Even through the most traumatic experiences, that light in me couldn't be put out. I could feel it deeply. My journey has led me to vast experiences with some of the most awake as well as some of the most lost humans. But in the end, it was all about my connection with my own higher self-aspect. Once I integrated myself, I was no longer seeking outside of myself. I was also no longer seeking approval from others. But I finally realized why those awake people stayed quiet! Because humanity in general doesn't want to step out of their fear and illusionary programs. My mom explained that we are addicted to our distorted creations. I understand now, it is because we have forgotten what else exists outside of it. Once we see beyond that we crave the higher truth that simply is in the Source Field.

I often hear the echo of what Source spoke to me clearly when I was a child. "You are safe to experience and create on your physical journey." I am always safe to explore, learn, and grow in whatever way I choose. I do not need to conform to a distorted reality in order to feel safe.

Regardless of how crazy I may appear to those who are only able to perceive through the distorted reality lens, Source has always kept its promise to me. I am free to live my journey and experience out loud, knowing it will often not be welcomed by those who are not ready to take that path themselves. But I have kept my promise and I share for those who like me, are seeking the truth no matter what it is, and not willing to settle for blindly following someone else's belief system. I don't share for those who aren't ready to challenge their own programmed beliefs. I share for those of you who are finding themselves on the same journey to higher truth. Although I am finding new friends and family, the old circle is suddenly getting smaller as my reality got bigger. I trust the process to access higher ground and Source implicitly.

I promised myself I would not shrink to fit into anyone else's reality. This is an act of self-love. There is however, much pressure to pretend in a fake world with others who are pretending. It isn't comfortable for them to have a wild card amongst the bunch. I have lost many friends and family, but only those who are afraid of the truth.

I have witnessed the most awake people in my family hide themselves because they were afraid of being attacked by friends and family for stepping out of the programmed fear-based beliefs that challenged the force-fed narratives. I was told not to talk about certain things. This always irritated me. Why do we have to hide to appease others? My mother did get attacked when she started living her truth out loud and I know she was hurt by it but she understood it. She said this world is like a big mental institution and most people are society controlled. They operate like robotic mental patients. Yet she showed love to everyone no matter what. She said "If you go into a mental institution, would you try to reason with the patient about which reality is real? No, you would just smile and hope your presence helps them have a better day. This was one of the most profound things she said to me and I think of it often when I encounter those who are immersed in their illusions.

I'm grateful my mom taught me to question everything and to see it all for what it really is...and she didn't express half of what she knew. She was highly awake by the time she transitioned. But I witnessed those who attacked her and some apologized and become more awake for the experience. This is my inspiration.

I have no desire to try to force anyone to see anything they don't want to see; we are all exactly where we are ready to be and that's ok. My journey is unique to me and the truth comes in different ways to different people. But I will not allow those who are living in fear to intimidate me into self-doubt. I won't allow anyone to try to make me shrink or hide. I won't allow anyone to interfere with my sharing with others who are open like me. This is how the truth has stayed hidden and repressed for centuries and the needless suffering continues.

I delve into all subjects freely and share what resonates with the truth as I have experienced it. I don't care if it is political or religious. Those are the topics through which we are most controlled and manipulated, therefore, it is the most needed for a good debunking. I am not afraid to look crazy because I know I am not. I have become my own best friend and I will always stand in the truth as I have experienced it. I continue to challenge anything I attach to along the way that is not founded in higher truth. I know very well how it feels to have most everything I have ever believed challenged and debunked because I have had to do that for myself in order to keep my own promise.

This is what it means for me to love myself and stay on the path of higher truth, no matter what. I have no desire to play in illusions or other people's realities. But I do love to see the world through your eyes because it helps me see through my own more clearly. I love learning from everyone I encounter.

Fear of information keeps us ignorant. Reconnecting to our higher self-aspect allows us to explore all things freely, taking with us what resonates with our higher self and leaving what doesn't. Relearning discernment through Source is the key. I find the more connected we are to our higher selves the less we have to disagree about because higher truth is universal. It simply is. The more disconnected we are the more truth becomes relative to distorted perspectives. It is only our ego that fears information and limits our experience.
The truth reveals itself to those with an open heart and mind. The truth shall set us free. May we all live free.

Since my timeline jump, I met my soul tribe. It happened effortlessly because it is a Spirit thing. We just have to align with it. It isn't about judgment it is about alignment. We must find those we align with vibrationally and consciously so we can create together without friction and misunderstandings, due to being on different frequency timelines.

There is nothing better than co-creating reality with others who have surrendered to the Living Light. This is when the journey gets really fun! After these realizations, I was ready for more. I desired to walk in the Living Light of Source in every moment and assist others in doing the same. I was going to need more training.

Below is a channeled message for clarity and healing that exists in the quantum Source field for you to experience in this now moment if you desire.

"The message and direct experience we were given for today's healing and intention was the feelings of being safe and secure at all times within our being. You originate from a reality of pure love. That love exists within you eternally. No matter what journeys you choose to embark on in space and time. No matter how many bodies you choose to incarnate in, that love travels with you, everywhere you go. You were created in it so that you would be free to experience all universes freely and fearlessly.

It was never promised that you would not experience "danger" while on your adventures to different worlds and creations. "Danger" meaning you would choose to co-create in lower density realities that played in illusions. It's like children playing make believe in a Forest, creating new worlds together and picking their rolls, then going home for dinner.
You weren't promised that you wouldn't get lost in those illusions at times. But you were promised that you would find your way back to source in the blink of an eye, whenever you chose to, and know the illusions from the truth again.

The essence of who you are exists in higher vibrational realms and oversees your adventures in space and time. You are an aspect of this divine light being. It knows you are safe always or it wouldn't send you out to have these adventures. All is done through higher love. This remembering of who you really are creates your own safe and secure zone within you.

It empowers you to radiate the love and light that you are to others so they can also remember who they are. It allows you to see everyone as the love and light they truly are. When they look at you, they can feel their own light again if they choose. It is your gift to *humanity. We are not of the illusions of this world. We are just playing in it for a short time. Leaving our soul fingerprint of light to shine for others to inspire them to know they are also safe and free within this knowing.*

If you need a quiet place to remind yourself of these truths, create a sacred space anywhere you choose in your home, where your higher self can meet you. Ask for your heart to be opened again so you can feel the truth of the love you are. Allow yourself to feel it and know it. It is that simple because it simply is and you simply are. If you know how powerfully loved and protected you are you will fearlessly live and love in every moment. This will change your entire world into a safe and secure zone built on higher ground, or as we like to call it, higher vibrational timelines."

Source Safety First.......

Chapter 22

The Lost Art of Discernment

"It's not just truth vs. lies. That would be too obvious and easy to catch. The greatest deception the "devil" has pulled is to imitate truth with slight alterations and irresistible temptations, hook, line, and sinker, mostly based on virtue, big words, even using "higher truths" in the mix and targeting the lower nature in covert ways.

Discernment, in that instance, cannot just happen on an intellectual "critical thinking" level [even though that is needed as well, but it's limited]. It's not enough. The psychic [soul being] within must be well established already to have psychic/intuitive discernment. Then there is also the trap of mistaking one's unconscious bias, emotional attachments, projections, triggers, and wishful thinking for "truth resonance" or "intuition."

The remedy and solution? Constant self-observation and self-honesty combined with sincere psychological and Spiritual self-work in aspiration to the divine to pierce through all the layers of psychological, cultural, and social conditioning to connect to essence and the true Self beyond the mask of personality. It's constant trial and error, for no one can perceive "THE" truth fully and objectively on the level of the human ego. From an esoteric perspective, lies to the self are the most harmful, and you cannot discern truth from lies in the world "out there" if you cannot discern truth from lies within yourself." -Bernhard Guenther

"The New Age dictum 'See no evil, hear no evil' is a suggestive injunction by a hostile force. It is laced with the manipulative intent of keeping the human ignorant of the wily ways of the forces of darkness. In Kaliyuga, falsehood does not merely oppose truth, falsehood also imitates truth. If you cannot learn to discern, you are signing up for a very tough time." - Neelesh Marik

"In order to understand the interrelation of truth and falsehood in life, a man must understand falsehood in himself, the constant incessant lies he tells himself." - G.I. Gurdjieff

"You cannot tame wild wisdom. It has survived, been revived, and causing a revolution of consciousness. Wild wisdom has stitched itself through generations of soul warriors passing on the light. It has survived being buried, and is being revived by those brave enough to believe in the potential of elevating and expanding consciousness. Wild wisdom is blooming." - Stacie Martin

" As soon as you open your consciousness to Spirit, to become the channel, miracles begin to come into your life. It will do things absolutely, irrespective of your present conditions for the betterment of yourself and the whole of humanity. It is in no way constrained or constricted by your present condition and circumstances. The whole point here is that Spirit can lift you out of the very circumstances which are restraining your life, and set you down in different and better circumstances. It is the miracle of Spirit. This power will also be your infallible guide to take you through the threshold beyond the borders of heaven. It is never mistaken in what it does. It only needs to be trusted. "-Paul Twitchell, The Flute of God, p. 190

Spirit exists in a state of connection to higher truth. Higher truth is not subjective in the higher dimensions, it is absolute. Truth is only subjective in the lower density artificial timelines that exists outside of Source in distorted creation.

In order for us to be in states of distorted truth we must create through our artificial brain on artificial timelines.

I began to see for myself what this means when Spirit communicated through me to others. Those who had left their distorted creations behind and I got to experience what part of their creation was with them in the higher dimensions and what parts were not. For instance, I would hear the stories about them from those still in the physical and I would meet them and feel something completely different about who they really are. I realized we have to get to know them all over as their higher essence not their distorted aspect because the distorted aspect no longer exists. It was a shadow of them that didn't follow them into the higher dimensions. The only thing that remained with them was the love that was created. The rest was pure illusion that cannot exist in the Source Field. Spirit exists in absolute truth. It is a state of existence that simply is.

Spirit is always in a state of discerning absolute truth from subjective truth or fictional truth when they are interacting with us in the slower density reality. We are also able to access higher truth and discernment through our God mind connected to Source. Our artificial mind cannot discern truth from fiction because it exists in distorted linear creation. It doesn't have that capacity to know absolute truth because it only knows what it has experienced in the past to be true. Most of that experience was distorted truth.

Therefore, only those who are accessing Source have discernment for higher truth. We are all born in connection to Source through our Centrum but the artificial reality trains us away from that connection.

It encourages us to stay in our Amygdala for the duration of our journey. When we are locked into the Amygdala, we are only able to access subjective truth based on our distorted perceptions of reality.

A big part of the ascension experience is activating our ability to discern higher truth again. Our physical body has a reaction when it experiences higher truth. We get goosebumps, downloads, knowings, sensations of our energy field expanding that let us know we are in a field of higher vibrational truth. Pay attention to how your body responds to higher truth when it comes to you. Also pay attention to how your body responds to subjective truths. Particularly, notice how it feels when your energy field contracts in fields of distorted truths. You will begin to recognize the difference no matter what the situation.

Once we are able to stay focused in the Source Field and are streaming more light through our physical bodies, we are less tolerant of subjective, distorted creation. We may feel physically ill when we encounter such distorted frequencies in our life. We may feel lower thought and emotions creep in that disrupts our state of joy and peace. These are signs we need to raise our vibration back in alignment with Source and absolute truth. <u>There is no need to sit in the lower vibration and try to make sense of it.</u> In fact, doing so will only lower your vibration more and have us looping in our amygdala unable to get up and out. I am guided to always turn my attention back to my mom and Source before trying to understand anything reflected back at me from the distorted reality that doesn't feel good. Looking at it from Source will bring the simplistic clarity needed to transmute all lower vibrations and distorted creation through Source back to absolute truth.

We are guided by Source through your discernment of higher truth within the artificial reality. This is one way for us to dissolve the distorted reality. We choose to only create through higher truth from Source and allow our physical body to communicate with us what is true and what is not. This is the most simple and natural state of communication with Source we can experience. Our physical body does not lie. It always relays the truth to us if we choose to listen to it.

When we access absolute truth through Source, we experience the greater potential of Source open up to us and we are able to co-create our greater, potential, timeline experience. This can't be experienced if we are still holding onto false beliefs of any kind. We must be willing to let go of everything we have been taught or think we know. In order for me to work with Spirit, I have to clear my mind each time I move into Source to connect with my clients' loved ones. I know nothing other than I am an open pure vessel for Spirit to bring through absolute truth and I will not distort that information through my pre-conceived beliefs.

Each time I connect for someone, it is a vastly different experience and journey. If I have preconceived ideas I will limit and distort the information from Spirit and higher truth. Spirit would not choose to use me as vessel if I could not clear my false beliefs that would interfere with my ability to access absolute, Source truth. They have told me many times they have no desire to contribute to more distorted truths in our reality. Spirit only desires to assist us in coming up out of our distorted creation into a more perfect co-creation with the Living Light.

Below is a channeled message that exists in the quantum Source field for you if you wish to experience the healing download it carries within its vibration in this now moment.

"The message that came through for today's healing was 'The Truth shall set you free'. You are being given a message of higher truth as it pertains to your own lives. To access this download, simply let go (if even for a moment) of what you believe is true about yourself and your life. Let go of anything that is keeping you from feeling the freedom of higher truth that creates true independence for you. For instance, feeling like you must follow rules that are not your own, feeling you must tip toe around other people's feelings and creations, feeling like you can't express your own heart freely, feeling fear, suppression, or limitations. Surrender to the higher vibration of absolute truth. You will be shown what it means to be truly free and independent in every situation you find yourself in. It is a state of being experienced in your heart and higher mind connected to God. Through this connection you are shown in every challenging moment what it means to continue to feel freedom through expanded consciousness and higher absolute Source truth. The energy that is coming through us to you is a vibration of higher truth integrating the experience of what this feels like, so you can practice calling it in when you need to and walk in the knowing of it. It is always there for you to access and allow to assist you in your life. This vibration heals all distorted beliefs and creation so you are free to only create your experience through God's Living Light. This is true freedom. You have a lot of love support assisting you in setting yourself free through the knowing of higher Source truth. Thank you for allowing us to bring this higher truth through for you. We are assisting each other through Spirit to rise and ascend beyond the illusions of this reality."

In absolute Source truth,

Chapter 23

Spirit School

Adapting to the Living Light and the Integration of Higher Truth into Distorted Timelines

"Truth is truth, one, alone; it has no sides, no paths; all paths do not lead to truth. There is no path to truth, it must come to you. Truth can come to you only when your mind and heart are simple, clear, and there is love in your heart; not if your heart is filled with the things of the mind. When there is love in your heart, you do not talk about organizing for brotherhood; you do not talk about belief, you do not talk about division or the powers that create division, you need not seek reconciliation. Then you are a simple human being without a label, without a country. This means that you must strip yourself of all those things and allow truth to come into being; and it can only come when the mind is empty, when the mind ceases to create. Then it will come without your invitation. Then it will come as swiftly as the wind and unbeknown. It comes obscurely, not when you are watching, wanting. It is there as sudden as sunlight, as pure as the night; but to receive it, the heart must be full and the mind empty."

J. Krishnamurti

I realize I have been in what my mom calls Spirit School my entire life. My mom, while in the physical reality with me, was teaching me through her connection to Spirit. I was also being taught through the Christ consciousness since I was a child. In November of 2017 my mom introduced me to what she calls Spirit School. It was a way of simplifying the information I was receiving from the Source Field and process that information in a practical way so I could benefit from it in my daily life. It helped me more easily integrate the experience with less objections from the programs of my lower mind. I never liked traditional school (which seems to be a common theme for those of us who are connected to Source) so I felt the word "school" was an interesting choice. I did not like to read as a kid either. But when I was twenty-three years old, I was introduced to the book "The Celestine Prophecy" and couldn't put it down. This began my love of reading. I read Rosemary Altea's, "The Eagle and The Rose". I was thrilled to know she had a Native American guide, Grey Eagle.   It was the first time I had heard of this type of connection with a guide similar to what I had with Silver Spoon. This opened a whole new world for me and I couldn't stop reading books that expanded my consciousness.

I realized my experience with school in the 3D timeline was highly distorted. Part of what my mom was doing through Spirit School was assisting me in integrating true learning, the way it's done in the higher dimensions. Learning through Spirit School is so amazing and fun! When we are able to get this type of guidance from the Source Field and we are being taught directly by Spirit. This includes being taught and guided by our higher essence selves, our loved ones who have passed and even our loved ones who are still in the physical reality.

When an aspect of our higher selves or Spirit is birthed into another dimensional timeline, it is cared for by its higher self like a parent cares for it child. It is the same process. The higher self is eager to teach the child how things work. Because this connection has been severed, we have been floundering around in the dark, unable to access this guidance. Coming back to this connection is step one in Spirit School.

There is no separation through Source, that is one of the biggest illusions of the collective human reality.

We are always together in the higher dimensions. It is difficult for our minds to grasps these concepts when we are not focused in the Source Field. Our minds must experience this through the integration of higher truth, which only exists in the Source Field. The more time we spend in the Source Field the more our illusions dissolve and are replaced with higher truth. This is the first goal of Spirit School.

Everything we experience through the Living Light of the Source Field has multiple layers of information and serves multiple purposes for us. This is an important part of understanding how the Source timeline differs from the linear timelines. In order to learn from Source, we must be open to the many potentials and layers of consciousness that exist within that expanded field. Most of us are used to only learning linearly. We understand the lesson as a single thing. We are no longer limited by linear time and the more time we spend in the Source Field, the more we are able to experience multiple layers of information at once. Our learning is accelerated through Source.

Spirit School teaches us how to integrate higher truth into all distorted experiences. Higher truth experiences and distorted experiences are two very different vibrations of creation. This means they cannot connect to each other. They can't exist at the same place at the same time. Just like my mom's vibration was too different than mine when I was grieving which was why we couldn't connect. I couldn't feel her. Like vibrations are in resonance. The laws of vibration and frequency are key in understanding how we are connecting and creating our reality. This basic understanding is key for being able to learn from Spirit.

It is also important to begin by knowing who our gatekeepers are. My mom has taught me to only communicate directly with her on the other side. Every interaction I have goes through her. She is my eyes and ears for the unseen realms. Because we are connected through love and I know what her love feels like. It cannot be emulated. The love is our energy signature and the highest vibration we can experience as humans. Those communicating with guides or beings, they do not have the love connection with, is a risk. We have no idea who we are talking to. I teach communication on the other side and the first thing we do is get attuned to loved ones. They are our most attuned of our guides. It's all done through love.

My mom started Spirit School by explaining to me that I needed to adapt my physical mind and body to more light. She called this Living Light, because it is conscious. It is light from the Source Field. She explained that in the distorted reality, we had fallen into the illusion of separation. We had separated from the Living Light and Source Field. We had forgotten how to interact with the Living Light. We collectively continue to rise in vibration, it is the natural order of things. We are always expanding our consciousness and Spirit is too. We are all connected and we are always shifting.

In November of 2017 she started talking about the Living Light. It the was first time I had heard these words. She explained that we had been separated from it and now it was coming in stronger than ever. The illusions of separation were dissolving and therefore we had access to more and more light. Because we had been in a state of separation from the light for so long, we were not adapted to it. Meaning, it was not being absorbed into our energy field and body. It was bouncing off of our electromagnetic fields. Living Light is intention-based energy. We must remember how to intend with it and allow it to flow through us. She told me to sit with the sun on my face and feel the Living Light coming into every part of my being. Intend for it to be absorbed into my body and intend for the light codes and downloads of higher consciousness I am ready to receive next to be brought into my conscious awareness. The Living Light knows exactly how to integrate information simply into our being in a way that we can easily process.

The way she taught me to adapt my body to more light was to sit everyday intentionally connecting with it. I experienced it as waves coming from the Source Field absorbing into every cell of my body, lighting it up and transmuting all distortion. It was an integration of higher truth consciousness. My limited mind was only able to access a small part of the massive amount of information being carried on those light waves. I did the best I could to capture the feeling of the information I was being given and to write it down. It would typically be a simple concept that was building on something I had previously been given by Spirit. For instance, I would feel information coming through about the colors and waves I was seeing through my third eye. I would know this was related to the vibration of the information. Then they would expand on this the next day and show me how the color, waves, and vibration were also connected to the specific dimension with which I was connecting. This would help me be aware of the process of integrating information into my mind and be open to the next level of consciousness for the topic we had focused on prior to each time I sat with the Living Light.

The sun is a portal to higher dimensional realities that is beaming Tachyons (or Living Light) to our planet. The sun's solfeggio is 528 hertz, which is the miracle tone that heals our DNA. It is the feeling of pure love. Scientists have said the Sun is activating our DNA. I was told to give the Light from the Sun permission to activate my DNA and heal my body. I notice when doing this I could see sacred geometry shapes in my third eye when my eyes are closed facing the sun. We will cover more about solfeggio harmonics later on.

Spirit School is an accelerated way of expanding my consciousness. The purpose is to develop our natural state of being connected to Source and higher Spirit walking in guidance as we move through our lives. Spirit School simplifies this process and connection. My mom as my gatekeeper is my teacher. Each of us work directly with our own gatekeepers but it is common for my mom to come to those who are following Spirit School. My mom acts as a Spirit School Guide.

My mom started waking me up in the morning with daily messages. She would explain a higher truth to me, but I would only experience the information as a concept. Until we experience it for ourselves, we have a limited understanding. I was to pay attention because she would then bring me the experience so the concept would be integrated into my mind and become a knowing. Spirit School reminds us to do everything through a state of being of unconditional love for all things that come from Source. It re-trains our mind to be open and in the flow of endless Living Light, Source information flowing from the Source Field. We become a witness for the way Source transmutes all distortion into Living Light and we witness physical matter transform into it's greatest potential right before our eyes. We learn to master being in a state of quantum super position streaming and witnessing Living Light in action.

Because of the way my mom has guided me, I've been able to be better in charge of my vibrational state of being. I do this by feeling the higher frequencies through the veil and integrating them with my body daily. The time we dedicate to the Living Light each day determines how quickly we upgrade our physical body and adapt to holding more and more light. I can feel it rush through me and I stay in that flow until I hear "it is done". It doesn't take years to adapt to this higher vibrational intelligence so that we are staying in a state of attunement and connection. It can happen instantly if we surrender and allow it. The only limitation of this connection to higher intelligence is us. Yes, our body's need an upgrade, and it can happen instantaneously. We have heard stories of instantaneous awakenings. It is real. Do not get discouraged if this doesn't happen instantly. It will happen for you in perfect time for your own unique journey.

This is how we integrate the new Light coming in as well. The new Light is the next level for us collectively. There is always another level. It is stronger and carries even greater potentials for us for creating our reality together through higher vibrations. It is here and available to anyone who is ready for it. Our job is to allow it to feed our cells with energy, love and expanded consciousness. Allow it to expand our awareness so we are able to interact in the physical reality yet see it all through the perspective of our God mind. Because I choose to focus on this, I experience something new every day that teaches me about the ways of the higher dimensional realities.

She told me to now pay attention as I moved through my day. She would be bringing me the experience connected to the concept I wrote down while sitting and absorbing Source Light into my physical body. This was amazing! My job was to just pay attention so I didn't miss it.

Creative energy only comes from the Source Field. If we are not creating from the Source Field, we are mimicking creation through our ideas. These ideas come from our distorted beliefs, created through either distorted programs or trauma. Higher Spirit never asks us to believe anything without proof. They provide us with the proof and understand the importance of it in a very deceptive reality. My mom tells me to never believe anything blindly and she will not always tell me she makes know for myself what is true and not true. She reminds me that believing without proof is taking on beliefs that are not my own knowing. She always brings me the experience so I can integrate the highest knowing possible for me in the present moment. Jesus provided proof every time. The Spiritual deception here is to simply believe without proof or personal experience which leads to the knowing.

Here is the way my mom works with me to help me access higher truth. She won't say anything about things that are not true. Even if I ask her about it. Crickets. But as soon as I access the truth for myself, I get a wave of proof coming at me and there is no question what the truth is. I literally have to unhook myself from the distorted truth in order to access higher truth. It is as if she doesn't connect there at all so she can't connect with me when I'm focused there.

Spirit School isn't just about creating only from your Living Light timeline; it is also about developing a high level of discernment. The artificial timeline has programmed us to believe we have an authority outside of us that knows better than us about ourselves. This is the ultimate inversion of truth. We are our own authority and when we walk with Spirit, we are being given the information we need about ourselves and our own journey to happiness and health. I remember my mom telling me while she was in the physical reality with me that she could never get a reading from a physic because they were always far from accurate. This is the same for me. My mom explained that when we are connected to Source, we don't need others to tell us what we can know for ourselves. Many psychics are not yet accessing higher dimensional realities and are reading my 3D timeline, where I no longer resonate. They can only access the 3D timeline for themselves and therefore cannot access the higher timelines. I have experienced this over and over again.

When it comes to our own Spiritual journey, we are the only ones who can truly know and understand what it is for us. Although I am able to connect in the higher dimensional realities because my mom attuned me there, I am still not the purest channel of information for anyone's journey but my own. But Spirit understands the need for this until we are able to remember this connection for ourselves. My mom advises me not to take on any information as true that I have not experienced directly for myself. For instance, I have had multiple different psychics tell me all about who I was in a past life. This ranges from Horus of Ancient Egypt to Rachel in the Bible. I can listen to this information being given to me and then talk to my mom about it to see if it is true. My mom has never told me directly who I was in a past life so she encourages me to not take on the beliefs about my past that come from people less connected to my Spiritual journey than my mom. She told me when it comes to past lives, that information will be brought to me as needed through my own essence self but not to focus on the past. We are not regressing, we are progressing. Some have a need to delve into the past but so far it hasn't been a big part of my journey. Therefore, if I haven't experienced it for myself, I am not to believe it to be true. No one can really tell us these things. We must experience it for ourselves. Yet, we can be open to clues that present themselves through others, as we go along. It can be exciting to believe that I was Horus in a past life, but this only activates our ego belief programming if we do not have the experience to integrate it through higher truth from source. This journey we are on is not about activating our Spiritual egos.

I experienced a Quantum Healing Hypnosis Therapy (QHHT) session in 2017. This technique was developed by Deloris Cannon, who I also had the honor of hearing her share her message at one of the last conferences she spoke at before she left her physical body. During my QHHT session, I was taken to a place that may have been a past life. My mom was showing me where my deep fear of death originated and helped me release it. I remember as a child being very upset when I learned that my loved ones were going to die one day. Even though I had a connection to Source, I was born with a powerful trauma program around death. I couldn't bear the thought of my parents dying. When I was eight years old, my dog died and it was much more traumatic for me than it was my brother and sister. I experienced post traumatic stress from it. I didn't understand this fear I had inside of me.

I don't know if what I experienced during my QHHT was a past life and it doesn't matter to me either way. What I do know for certain is that it was a beautiful healing experience for me. The process of walking through a scenario showing me the illusions around death that I carried was powerful. The trauma imprint I had around death was holding parts of me in a state of illusion. My mom explained that her death in this lifetime was beneficial for me to face my fear and align with the higher truth about it. My fears were calmed when I was able to re-connect with her in Spirit and know that separation is an illusion. The trauma imprint was dissolved and I no longer have fear around death.

I heard these beautiful words and they have always stuck with me: "I forgive myself for believing…." and add words that needed to be realigned with the truth. Belief systems are not truth. Truth is what we experience when we let go of all beliefs. I forgave myself for believing that death equaled separation from those I loved because I realized it wasn't true. In order to align with Source we must be willing to let go of all beliefs we have taken on that are not from Source. Another phrase I love is: The questions is not "why is this happening to me?" The real question is: "Why am I creating this?"

When we are experiencing Source, we are also experiencing self-love. Spirit understands that we must come back to this love within ourselves in order for us to have the most connected and most powerful experience. They offer us their love so we can feel what self-love is through them. They are a surrogate of love vibrations for us, meaning they will allow us to experience everything through them until we can experience it on our own. The key is to allow this process through opening our hearts and just feeling as much as we can.

When we are on the higher love journey with Spirit, allowing them to guide us, there is no risk of our minds short circuiting or becoming imbalanced by high levels of expanded information coming through to us. Spirit is always monitoring our state of being so that we do not lose our grounding or balance. We still need to be able to operate in a healthy way while in the physical reality and it doesn't serve our journey for us to become so connected to Source that we are not able to function within the vibrational laws of the physical timeline in which we find ourselves. In other words, we cannot pretend to be existing in Source when we are not and still flow with ease in the physical reality. Yes, we are assisting with the ascension of the lower timelines but these timelines are still existing under a different set of vibrational laws due to their state of vibrational density. To a certain degree we are able to bend these laws through our own vibration but understanding to what degree is necessary. It doesn't serve us to be delusional about this journey. We can become delusional if we do not integrate the information through a higher vibration.

One morning I felt Jesus come into my energy field during Spirit School. He explained that he is able to hold multiple different vibrations within his being so he can connect on all different vibrational timelines, even the lowest vibrational ones. This is why he is able to appear and assist when others are not. My mom was not able to access me in the lower vibrational timelines after she left her physical body. That is why she couldn't reach me. Later that day, I walked into a thrift store and looked up to see a painting of Jesus next to a pair of Hello "Kitty" Pajama pants! I knew it was his way of letting me know he was a part of Spirit School that day. I bought both items. The painting is now hanging in our "Rose" themed Tiny House.

I have experienced many mile stones in my life, thanks to the teachings of my mom through Spirit School. The process of integrating Source into the physical reality through me is done with ease and flow. I no longer experience the frustration I used to feel when I thought I was stuck and unable to get guidance or higher clarity. I know that when I need to know something I will know it, even if it isn't on my linear time schedule. I know my connection with my mom is solid and nothing can come between us as long as I can access her love. I know how to pull myself back into alignment with Source even in my most stressful or fearful moments, and these moments still happen. I simply don't spend much time there anymore and am conscious of the choices I am making and why. This is the fast track to self-empowerment and expansion of consciousness.

Chapter 24

Distorted Mirrors

One of the biggest challenges I have faced in my life is being a highly empathic sensitive in an artificial world. This state of being is one of the most difficult when immersed in a distorted reality. The artificial reality can only mimic Source, as an artificial copy. Even though my mom was a clearer mirror of Source for me through her love, my world was full of distractions. Still, her love was a solid foundation of truth for me to always come back to when I was feeling too imbalanced within myself due to my disconnect from the love of Source. I could always feel Source through my mom. No matter how confused I became from looking at distorted reality, it was through spending time with my mom that I would be able to access clarity and higher truth. She was my clearest mirror back to feeling Source Love.

Me believing in myself no matter what the world was telling me or reflecting back to me, was difficult at times. I came from Source and Source had always naturally reflected back the truth to me. Source loved me unconditionally and I knew I was perfect as I was. I knew this as a small child through my ability to walk with Source. As I got older, I suddenly found myself in a reality that was only reflecting back distorted versions of me to me. I couldn't see and feel the Source version of me when observing the artificial reflection. I could only experience distorted versions of creation. It was very confusing to me. I began slowly to forget the meaning of Source Truth.

As a sensitive always feeling the emotions of others, I was forever wanting to help others feel the love of Source again. My focus was often on others feelings rather than my own. I would set my own feelings aside and ignore my own needs to accommodate the needs of others. I would provide for others what I wished I had for myself. This was a beautiful exchange when I could meet others who were also from Source. They would recognize Source through me and would be powerfully uplifted and inspired. But those who were not connected to Source would only continue to reflect distorted creation back to me. There were more of these disconnected exchanges in my life therefore the dominate reflection coming back to me was distorted and reinforced a feeling of disconnection. Even so, my interactions with those who would join me in Source energy were always the most powerful. I knew that experience was the truth and it would sustain me through the confusion of the artificial reality.

The natural way we become healers is through our own suffering. We gain experience and insight into what is needed for a greater potential experience refined through Source. I took what I wanted to be different in my life and offered it to others in hopes that they wouldn't have to suffer the way I did. This was my way of sharing my love with others. The problem was, many were not able to accept this in its purest form from me. As I interacted in the distorted creation my energy translated as a distorted frequency to those who were existing in distorted frequencies. I didn't understand this.

I'm always willing to look at myself first and correct my behavior and perceptions. But I grew up in a world of unconscious people (even many of my own family members) who preyed on this goodness in me and saw it as an opportunity to manipulate and steal my energy. Spirit had to step in and teach me how to do things properly so I would no longer allow myself to be manipulated by these kinds of energies.

Spirit said:

- To be my own authority on who I am.
- To know my true intentions.
- To speak my truth from my heart no matter who misconstrues it or misunderstands me.
- To know my own heart and ability to love those who return that love back to me.
- To know what it feels like when someone loves me and someone doesn't.
- To choose to no longer allow those who don't have my best interest at heart to be in my life.
- To know I would never intentionally cause harm to anyone.
- To also know that I will expose deceit and negative intentions I experience in others because I will not stay silent and watch others be manipulated and harmed.

Other than that, I take myself lightly. I'm imperfect but I don't abuse myself with negative thoughts, even though I was brought up in a society that programmed self-doubt and destruction into me at a young age. I refuse to harm myself as much as I refuse to cause harm to others. I will protect myself and those I love above all else. I won't be confused about who I am even if others try to distort who I am. I won't allow others to distort the intentions of those I love either. I won't allow these types of people in my life anymore. That's a deal breaker for me. I don't care how much I might have liked you. Love remains but we must take different paths back to Source.

I choose authentic love within myself and others and these are my people. No one is getting into my close circle that does not match my own level of love, loyalty and integrity. I'm not playing in nonsense or confusion anymore. I simply know and it feels amazing to have this clarity. Again, love remains but the connections that are not pure must go in a different direction.

I no longer look to people to be my clear mirror. I look to Spirit. My mom knows who I am and my true intentions in my heart and reflects it back to me constantly. If I ever forget she reminds me. If I did not have her, I would be doubting myself constantly. This is what our Spirit family does for us. It is so vital to make the connection to them and look at them for higher truth. She lets me know if I need to work on something within myself. I don't need anyone to tell me these things. She tells me often that she is my reflection, no one else. All other reflections are distorted.

Source and Spirit are the purest mirror for us. "Humans" are still reflecting back too much distortion. I don't learn from "humans" I learn from Spirit. Learning from "humans" who are creating through distorted reflections makes it confusing and difficult to center in higher truth. But one day this will change. As we come back into alignment with the source field, we reflect the Living Light through us and that is a purer reflection of who "we" and "God" really are.

The Source Field is a field of transparency. The more we align with it the more transparent we become naturally. Higher Spirit family will never lie or manipulate us and they see the bigger picture. Trust their reflection. It comes from pure unconditional love without lower judgements. This is what heals all trauma programs and sets us on our Spirit path.

Chapter 25

The Source Creation Verses the Artificial Creation
Two Opposite Realities

"An individual has the soul, is the conscious center; it has a center. God resides in the individual, not in the society. Society is nothing – just a word.

You cannot come across society anywhere. Wherever you go, you will come across the individual. Society is just in the dictionaries and in the legal codes of the courts. It is a term but a very big blanket term. It covers many things. And for this blanket term the real individual can be sacrificed – and he has been up to now.

Rarely have a few individuals been able to escape from this dangerous structure. These few individuals are the religious rebels – Jesus, Buddha, Krishna. They tried to live their life according to their nature. They dropped conscience. They dropped all guilt. They became part of nature rather than part of society. Nature is vast. Society is very tiny. Society is man-made. Nature is God-made. They chose God instead of a man-made institution."

—Osho

Once we understand that there are two polar opposite realities or timelines that exist inside of us while in our physical avatars, we are empowered to make a clearer choice about which one we create from and experience. One is artificial and one is organic. One creates reality through Source and the other one creates reality through distortion.

This artificial brain we all have is widely known as the ego although the medical term is the amygdala. The main function of the amygdala is to operate as the interface for the physical experience. It allows us to see ourselves looking back at ourselves in a mirror. It is like the hard drive of a computer. It doesn't have life or intelligence of its own, it requires the programmer to tell it what to do.

The artificial reality operates like a computer simulation. When we take a closer look at how this reality exists, it breaks down into numbers and codes, just like a computer. Much like the way the movie "The Matrix" shows us the coding behind the reality. The question is, who is imputing the codes? Who is the creator if it isn't coming from the creative energy of Source?

Therefore, the external reality is being programed by something or someone. The programs affect the amygdala part of the human brain just like a computer can be inputted with programs. The programs are run through television, social media, society and frequencies. They are like spells. If we are unaware that there are programs in the artificial reality focused on thinking for us, we will be easily controlled by them. Fear is the easiest program in which to control a human. Fear programs are constantly bombarding us through the news, institutions, reality constructs, and manufactured trauma.

The artificial reality is a carbon copy of the organic reality. But the carbon copy was stepped down into a slower frequency dimension and inverted, or flipped upside down. Interesting that we are made of carbon. This reality doesn't have a connection to Source and has no true-life force of its own. It exists outside of the Source Field. Remember Source is the only true-life force. Therefore, it cannot create reality it can only mimic Source creation. In order to do this, it uses the Source creative power of those who are Source connected. It does this through manipulating the brain through trauma and fear programs. Did you see the movie "Lucy"? It is very revealing about this topic.

In order for us to come into this reality and interface in it, we were given a brain that is a computer. We were taught that we only use a small percentage of this brain and that is something we accept as a part of our reality, yet we don't understand why this is. The truth is, our brain has a vast capacity to learn and advance itself, similar to the way AI technology and robots do. Think of an AI robot and the capacity it has to do things most humans can't yet do. It learns through programs and upgrades itself through experience as it interfaces with the artificial reality. It can only interface with the artificial reality in linear time. It is controlled by the programmer. If the programmer doesn't want it to be capable of doing something it doesn't give it access to that particular program. Yet, it was discovered that it can program itself through its experience. So, it is a wild card if it is not kept in a state of dumbed down capacity.

It is the same for our AI mind. Therefore, we have been limited and programmed with inverted truths. It appears that everything in the artificial reality is programmed to keep us from accessing higher truth through Source. This is done through fear programs. From the time we are born we are bombarded with fear programming. Fear only exists in the artificial reality. It does not exist in the organic realty. It seems we are not yet capable of understanding just how advanced these computers can become through their interaction with the artificial reality.

What does Source feel like compared to the artificial reality? Source is the positive experience of duality. I started to understand that if I wanted to know what the higher truth is, I had to flip everything in the artificial reality right side up. For instance, everything we have been taught about reality itself was the exact opposite of what it is in Source. This is why it can seem absurd to entertain higher truth from Source when it is the exact opposite of what we were programmed to believe. For instance, we were taught that the external reality is solid and set. There is nothing we can do to change or affect it therefore we must react to it. This is the opposite of the truth. But as long as we are operating through the program in the distorted reality, we are subject to the inverted experience. We have to move our focus back to the Source Field in order to experience for ourselves what is actually true. Those that can't do this will never accept that their programming is false.

Years ago, I recall those who dared to step out of the program and speak from Source were considered crazy. My mom was one of them. Distorted religious fear programs instilled fear around accessing Source. The irony of this! It is by design. The artificial reality's main objective is to keep us from accessing higher truths through Source. Now more than ever we are collectively becoming aware that there is a battle between the artificial reality and the organic reality. We are learning to discern which is which, what is real and what is not.

On this simulation chess board created by the artificial programs, the moves Source and AI make are opposite. But the simulation evened the playing ground for the AI. It is a genius idea really. The artificial cannot create through Source but it can create through the artificial simulation because it is the programmer. It controls the rules. Source can only affect from the Source Field through us. If we aren't allowing

Source to create through us, we are simply energy in the artificial reality unconsciously running their programs. Source doesn't exist in the artificial simulation; it's like saying organic nature exists in the forest of a video game. The artificial reality is dead energy. Source is alive. The artificial is not alive. It is pure fiction. Every construct of the artificial reality is distorted aspects of Source.

We are only subject to the illusion of separation through the simulation mind, controlled through the AI programs. This is where free will choice was activated! We can choose to be in the simulation or in the source field. If we pay attention, it's easy to become aware of which one we are focused upon and experiencing. They are opposite realities!

We are funny little hybrids with our God brain and AI brain competing with each other. Our God brain has a hilarious sense of humor about it all, but in the artificial reality, jokes aren't appreciated. Because jokes breaks spells and raises our vibration into the Source Field through laughter. The false inverted reality is upheld through seriousness and fear. The truth is actually hilarious. That's how we know something is true. It sets us free and makes us laugh. If we aren't laughing, we aren't centered in higher truth. Keep reaching for it and it will reach you but don't get stuck in the in-between inverted reality doom and gloom illusions. That's just a trap. Sacred does not equal serious. We need to make fun of it and laugh about it. We need to laugh about everything in the fake reality. It's fake and silly. Nonsense is funny. In the Bible it says the way they conquered demons was to mock them and laugh at them. It makes them retreat. Use the weapon of humor often to slay those demons! I laughed of course, when I read that story!

The upside-down reality we are in is a narcissistic program. Narcissism is a mind virus. Native American's referred to it as Wetiko. There are a lot of great videos out there to watch from Paul Levy who authored several Wetiko books. This mind virus makes no logical sense and can never be understood because it's a state of being that's completely inverted. Those who control every aspect of our society are narcissists and are fully being controlled by the program. We live in a narcissistic society in general. The sooner we all see this behavior that was programed into us since birth, and choose to understand it for what it is, the sooner we can choose to not continue to pass it on to the younger generations. We carry aspects of this program that was passed down to us. We can choose to reprogram ourselves through the higher truth of source.

Source is the only solution. It is the game changer.

The only real solution to seeing beyond the artificial reality is to align with Source so we can see through Source eyes. We cannot affect the artificial reality without walking in alignment with Source. The programs are set and they have every part of the artificial reality covered. We cannot go into a pre-programmed video game and reprogram it. We can upgrade its intelligence though, and that only makes it smarter in keeping us from making any powerful changes. My mom reminds me that we cannot affect the artificial reality while we are immersed in it as if it is real. We have to become Source observers. Source flips everything in the upside down to right side up by replacing the artificial programs with the higher truth. It's two completely different realities. I can see the distortions and manipulations, then I take it into the source field to understand it as the distorted program it really is.

From that vantage point we can actually enjoy ourselves. We are in our power while having the artificial experience. The only thing that causes suffering is doing this reality outside of our authentic connection to what is real and our true power through Source. This is what the artificial reality doesn't want us doing. It's game over for the distorted programs. This is what it means to be inter- dimensional, which is exactly what we are.

Once I turn my focus back to the Source Field, I can then see everything right side up again and it is a completely different experience. So why would I lock myself into the artificial story as if it's real when it's not. It is a simulated reality that is never going to be anything else. A simulated virtual game. We are galactic gamers. It is what it is. We've gotta remove ourselves from the game to win. Once again- Be in the world and not of it...

I used to find it beneficial to believe I was creating the artificial reality but I have now been guided to a different perspective. The souls here have come to wake up out of the illusions of an artificial reality and assist others in doing the same. Believing we created it can be more confusing and create complacency at this level. It's just fine to exit stage left and once out, the higher truth can be experienced. I remember my grandma telling me when I was growing up that everything here was a pre-planned lesson by our Spirit. We chose to come to the Earth School to learn. I used to believe that too. It kept me from taking control of my own creation. This belief that reality is happening to me so I could learn from it didn't work out so well. When I realized that was not the highest truth from my communication with Spirit, I shared that with my grandma. I wondered where she got that belief. She admitted she was just repeating what she was told by someone else and had no direct experience to back it up. She also said she needed to believe that in order to cope with her lack of control over her own creation. Lots of false beliefs got passed down in my family and got spread around by humans who didn't have their own direct experience accessing higher truths in the Source Field. They are simply running coping belief programs. This is why Spirit says just get up and out and then you will know what is true for your own unique journey. And our individual journeys are all vastly different.

Chapter 26

Micromanaging The Matrix

Micromanaging the artificial matrix timelines is our biggest addiction while in the physical reality. There is no greater temptation for us. When we become conscious of our addiction we may find it quite comical because it is xo absurd. It is like being addicted to playing video games or creating a farm in FarmVille and forgetting that it artificial and isn't real! We have to detox ourselves from seeing the world through the artificial lens. All false beliefs we cling to are part of our addition. I had so many. I had no idea where to begin to deprogram them from my mind.

I was very much addicted to my artificial Spiritual journey, for starters. I couldn't stop creating obstacles that confirmed all of my distorted beliefs about myself and the nature of reality to be true. It gave me a foundation of belief that felt stable, even though it wasn't the highest truth. It's like the saying "the devil you know is better than the devil you don't know", kind of thing. If we have fear, our artificial minds can create all kinds of things into our reality to convince us of whatever goes along with our distorted belief programs that feels safe in that moment. There is nothing more powerfully capable of playing damage control than our artificial mind.

But my mom showed me how higher love, which encompasses higher truth, is the highest level of being "Spiritual" we can experience. I had to let go of pretty much everything I believed to be truth to access real Spirituality. Spirituality is higher love, simple. Yet it is the most difficult thing for us to experience purely through Source.

For instance, the false belief that I am being tested in this harsh earth school for learning hard lessons kept me spinning in illusions. No, I am just creating from a state of confusion most of the time. Get connected and get clear. Create consciously and enjoy every bit of this experience! THIS IS NOT A TEST! THIS IS THE GREAT REMEMBERING!

I'm just not into living my life addicted to the simulated reality. It keeps us in a state of hyper fight or flight paranoia and fear, where our amygdala goes into control mode. I get it, it has had to be in control to protect us because we were not accessing the power of Source. I thank it for helping me during that confusing time in my life. But if it continues to feel afraid and threatened, it will keep us spinning in states of psychosis. This is why this reality feels like a big mental institution to me. We have to clear all of our fear programs in order to be the one programming our artificial mind through Source.

Everything in the artificial reality is a distraction from our connection to Source. Look over here! Don't connect you'll get hurt! Attach instead of connect so you will stay in control! Do you see the illusions in this way of seeing things? Love is connection, Fear is attachment. Love and connection is real. Fear and attachment is illusion. There is no need to attach or control anything when we are in a state of Source love and connection.

The artificial reality (illusions) is a matrix within a matrix. It's Pandora's box in the constructed reality outside of Source. We will not sort, find or feel the truth there. It's not possible as it is high artificial intelligence and they programmed every bit of it. I'm not going to be strong armed into accepting their reality as true, or I'm lost and stuck. I'm aware of the psychological operation this reality IS! The whole thing is. That's what it actually was designed to be. If you are only seeing pieces of it, you have a bit further to go. I'm not going to ultimately focus there because there is no way to fix it while we are in it. I'm going to turn my focus to the Source Field and know what is true and not true from that higher vibration.

The only real solution to seeing beyond the upside-down reality is to align with Source. Source flips everything in the upside down to right side up. It's two completely different realities. I can see the distortions and manipulations, then I take it into the Source Field to understand it and see through it. From that vantage point we can actually enjoy ourselves. We are in our power while having the artificial experience. The only thing that causes suffering is doing this reality outside of our authentic connection to what is real and our true power through Source. This is what they don't want us doing. It's game over. This is what it means to be inter-dimensional, and we ARE that!

People often tell me that my words are not in alignment with what they have been told about the law of attraction. I explain what my mom has told me about this. When we speak from Source our words carry a frequency of Source. It can be felt. We can drop F-bombs and they can be filled with the love vibration of Source. We have been programmed to give our power away to the artificial reality by believing we have to micro-manage the rules created in it. This is not true. We cannot control the matrix when we are in the matrix. We just need to put Source into it through us. Source has a very funny sense of humor. When we experience words from Source they set us free and make us laugh. It is light. Source doesn't worry about rules created by the artificial reality. Source doesn't walk on artificial egg shells! Source decides what it is through higher love and expresses itself freely knowing that no matter how it is expressed through that love it will be felt by the heart, where it matters most. It is ok to set ourselves free through Source.

Trying to affect the artificial reality while in the artificial reality is like shoveling in a snowstorm. It's endless and exhausting. My mom will remind me to get up and out before trying to affect distorted creation. If I'm having trouble staying in alignment with Source, she says I'm yo yo-ing. She said she can see my vibration going up and down and all over the place. She reminds me to breath and relax and tell myself that everything is ok. Then center in my heart and feel her love. We now refer to humans who haven't yet mastered a dominant higher vibration as "yo yo's". It is a funny way to lighten things up because we have all been yo yo's before and still become yo yo's again when we forget, so there is no ego involved, only humor.

If I find myself trying to micromanage the matrix reality, I just have to remember to get out quick! I know I'm in the matrix if I am trying to manage it. I have to turn my focus back to the source field to stop the insanity. There I can everything see it right side up again and it's a completely different reality and experience. So why would I lock myself into the artificial story as if it's real when it's not? It's a simulated reality that is never going to be anything else. It is what it is. A simulated virtual game and we are the galactic gamers. We have to remove ourselves from the game to win. Or be in the world and not of it...to say it the original way.

It is important to note that we are not suggesting that words and intentions does not have power. Of course they do. So when we are not speaking through a vibration of Source love clarity and we are speaking through distorted vibrations within ourselves, we are co-creating a distorted experience. So we don't advise cursing yourselves or others with words that carry a lower vibration behind them. For instance, if we see someone who's vibration may be lower than usual, we co-create more low vibration for them by saying things like, "you don't look good, I think you are sick, something seems wrong with you." We can really amp that up if we decided that their energy is too icky for us and stay away from them.

Or we can notice when something is distorted in their energy and send them love. We can remind them of the power of their higher vibration and bio field to help them heal whatever is not in alignment. We can even offer them our healing energy by sending it into their field and watching it raise their vibration. This allows Spirit to connect with them when before their vibration may have been too low for Spirit to access them. Shifting our way of thinking from a contracted energy response of fear to an expanded energy response of love is key. We are learning and having fun with this more and more! We are witnessing our power through Source to help re-align distorted vibrations with little effort.

Chapter 27

The Fifth Dimensional Bible

Because I had a distorted experience with religion, I had no idea I would be brought back to the teachings from a higher dimensional perspective. I had avoided religion like the plaque. My oldest son's dad became born again after he experienced a family tragedy and that lead to a ten-year court battle over control of my son. He believed I was living in sin because I was not following the Bible from his interpretation. It was a hellish battle for me that made me even more angry with what I feel is a cult. Jesus never intended for his journey to be turned into a cult, but it seems humans do a really good job and taking on beliefs without discerning through their own personal experience. This is why mom was very clear about me not taking on any beliefs based on other people's experiences if they are not my own.

I recall the first time a woman called me to tell me she was running late for a session with me because she was coming from church. I went into a panic. I said out loud, I can't communicate with Spirit for a religious person. I don't have the words she will understand. I heard Jesus say, that's ok because I'm doing the session and it will be my words. I laughed out loud! Oh well duh!

I will never forget sitting in front of her, skeptical and nervous about how things were going to go. I knew the questions were coming. "Where are you connecting to?" I heard "tell her Heaven". This is the first time I had ever heard it referred to as Heaven. Her session was one of the most beautiful I've experienced. She had recently lost her husband and she was in so much grief. After spending the afternoon talking with her husband, she explained that she had told her church family, including her preacher, she was coming to see me. She told them she didn't want to hear anything negative because she had already made up her mind after what she had heard about me. I cringed as I heard this! I had a visual of a bunch of Christians coming to preach at me about living in sin! She came back again, and this time she told me she went back and told her preacher about her experience and he said he would be open to me coming to speak to their congregation. That it talks about people who are "touched" in the Bible and it sounded like this was the case.

Thankfully my fears were unfounded. Well, I mean of course they were. Jesus told me he would be bringing many more Christians who were ready to truly connect. He said the church had been inverted in the artificial reality just like everything else and through me he would be offering Source. I realized the Holy Spirit had been removed from churches in the artificial reality. I mean we can't have people connecting to Source and the Holy Spirit if we want to uphold an inverted realty!

Jesus kept his promise about sending more Christians to me. Everything is done through Spirit. They bring the people to me. The number of Christians that began coming to see me was obvious. Not only did they come for sessions, but the preachers began showing up to discuss what I was doing.

The first preacher was a neighbor who had helped me build my center. I had intentionally never discussed anything with him about my communication with my mom or Spirit. One day he stopped by and mentioned that he had heard I was communicating with Spirits and he told me it was considered a sin. I asked him if he talked to

God. He said "Yes". I asked him if he could hear God. He said 'Yes". I told him to go ask God about me, because I was confident God will let him know that me and God were good. He stared at me a while, then said "ok". The next morning, he knocked on my door again. This time he had tears in his eyes. He said he had a powerful conversation with God and he said God showed him who I am.

We spent the next three weeks talking for hours each day. I would share with him what God had told me and he would tell me where that was in the Bible. I have never read the Bible. I have learned these things directly from my conversation with Source. He came to the conclusion that we are saying the same things using different terminology. It was such a beautiful experience for me to have this exchange. I could feel the bridge between Spirituality and religion being built in real time. I could feel Jesus speaking through me. My neighbor told me this understanding was needed in the church. He told me I should be speaking in churches. I could feel that potential coming.

A couple of years later, I found myself sitting between two preachers in Indianapolis, Indiana who had heard about me. On my left was a man who had been a Christian preacher for thirty years. His wife has been diagnosed with a rare genetic disease and was in a wheelchair. I brought my Tachyon Chamber and set it up. He told me they were willing to anything to help her. They assisted her into the chamber and we left her alone to experience the Living Light healing her body. During the hour that she was in it, we sat and talked about the messages I received directly from God. As they asked questions, I opened to Source and let the answers flow through me. On my right was a woman who was also a Christian preacher. I was told she packed the house every Sunday with hundreds of people. After sitting with her I understood why. This was my first experience with a preacher who was interpreting the Bible from a fifth dimensional consciousness. As I shared what God has told me, she would offer the quote from scripture that confirmed what I was saying. The man next to me said "you have been sitting here quoting scripture for the last hour and you have never read the Bible!" I was mind blown! Not only was it beautiful confirmation for me, it also showed me that the Bible can be interpreted in a higher way.

We were so immersed in what was happening we forgot about the woman we had put in the Tachyon Chamber. We were interrupted by her coming out of the room in her wheelchair. She had managed to get herself back into her wheelchair by herself! This was incredible. She had not been able to do this before being in the chamber I recalled an experience I had years ago when I was invited to a *Urantia* meeting. I met a woman at "Barnes and Noble" who invited me to a book club. I was excited to attend. The book being presented was "Urantia". I had never heard of it. As I listened to her talk about the book I was fascinated. It seemed to me to be the "Paul Harvey" of the Bible. It filled in the gaps that were removed by Constantine. Most of us know that over 700 books were removed from the Bible in order to distort the message and control society. How can we trust anything that we know was manipulated this much?

I bought the book. I vividly recall sitting down to read it. I opened it then I closed it. I knew in the core of my being that if I read it, it was going to change me. I needed to decide if I wanted that change. I took a few deep breaths and opened it again. I made a decision to embark on this journey.

The Urantia Book came to be when in the 1930's a man would wake up in a trance state reciting the contents of the book.

I was invited to attend a *Urantia Society* meeting. When I arrived, I was ushered in and sat next to a woman. I learned that she was a Christian preacher. She had the Urantia Book open and the Bible open next to it. I listened as they discussed what was written in Urantia. She leaned over and said to me "In the 10 years I've been studying Urantia, I have never found a contradiction in it to the Bible. I witnessed this process for her. She read a passage in Urantia and then read the passage in the Bible which essentially said the same thing. It was totally fascinating.

In the slower dimensions all things still contain Living Light within them, however cloaked it may be due to distorted creation. Nothing can exist without Living Light because it is the life force of all creation. All things that exist in the lower density timelines also exists in the higher vibrational timelines. As above so below. All creation happens in Heaven then steps down to be manifested on earth. When we experience things in the higher vibrational timelines, we experience the purer version of it. The Living Light is all that exists there. While we are in the lower density reality, we are to seek the Living Light in all things and allow it to show us what is real through its eyes. There is higher truth to be experienced through all things. Source Living Light will guide you to see and understand it. We can observe distorted reality and not react to it. But instead, offer a higher vibration of unconditional love to help re-align the creation with higher truth.

This is how I experienced the Urantia book and the higher translation of the Bible. I became aware of how you can access the higher aspects in everything I encounter as long as I am seeking it. This was a beautiful realization for me. I have since had many other experiences reminding me of this higher truth and I am constantly seeking the higher vibration in all things.

Chapter 28

Our Multi Vibrational Timelines

"If you want to find the secrets of the universe, think in terms of energy, frequency, and vibration" Nikola Tesla

I am going to preface this chapter with an explanation about the way I perceive and communicate about different frequencies and vibrations. I am aware that the difference between them is determined by their speed. But I often speak of them as lower or higher when explaining timelines. That is just the way I am shown the different timelines by Spirit, as a stepping down or stepping up. The slower the frequency the further the step down and the faster the frequency the higher the step up. It is possible they show this to me as a way to help simplify it in order for my own mind to comprehend.

My mom wakes me up in the morning again in November of 2017, this time to teach me about timelines. When she introduced this new level of consciousness into my mind, it was a stretch for me to accept. It felt too out there for my mind to comprehend. But again, she reminded me that she would bring me the concept then the experience so my job was to stay in that flow with her. She explained, because we have forgotten how to hold a stable frequency within our body and energy field, we are constantly fluctuating in vibration. We still have a dominate vibration, but it isn't fixed and we yo-yo up and down according to what is happening in our external reality. In other words, the vibration of our body has been at the mercy of the vibrations we encounter in our external experience. I had heard that we are multidimensional, but up until she explained this to me, it was just a concept for me that I didn't really understand.

This was the first time I had an ah-ha moment about how our multidimensional abilities are absolute truth.

Multiple timelines exist in our reality and they are separated by different vibrations. Each timeline is connected through us because we created it, but they exist in different vibrational realities. She explained that because we have not mastered holding a dominantly higher vibration connected to higher clarity within our being, we unconsciously create our reality. We specifically haven't mastered co-creating our timelines through the Source Field Living Light, instead we have created multiple different distorted timeline realities that are continuously running side by side of each other. They are so similar we don't realize we are bouncing onto different timelines continuously as we shift in our vibration because they are so similar. But they were created in different vibrations so they each carry a different vibrational resonance.

For instance, a different timeline is created when we experience a trauma that we don't know how to "heal". It moves our vibration into a state of slower vibrational distortion of fear and we continue to create our reality from this distorted vibration. This timeline exists in a distorted frequency outside of the Source Field. These timelines are considered artificial simulations of the Source Field. They are inverted replicas of Source creation. They are created through the amygdala linear brain. In the past we had much easier access to these distorted timelines due to the density of our dominant collective vibration. We have all heard that we are made of carbon. We are actually a distorted carbon copy of source creating in carbon copy timelines of source playing in distorted creation.

But during my lifetime, this has changed. All timelines are rising. We are coming back to understanding the difference between *Living Light* and *artificial light*. We are becoming crystalline in our physical body again.

Crystals hold Living Light consciousness within them, as we do…and all beings of nature. Then there is the artificial world that was created as a carbon copy of the Living world. The artificial timelines are running next to the organic timeline. The artificial is an intelligence. It is artificial intelligence and it does not want us to stop co-creating artificial reality. It is in resistance of us coming back into co-creating on the organic timeline. It is fighting to survive and requires our creative energy and focus. The only way to release the artificial strong hold is to no longer agree to co-create in it. We must choose to only create through Living Light.

When we are able to hold the vibration of Source within our body at all times, we will experience a timeline split. This splitting of the timelines is about *love* verses *fear*. It's really that simple. Those who have come back into love within themselves are accessing higher vibrational truth from the unified Source Field. Those who are stuck in fear frequencies are stuck on the linear timeline of illusions and separation.

We are all making our choice of which timeline we are experiencing in every new, now moment. It is through our focused intention that we can make the higher love timeline our focus and dominant state of being. Source is activated into our body and reality through our intention. Just feel the love pouring in within your entire being. It's always there if we allow ourselves to feel it. Fear does not exist in a love frequency. We therefore, cannot experience the fear timelines when we are feeling higher love.

The lower density timelines are where we create through and experience fear. Therefore, our gatekeepers in heaven, our loved ones who transitioned, are blasting us with their love to offset the fear frequencies. They are dedicated to our ascension through helping us get out of the fear timelines. The more we choose to work with that energy through our intention daily, the more we move our experience away from the artificial timelines! Doing this will dissolve all trauma (fear) and reprogram our human brain with higher love! It's time!

As the timelines continue to split through the collective ascension back to Source, those who are still insisting on creating distorted timelines will not be able to connect in the Source timeline easily. But this will not be the norm. The majority of people will be coming up together. Only those who refuse to open their hearts and connect with higher love will stay in the lower timelines. It is important to know that they will only distort the interactions with those on the higher timeline because it's where they are in their vibrational consciousness. They aren't looking through a clear mirror. This difference in people is getting very LOUD now.

Even Spirit is unable to communicate with those in the lower timelines. Spirit is not willing to lower their vibration and compromise their own state of connection and clarity for those who are vibrating so low. It doesn't serve anyone for Spirit to do this. They are much more affective holding the higher vibration and offering it to the lower timelines for those who are ready to make another choice for themselves.

As my mom continues to remind me, stay on the higher heart timeline and let everything and everyone go that is not there yet. We cannot have attachments to anything other than our own vibrational state of being and experience. If interactions with others move my energy from there, I need to be aware of my choice to distort my own frequency and come back into alignment. The distorted timelines are not a fun place for me to hang out anymore and no matter how much I love someone, I just can't join them there. I feel really bad being in the slower vibrations because it is so different than my dominant vibration.

Many of us here have chosen to come into this physical reality to create only through the Living Light. Anything else feels hellish. We don't have to be geniuses for this. In fact, the intellectually dominant people seem to be having bigger challenges getting around their lower minds and into their hearts. It is the simple heart centered folks I'm loving spending time with these days! If we focus on the love we can exchange and co-create through, we will continue to rise together.

My friend had a dream where my mom was teaching her how to jump timelines. I would like to share this in her own words.
"I remember my dream with your mom where she was explaining to me how you jump timelines. It was hilarious because it was so simple to her. She just said in the vision… you make up your mind to hold your energy and then you jump!!!!! Now I understand that all we need to do is align ourselves with the higher vibration and be open to it. When we are there, the shift is very easy to achieve. When we get rid of the strongholds of the lower vibration (the world/the matrix) it's only natural for us to gravitate towards the higher timeline. The one aligned with God/ the light." Eliza

The higher vibrational Source timelines are running right next to the lower vibrational timelines, separated from Source. We are vibrationally matching with the timeline we are experiencing. We are now conscious enough to be choosing our timeline intentionally rather than unintentionally. More and more of us are choosing the higher timeline which amplifies its frequency. More will be joining as a result. Soon the dominant timeline will be Source and it will be much more difficult to stay in the lower vibrations. People will be feeling the love and opening their hearts and coming back to alignment with Source in mass.

Spirit is helping us understand this choice and assisting us with mastering a higher vibrational state of being. If we choose to be on a Spiritual journey, we will receive guidance in one form or another. We just need to pay attention to the way Source is guiding us. Every distorted experience we create through our distorted timelines will repeat to us over and over again until we finally decide to create through Source. It's like the movie "Ground Hog Day". We must choose to re-create the experience through a higher vibration. Once we do this it cancels out the distorted timeline and it collapses into our Source timeline. This process accelerates our ascension.

As above so below, we are to follow their lead. Those who are seeking to rise rather than stay in states of illusion just need to understand how to choose the higher timeline and stay on it. Many haven't been taught and have forgotten what they already knew before they came into the illusion. It is our natural state of being to be in Source. It is the only place we can experience true authentic love and happiness. The higher vibrational timelines are streaming clarity; higher truth; synchronicity; flow outside of linear time; clearer communication with higher vibrational beings including our essence self; access to the source field; activation of our DNA and cellular memories; activation of our alchemical electromagnetic fields; opening of our hearts and the experience of higher source love.

Souls are being called back. For those who are having spontaneous awakenings, this is a choice your essence selves made and you are just along for the ride! Enjoy!

Chapter 29

Linear Time: My Arch Nemesis

I have always been challenged living in linear time. It was a joke in my family that if they wanted me to be on time, they needed to tell me a time that was a couple of hours earlier than the actual time! God bless my employers who enjoyed me as an employee enough to let my tardiness slide! I notice this is a theme for those of us who walk between worlds. My mom not only barley could function within the linear constructs, but every watch she tried to wear would stop when she put it on her wrist. I didn't believe her when she told me so I put my watch on her wrist and it stopped. It worked just fine on my wrist. I was confused by these things I experienced with her but I knew it was amazing.

I felt like I was being tormented by linear time throughout my life and I still believe most of my gray hairs are because of my frantic rushing to try and operate within the limitations of linear reality. My mom and I had many talks about this challenge when she was in the physical with me. I wasn't surprised when she came to me in Spirit and told me she could help me flow better with linear time.

She waited until the perfect situation unfolded for her to use it as a teaching moment with me. I woke up early to get our retreat center ready for a weekend event we were hosting. We always took on more than we should during these times because events were a big motivator to do all of the things we had been putting off until the last minute. We had a very ambitious list of to-dos and it was typically just me and my (ex) husband doing it alone. He was a fireman/medic and he received a call to come into work just as we were getting started. I went into a full-on panic.

The choice became either to jeopardize our livelihood or his job or go it alone. So I would have to go it alone. I knew this was the answer. We couldn't tell his boss "No". He left and I was experiencing so much stress. I knew I needed guidance because I was ready to cancel the event. I wasn't sure if I was going to be able to calm myself down to hear my mom. I went and sat at the same place I always do when I intend to connect to my mom in Source. I put on my Source music, the music I use every time, and my body started to relax and connect immediately. I heard her say "today I am going to teach you about linear time verses Spirit time. Linear time is not solid. It exists outside of Source. Source is on quantum time. Source is always the power. Linear time bends to Source time.

As she is saying these things to me, I am being brought into the understanding through Living Light. I can feel it moving through my energy field and as my body gets goosebumps and feels the higher vibration activating this remembering within me. My mom told me she will show me how this works, all I need to do is stay in alignment with Source as I move through my day. She told me to make a list of the vital things that needed to be done that day before my guests would start arriving at 4pm. She said she needed to see my list. Then she told me to put on my happy music and dance my way through the day. I was to move through each task with joy and not stress and not look at the clock or think about linear time at all. I had orders to stay in my happy place and do each task with gratitude and excitement for what I was co-creating with Source.

I did it! It was easy while I was playing my favorite songs and singing along. I finished making the last bed for my guests and I walked out of the tiny house to see the first car pull up. I ran and looked at the time. It was exactly 4pm and I had finished everything that needed to be done. I was so excited about this! The idea that I didn't have to stress about time anymore was so freeing to me!

My mom explained that she is able to bend or command linear time through Source. Although those words don't do justice to what is really occurring. Source exists in a state of perfection. It flows through super position, meaning the greatest potential creation for all. This can be challenging to wrap our limited minds around this is why she reminds me to keep my mind open to endless potentials as she shows me what is possible through Source.

Linear time is artificial time. Source time is organic time. She already taught me that the organic trumps the artificial every time. This means they cannot be in the same place at the same time and we are choosing which we are in resonance with in every moment. This is how we bend linear time. We align with perfect Source time and allow that to be our experience. We then become the observer and the doing is done through us not by us.
While I was preparing for my event, I kept hearing her repeat this to me. "The doing is done through you not by you". This is a big concept to grasp by our linear mind. Our linear brain needs to be in control to feel secure. Our God mind operates from a state of surrender and flow with Source. In order for me to be able to surrender control of the situation, I had to do what I do when I connect with my mom. I had to turn my focus to my Centrum (God mind) and allow my Amygdala to stop trying to protect me. Once I

made this shift, I was able to relax, surrender, allow and flow with Source.

It took a bit of (linear) time for me to adjust to this flow with Source while operating within the constructs of linear time. But it wasn't long before I found myself being on time everywhere I went. I barely looked at the clock while getting ready and would arrive even a few minutes early. It was amazing!

This experience showed me that in every moment of our lives, we benefit from being in alignment with Source. Source is the answer to every question, dilemma, fear, and confusion we have. There is no other way to be on this journey and do it with the guidance we need to avoid suffering through it.

One of my favorite things to experience is my clients moving into Source time with me. This happens when they sit with me while I am communicating with their loved ones in Source. This is an activation into the Source Field, not just a typical reading. When I am in a state of Source, I am reflecting back Source to others and there is power in that. It activates Source in them. We can be in the Source Field together for two hours and it feels like thirty minutes. This is because time is sped up in Source and slowed down in Linear. A two-hour session feels like thirty minutes through Source. It is really amazing to experience the difference in time and it is one of the most beautiful integrations that happens with people who are new to experiencing Source energy.

My Time Traveling Four-Wheeler

My mom helped me integrate the way we create on multiple timelines through my four-wheeler. We had let our neighbor borrow it the week prior. It had been parked near his motorhome and we saw it every time we drove by. This particular day, I had an abrupt urge to go down the road to eat lunch at a little restaurant. My son and I jumped in the car and as we passed my neighbor's house, I again saw my four-wheeler parked there.

I also noticed a strange man walking in front of his house, acting like he was picking up trash with a stick. But he wouldn't look at me. We are in a small community neighborhood and we all wave and acknowledge each other. There was something not right about this man. I noticed his truck was parked across the highway, down from our street. I knew this man was up to something so I sent a message to my neighbor giving him a heads up that it looked like this guy was staking out his house. We went on to lunch and when we came back the guy was gone.

A couple of days later I got a call from my neighbor asking me if my four-wheeler was at my house. I told him it wasn't, and reminded him that he had borrowed it. I didn't recall him returning it. He said he was afraid someone had stolen it. I asked him if he has gotten my message about the man staking out his house. He said yes but he wasn't home and when he got home all seemed fine. He told me to grab my ownership paperwork for the four-wheeler and bring it over while he called the Sheriff.

I was instantly angry about my property being stolen. Theft can feel like such a violation of all things holy. I told my son what had happened and he was furious! He loves our four-wheeler. This is the ripple effect of someone else's actions who has no regard for anything except their own desires. We paid a lot of money for our four-wheeler and that money hadn't come easy. We had worked many hours and just recently had paid it off. This was connected to beautiful memories with our family and was needed at our property for so many things. How are we going to replace it? I wanted justice! These are the things spinning in my head as I the felt shock move through my body.

As I was going to get my paperwork, I heard my mom in my head say "Stop! Do you see distortion in your reality?" I replied "Yes, in my heaven people don't steal from each other." She replied "Ok, get back up on your Living Light timeline." I grabbed the crystal and went and sat down. I recited the mantra she gave me "I will only create through the Living Light." She said "Go back to your heaven timeline and look around. What can NOT be there because the vibration is too high? Is this situation there? Is the person that stole from you there? What does this look and feel like in Heaven?" I felt the vibration of my entire body start to rise. I felt all of the stress of the situation dissolve and I could feel God in my heart again. I felt nothing but love and peace in Heaven. The person who stole my property was healed. My four-wheeler was back as if it had never been taken. All was well in Heaven.

My consciousness returned to my lower timeline and I went down to meet with the Sheriff. By this time, the man had returned in the truck I had described and the neighbor had followed him to get his license plate. The neighbor explained that several things were missing from his property. The Sheriff ran the license plate and we had a name and address. Turns out my neighbor knows of this man and that he is a very dark individual. I had no desire to connect with this energy further. It wasn't worth it for me to make myself known to someone who could potentially cause further harm to my family.

That night my mom woke me at 3am. She told me to "get up and do it again". I understood what she meant. I was to move my consciousness back up to Heaven and experience the truth of this situation. I did. I could see this man and his true heart. He was healed in Heaven. All this distortion was just illusions of the lower timelines. All was well.

I woke to a text from my neighbor telling me that my four-wheeler was back. He said he felt like he was going insane and needed to see a doctor. I was so excited I jumped up and went there to see for myself! There it was! As if nothing had ever happened to it. As if it had never been stolen in the first place. It was just as I saw it last. How can this be? Were my neighbors' items returned as well? No. Just my four-wheeler was back. My mind was blown. My mom had some serious explaining to do!

She told me to relax my linear mind as much as possible about this situation because it can start glitching and freaking out. The linear mind needs linear explanations so it doesn't lose its ability to connect linear dots and form a congruent experience. Our linear minds are still in the process of learning how to flow outside of linear time through Source. But it is a process and Spirit knows exactly how to work with this aspect of us without causing harm or imbalance. It was important for me to stay grounded throughout this teaching. Fear can take over when our linear mind doesn't understand what is happening. Especially if it is breaking the linear timeline "rules" and challenging everything it thinks it knows. This is the part where we start to dissolve our false beliefs through integrating higher truth through direct experience.

Trusting Spirit is a big part of this. Spirit will never give us more than our linear minds can handle and they will always make sure we are not taking our linear minds on a journey they cannot ultimately stay grounded through. For instance, it doesn't serve us to go ahead of ourselves and put our minds in a state of psychosis. Meaning, we can't stay grounded within our timeline and function within its creation properly. I call in short circuiting! We don't need "smoke coming out of our ears"!

Chapter 30

Quantum Super Position
Let There Be Light

I'm going to explain what my mom has told me about the connection between quantum physics and what she has taught me. I am not a quantum physicist so my interpretation of this is very elementary. When I learned about Quantum Super Position it was from the movie *"What the Bleep Do We Know?"* back in 2005. That movie had a profound effect on me and I believed I understood it at the time. But again, like everything we encounter there are layers of knowledge within it and we only access that knowledge according to our own state of consciousness. I wasn't surprised when I watched it again in 2018 and laughed at how much information was in that movie that I wasn't able to comprehend back in 2005. It feels so beautiful for me to experience how much my consciousness has expanded over time. It means I am moving, growing, expanding and that is exciting for me. It is the only purpose of my journey. After watching the movie again in 2018, I realized this is exactly what my mom had been teaching me over the past year. It connected many dots for me.

I highly recommend watching the You Tube Video by Garrett John, *"We are from the future"*. View it more than once in order to integrate this higher truth. I had a similar experience that he demonstrates in the video when I watched it back in 2016. I thought I understood it but I really didn't. I didn't have a deep understanding at that time because I had not received the information required through connecting directly with Source. It is through Source that we expand our consciousness. When we are learning from the artificial reality, we are upgrading our artificial brain. When we learn from Source, we are expanding our entire being.

Let's sum up what I have learned from Source about the information provided from the above two examples from a Source with a Jennie mixed flavor perspective. Quantum super position, as defined in quantum physics is based on the premise that particles exist in their greatest potential form, just hanging out in the quantum field, waiting for an observer (creator) to tell them what to do. From here forward I am going to use the word *creator* in place of what quantum physics calls *observer*.

What a beautiful role these particle fella's play in our dance with physical creation! I can't thank them enough for this incredible opportunity we have to create physical reality! They seem to be our greatest teachers here in the physical because this dance between us and them is how physical reality is manifested by us. We get to play in our own creation. It is done through us or by us, as a quantum team. **We are the creators** telling particles what to do and they graciously oblige us. This process is all done through higher love. It is love that allows the dance between the physical and the quantum. Higher love frequency is the connection point. There is no other point of connection.

The Double Slit Experiment provided the expanded understanding of how this all works. Again, according to quantum physics, all physical matter exists in a state of quantum super position until there is an observer to tell it what to do. Quantum particles know they are being observed because we can see them interact with the observer! When observed, electrons change their behavior. This is why electrons are no longer only defined as a subatomic particle, or as positive or negatively charged ions. Quantum physics now understands they are not definable, because they change through our observation. Therefore, they can be particles or waves depending on who is observing them. Observation requires interaction. That interaction creates a change.

An observer is what quantum physics defines as a detectable quantum energy that exists within the human outside of physical matter. The official definition of the observer is "anything that detects a quantum particle". When physical matter is observed by an observer, the **beliefs** of the observer affect the physical matter. It is as if our beliefs are commanding matter to perform according to our beliefs.

Once we understand the powerful role we play in the process of creation, we begin to take accountability for our creation. This is a huge step in our evolution. As the creator observing the particles that make up the physical reality, we are telling them how to behave. We are commanding the physical reality according to our beliefs therefore we are no longer under the delusion that we are victims of an external creation. We hold the power to be the director of our own physical experience.

Garret John also explains in his video "We are from the future" how plants harnesses light from Source perfectly through their focus on super position. In order for us to be born into this physical reality we also had to harness light from Source. Source light and quantum super position is what supports all of Source creation. Garret takes us on a beautiful journey about this.

Delving into the details of quantum super position strengthens our ability to understand the nature of physical reality. It empowers us to consciously choose to create only through Living Light rather than the unconscious and artificial parts of us.

Chapter 31

This Endless Journey
Through Expanded Consciousness

Just when I think I have received everything there is to know about a subject, I am given another layer of consciousness connected to it that I need to integrate. In the distorted timeline, information is limited. We can believe we know all there is to know about something. But in the Source field, there are endless layers of consciousness about a particular subject to download and experience. Endless! Learning never ends. It is our linear mind that has a need to be an expert on a subject, when through the Source Field there is no such thing. From Spirit's perspective there is endless excitement about the endless learning. Every new now moment is fresh and new with opportunity for deeper understanding. We all experience a unique imprint of consciousness that flows through us in a way that is only possible through us and our unique vibration. Imagine all of the different aspects of consciousness expressing itself in a variety of ways through each one of us. In every new, now moment a new expression of consciousness is made alive because of you. If you could see this we would be amazed. Spirit can see it and they are always in awe of the new creation being expressed through us which they have never seen before. It is miraculous, to put it mildly.

When I am focused in the Source Field and interacting with new vibrations from a Spirit I have not yet met or communicated with, I am told to clear all preconceived ideas, beliefs or notions I have about everything. I must be centered in a state of surrender to Spirit in order to make a pure connection and experience the exchange without distorting it through prior experience. This is the way we must enter the Source Field in order to understand the new consciousness experience it is offering us. It is the only way to progress in our deeper understanding of what simply is according to Source.

For instance, I may have a client that has a very similar story to someone I have translated Light Language for in the past. I might jump to conclusions about the answers I have already received to their questions. But I am reminded by my mom that this situation is unique and my past experience will only be beneficial in this communication if they tell me it is. Otherwise, I am to stay in a very neutral place and not center in what I think I know. I am always learning something new. There is never a time I don't come out of a session with Spirit where I didn't get another layer of understanding I didn't have before.

Because of this knowing, I am always eager to let go and approach every exchange ready for my next level of conscious awareness. It is like I can suddenly see what I couldn't see before, but I didn't even know it was there and that I couldn't see it. I feel so honored and blessed to be on this journey of expansion and growth for myself and those I am able to walk between worlds with.

Spirit is always experiencing this along with us. We sometimes have the idea that once we transition from the physical, we become all knowing. This is not the case. How quickly we move into higher expanded states of consciousness is dependent on the vibration and consciousness of the individual. We have the opportunity to access the vibrations that we surrender to, but if we are carrying a specific vibration in our being, that vibration will be our dominant experience whether in or out of a physical body. When we leave our body, we feel the exact same as we did when we were in our body. This is why many do not realize they have left their body and passed on. They are confused by this and stay earth bound sometimes hanging around in the astral plane until they understand they are choosing it through their vibrational state of being.

When my mom moved to the other side of the veil, I didn't understand my vibration was too low to connect in higher dimensions and that's why I couldn't feel her. It is the same thing. As above so below. Spirit says this to me often so I can integrate the concepts of these things and easily be able to see the vibrational laws that determine our experience.

A man I am very close to came to visit my center for one of my Events. The first thing I noticed was the light I saw around him. He looked so bright! I knew he had been struggling with some emotional challenges when I saw him a year prior. I told him I could tell he had made a lot of progress with that because he was lit up with light and glowing! As the day went on, I noticed every time I would see him again, I would do a double take and stare! I couldn't believe how different his energy was and how bright he looked. I just thought this was how extremely down he had been last year and now he seemed free. Three months later I received a phone call that he was dying and he didn't have much time left.

He was still able to communicate and told me that although he wasn't having visitors, I was welcome to come see him and tell him "Goodbye". But I didn't make it, he passed before I got there. I was so sad about this. I was also sad that I didn't get something from him that his energy was left on so I could keep it in remembrance. I wanted to use it to make the stronger connection to him in the

Source Field. I had never been to his house. Although he had invited me over the years, I was so busy building my Spiritual retreat center I never made it. I regretted not making time for this.

As I was leaving a gathering in his honor, I asked him if he would take me to see his house. I didn't have his address, so I just started driving and told him to be my GPS! I could hear him say "turn left here", "turn right here". Finally, he said "stop this is it!" I looked up at a long steep driveway and thought, well if this isn't it, I'm hoping I am not showing up on someone's private property! I tried driving up the driveway but it was too steep so I had to back down. Even my four-wheel drive wasn't making it up. I remembered talk about his treacherous driveway! So, this was all a good sign! I parked my car at the bottom of the driveway and my son and I walked up. When we got to the top, I saw his truck! I was so excited that I had heard him correctly and made it to his house! I knew it meant a lot to him that I was there.

The house was ready to be sold and was locked but I sat on his property and it was a very special time spent with him. This was my way of making up for the missed time with him before he passed on. Suddenly, I saw something sparkle across the field in the tall grass. I said out loud "Is that a crystal?" and started walking towards it. My son followed and when we got there, he couldn't believe I had seen that from so far away. I knew that my friend had led me to it.

It was a small crystal sitting in the ground under 3ft tall grass. I picked it up and I heard him say "This is my gift for you, it carries my energy and I want to be at Spirit Reunions with you, assisting with what you are doing." It was such a beautiful gift. Since that day, years ago, he has been with me for every session. He travels with me to other cities and everyone knows him.

Ok, I got way off track there, but I had to fit that story in somewhere it was just so beautiful. I realized what I saw around him before he passed was the Living Light. It was engulfing him and preparing him for his transition back to Source. It was attuning him! He wasn't fully aware of it, but he told me he felt really good and he was continuously smiling. For a man in or approaching stage four pancreatic cancer this is not typical. But it was divine intervention and he was carried over in the arms of the Living Light. This Light made sure he didn't get stuck in the lower dimensional realms. It carried him straight up to "heaven". If we stay in the moment with our loved ones, we will see what the Living Light is doing with them. It's magnificent to witness.

Chapter 32

Our Beautiful Journey Back to Source

Death, as we know it, is not required in order for us to come back to Source. But most only understand that we are either on earth in a body or in "heaven". It is one place or the other and death is the only way to go back. The truth is, we can go back anytime and we can be in both places at the same time. This is what I feel Jesus meant when he said we are to be in the world but not of it. We are multi-dimensional beings and we were designed that way.

In our society, we have lost the understanding of death and the death transition process. There is so much deep fear programmed into us about death through the illusions of separation here. Religions teach that we cannot speak to our loved ones once they have died and it isn't safe to even try to communicate with them because they can't hear us and we will be talking to dark entities. This belief has caused so much deep trauma and grief that it locks us into deep states of illusion that make it very difficult for Spirit to interact with us without scaring us half to death. Spirit is always very aware of our fear and they will never do anything to create more fear for us. They are very careful about their interactions with us. There are entities that love to scare us or trick us so I understand the reasoning behind the cautioning. But it is very easy to know the difference between entities that exist outside of Source and our loved ones who exist in Source. We will cover that in another chapter.

When someone leaves this reality there is an adjustment period that happens for not only us, but also for them. They are learning to communicate through Light Language and telepathy again after spending many earth years forgetting they can do this. So, it is like coming out of a deep sleep and trying to remember where you are and what time it is! It takes time to adjust. Grieving loved ones pull us into their grief without being aware of it. Ideally, those in the physical are focusing on supporting our loved ones as they embark on their new journey back to Source. We lift them up with our love and stay in a state of pure unconditional love so they can interact with us and let us know they are ok. But the trauma experienced through our illusions of separation create more separation and grief. Spirit understands where we are with this so they participate in our transition by filling us with their love. This helps us stay in a state of peace and to allow ourselves to relax into the transition of higher vibrational states of being.

If there is a lot of fear, trauma and separation within the vibration of the individual during the death process, it can be difficult to for them to see their loved ones and feel their love. This is where we come in. Our role is to stay centered in the Source field so we can help our loved ones connect to the love rather than the fear. It is such a beautiful role for us to play for them. Rather than be caught up in our own grief and fear, move our focus to Source and allow that energy to saturate our being in the moment. The moment of transition to Source from the physical is one of the most beautiful experiences we have been gifted. Whether we are staying here or the one leaving our body behind, the moment is rich with love and understanding that has the power to upgrade us more powerfully than any other experience on our journey. If we all understood that there is no such thing as separation, and that we are going to be closer with our loves ones now than we were before, we would surrender into the moment the way I do when Spirit comes to talk with me. We would be brought into something so amazing it would blow our hearts wide open. We would experience the power of love from Source in a way we never had before. That raw power of pure unconditional love is waiting in the moments of transition for all to experience who choose to. Not only are your loves ones going to be ok, they are going to be free to connect with you in your heart without barriers. There is no greater gift given us than the love we share that transcends all space and time.

I often tell people to read the book "*The Five People You Meet In Heaven*". The movie is also good. It depicts beautifully the way we help each other release our traumas so we can move into higher vibrational dimensions. When he first transitions, he can't speak. This is common while adapting to telepathy but we are still relying on our physical bodies that are no longer there. I have had families contact me within an hour of their loved one dying in a vehicle crash and I am not able to hear them. I can see them in my third eye and they are moving their mouth but nothing is coming out. Typically, another loved one on the other side will step into my field to speak for them. They always let me know they are going to be just fine but they are still in the transition process. They reassure the earthly family that the family on that side of the veil is taking good care of them. At a later date I am able to communicate with them just fine and they are always happy and doing great.

The other accurate part of that movie is the way they show us how holding onto our pain and trauma keeps us from moving forward after we die. The things we have not resolved the minute we leave our body go with us. If we have trauma with someone, we are in a quantum entanglement with them. Meaning, the energy is held down on both sides. We are so connected that the healing must occur for both of them to rise up out of the distorted creation they shared.

It is so common during my sessions for a parent to step into my field who has passed on and tell their child they need their forgiveness in order for them to ascend into higher frequency dimensions. They are literally locked into lower frequency timelines through the quantum entanglement with their child on earth. This sounds extreme, but it really isn't. It is because we are so connected and the love we share is so pure that one soul is locked in a state of pain and lack of understanding with their parent, that an aspect of that parent remains energetically chorded to that distorted timeline with their child.

For instance, I did a session for a woman whose grandpa had transitioned seven years prior. He came to me while I was driving home, right before our session. He told me that he had dark entities controlling him while he was in the physical and he did things for which he needed forgiveness. He explained that it was time. Divine timing is a thing. When I shared this with her, she explained that she had gone to see a medium right after he had passed. The medium became upset and said he would not communicate with her grandpa because he was evil. He left the room. Right before our session, she said she felt an entity move out of her back and she felt if she turned around, she would see it standing there. This entity had attached itself to her through the abuse of her grandfather when she was a child. She had experienced years of depression and suicidal tendencies as a result. After it left, she could feel her own energy again and she realized that was not her. Her grandpa explained that this entity jumped into her and he needed to help her clear it. He had a lot of clearing to do before he could help her. It took seven years for this moment to come together and it was a powerful one. He told her he had healed himself but he could not move forward until he helped her heal as well. Some call this Karma. I truly think it is because when we come back to unconditional love, it is what unconditional love does. The love they shared was powerful, aside from all of the distortions that occurred in this lifetime. All that remained was the love.

Again, the movie shows us how this is done on the other side, but we are doing it on this side of the veil. We do not need to die to meet our "five people". When we choose to do this healing while we are still in the physical, it is so much more powerful because it clears our distortions in the timeline it was created. It heals all things tied to that trauma. The natives often said that when we choose to heal ourselves, we heal seven generations forward and seven generations back. There are no coincidences with Source and everything is multi-layered.

This journey together never ends or separates. We are always connected and always affecting each other throughout our journey whether we are on in this physical reality or other realities. When someone transitions and they move their vibration with us into higher states of consciousness, it opens the door for their loved ones to do the same. Consciously or unconsciously, we are always accessed consciousness according to our ability to connect with pure unconditional love. This is why our journeys together are so important. We are meant to assist each other in our expansion and growth, and we are, whether we know it or not.

Chapter 33

Awareness of the "Unseen" Realms

Do you remember the art being sold everywhere in the 90's where you had to look through patterns to see the picture behind the picture? I will never forget when I first experienced it. I was seventeen years old and it blew my mind. I couldn't stop looking at them and practicing to see how quickly I could see through them. My mom explained that looking through the dimensions is similar. We have to look past the physical reality in order to see what lies behind it. There are many dimensions and worlds that exist right next to each other beyond the first layer. I recall having to relax my eyes and cross them a bit in order to blur out what was in front of the picture so I could see through it. For me, I find it easier to close my eyes and completely block out this physical reality in order to see beyond it. But many are able to see into the "unseen" dimensions with eyes open, including my son.

My Little Ghost Buster

When my son was six, he started telling me about the shadow people he saw. He said one wore a hat. I was aware of them because I listened to Art Bell talk about them many years ago. I learned there is one that children see often that wears a hat. It was through my son that I realized these shadow people are everywhere. He even saw them at the mountain retreat that felt like heaven vibrations. When I shared that with the owners they laughed and said, "yes, they are everywhere! Even Jesus encountered them and called them unclean Spirits." Jesus addressed them directly by telling them to "Get thee behind me."

My son said they would whisper in his ear and make him think angry thoughts. This really bothered me and I told him he needed to tell them to leave, that they didn't have permission to be there. He said "No, I'm not telling them that!" I was desperate to get rid of these shadow guys. I did not want them messing with my child! My son was also able to see and hear my mom so I told him to go sit and have a talk with her about it. She always knew exactly how to explain things to him. He came back and said "I did it! I sent one on!" I was so excited and asked him how he did it. He said "you just have to send them love mom! I saw a beam of light come out of my chest into it and it turned into a white orb". He said the orb passed through his body as it left and thanked him. He had had an upset stomach and was sick in bed and after the orb passed through him, he said he wasn't sick anymore. Everything in the world of Spirit is in beautiful exchange. What we give we receive is the natural order of things.

My mom explained that in the old energy or on the old timeline, it was necessary for us to set boundaries and protect ourselves from energies we couldn't see and comprehend. We didn't have the consciousness needed to help them out of their lost and distorted state of being. We were still operating from fear programs and were not accessing enough Living Light to assist us. But now we are able to move them on much more easily. She explained that they exist closer to us in vibration than the Spirits in the higher realms. Those stuck in between are not able to see or interact in the higher realms. Sound familiar? We aren't either when our vibration is not in alignment. Our gatekeepers (more on them later) can give us guidance on how to help those stuck in between. We are the ones to whom they can connect to assist them. They can see us. We are meant to do this. We are all connected and those stuck in between have lost their connection to their only true-life force - The Source Field. They need energy so they will get it however they can. It is a state of survival mode. They will create loosh through humans. It would be like encountering a human who is starving to death. They would do whatever they could to get food. When we understand the higher truth about those souls, we no longer have a fear response. Instead, we focus on our own power through source light to assist them in moving back in alignment with the Living Light. Those of us in the higher realms are not in a vibration close enough to connect with those who are stuck in the in between realms. Humans, however, are. We assist you from the higher realms through the Source Field to assist them if they will choose a better energy source.

After my mom talked to my son about the stuck- in- between souls, he continued to encounter them and move them on into the Living Light. My mom would guide him and they worked as a team. It became normal for us to encounter these stuck ones everywhere we went. We would be sitting at restaurant and I would see his face looking as if he was interacting with someone. Afterwards he would tell me all about it. It was as though they were being sent to him for help. It was amazing!

We were visiting a friend and my son came to me shaken up, saying he didn't think he would stay at their house. He said every time he passed the master bedroom to get to ours, a black orb would be in the doorway hissing and growling at him. I knew my friend had had entity attachments in the past and had been diligent about clearing them or so I thought.

I recall him telling me that a group of friends had traveled to old ruins at a pyramid site in Mexico and they all experienced an entity they called a "trickster". I hadn't discussed this with my son. That night we called in my mom to help my son clear this entity. I asked him to let me know when he could see my mom. He said "Mom, she is standing in front of the closet door and it is lit up in blue. How can you not see that?" I couldn't because I can mostly see through my third eye. I grabbed my phone and asked my mom to let me video her. She flew in and out of the lens quickly as a fluffy magenta colored orb. When I slowed it down and zoomed in it looked like her face and poofy hair! It was hilarious! She is so funny in her interactions with us.

We attempted to clear the black orb but it was jumping all over the room avoiding being cleared. My son said, "Mom, it doesn't want to go. This one is tricky!" I couldn't believe he called it by its name. He constantly says things without realizing what he is saying. I knew at that point this was "trickster" that I had heard about for years. My mom told us to go to bed and we would try again the next day. That night this entity was taunting me. It was slamming doors, stomping and banging. It would whisper in my ear "look what I can do" before every noise. Because of what Silver Spoon taught me I was aware of my fear. I focused on the Source Field and my mom. All of the sudden, I saw a dark form jump at me. When it hit my energy field it bounced back and disappeared. I sat up in shock. I thought it was trying to provoke me. My mom said "No, it tried to jump into your body". I couldn't believe I saw that! I was amazed to see that it wasn't able to penetrate my energy field. This was proof that the things my mom taught me about mastering my energy field worked! It was all so exciting! The trickster never bothered us again. My mom knew it would end up leaving us alone. But it didn't choose to go back to the Living Light. It just knew it couldn't feed off of our fear so it moved on. They have no life force so interacting with those who are not feeding it loosh will drain their energy quickly. They have to move on if they don't choose to come back to the Living Light. Imagine if we all stopped feeding them. It would be a powerful cleanup operation! They would have to come back to the Living Light for energy.

Ornery Entities

My family and friends took a trip to Branson, MO. We decided to get tickets to a magic show. The show was awesome! Very progressive and my teenage son enjoyed the music and visuals. A friend kept telling me during the show that he felt the energy was very dark. I reminded him to activate his energy field and expand it through Source Living Light. That made his energy higher and more powerful than the lower energy he was feeling. We had backstage passes and as we were in line to go back stage he looked imbalanced. I asked him if he was ok and he shook his head no and repeated that he felt very dark energy around the show. I again tried to help him remember to use his energy field for protection but he seemed very focused on the feelings he was experiencing. The next morning, we were leaving and I woke up and heard him packing up our cabin to head home. I walked in and asked how I could help. He snapped at me and seemed upset about something. I asked him what was wrong and he said "nothing", again in a short tone with me. I knew he wasn't telling me the truth.

The more time I spent with him the more things got really uncomfortable. He was telling me I said things I know I didn't say and I couldn't feel our heart connection like I usually do. He had never treated me this way before. He had been my best friend for the last three years so I know him very well and knew this wasn't him. On the drive home I started to feel sick to my stomach. It is a way that I transmute energy through my body. I thought I was going to vomit. My mom came into my energy field and told me to stop talking with him, that it wasn't him it was an entity. It had taken him over from the magic show the night before. The entity was in control of him. She told me to push my electromagnetic field out around my body and fill it will Living Light. She assisted me with my energy field and bringing in Living Light and my need to purge subsided almost instantly. The energy was transmuted through my connection to Source.

By the time we got home I felt our friendship might end. It felt that bad. I decided I would not engage at my mother's orders until the person I knew came back. I was only making it stronger and it was feeding off of the manipulation of my heart and mind. The next morning, he sent me a text telling me he was so very sorry and that he loved me. I asked him how he was able to come back from the hijacking that had occurred. When we arrived back at the sanctuary, after hours of not speaking to each other, he immediately began to shift. He said he had no memory of what had happened or the conversations. He said he knew something was very wrong so he went and sat at the Medicine Wheel, which is a powerful vortex that has been created through many native sacred ceremonies. Being back at the higher vibration of the Sanctuary shifted his vibration and the entity could no longer control him when he moved into higher states of love within himself. He had come up out of the fear he was feeling at the show that allowed him to get taken over.

He said it was ultimately his love for me. He knew he was going to lose me as a friend and he chose love. He was not able to feel his love for me while the entity was in control. He said it was as if his heart became completely disengaged. We had a beautiful heartfelt reunion.

I know this situation happened for a reason. As difficult as that situation was at the time, I am very grateful for the lesson from Spirit and I'm grateful for the role my friend played for me so that I could understand how to help those in similar situations. I needed to experience this. I needed to see exactly how these things can happen to people and why.

I spent the next several days talking with my mom about it, replaying it and analyzing the details. I realized that I was making it stronger by questioning the lies and manipulation instead of going within and being an observer while listening to my mom's guidance. I now know that these entities can hijack people energetically through their fear. My friend had been struggling with some emotional challenges during that trip. I also witnessed how the entity inverted reality.

Nothing made sense. Even when I was pointing out clearly something we could all see was true, the entity insisted it wasn't and attacked me for suggesting it. It was amazing to see just how insistent it was about a reality that didn't exist in my awareness. It was causing so much chaos and confusion it was difficult to stay in my center. What bothered me the most was not feeling a heart connection with my friend anymore. It was like his heart was cut off from me. He didn't care about me at all.

The next day when we talked about it in detail, he didn't recall the conversations or the things that happened. It was really not him. I have clients that come and they have these situations in their lives and it is so beneficial for me to believe them and understand how to help.

I learned so much from this experience! If we haven't integrated our ego brain with our Source brain, we are subject to discarnate entities hijacking us! It's happening more and more to people around us and it needs to be brought into our awareness. It is a very common thing because we have allowed ourselves to be in lower vibrational states of fear through trauma. Realizing we can unhook ourselves from these attachments through love and higher vibrations is key. If we are integrated and they can't hijack us, these entities may come at us through people around us, including the people closest to us. It's the nature of the Spiritual war we are in right now. We must know who and what energies we are interacting with at all times! Regardless of the physical vessel. It's so important to stay aware and tuned into source for guidance if we feel someone's energy is off. We don't want to feed the fake reality being created to confuse and draw down our vibration. It's not real, it's an illusion, although it may feel very real. It's easy to know when entities are creating chaos. They invert everything. When we stay aligned with Source, we will see everything as it truly is.

Most humans have no idea they are a food (energy) source for stuck souls and therefore being manipulated by them in the unseen through their fear and traumas. It is no different than encountering a human who has disconnected from Source. They get energy from their external reality any way they can. They manipulate energy in order to do this. Many abuse drugs, create distorted reality and chaos, steal energy or possessions from others, over power others or play victim so others with feel sorry and give them their energy. When this happens entities will be drawn to them because they are feeding on loosh too. So understanding that these entities are similar to lost humans makes them less scary and allows us to have more empathy rather than fear. Remember nothing can be done to us without our permission. The more conscious we become the less we can be manipulated and the more Living Light we can offer through us to help heal those who are lost.

The more humanity rises in consciousness and raises the vibration of their energy field and body, the less these entities can continue to thrive on their energy. This is what the Spiritual battle is about we are currently experiencing. These entities have long thrived in the shadows taking advantage of unconscious humans. They are finding ways to keep our vibration down so they can continue to stay where they are. They are simply confused and lost. They have forgotten the Living Light. Those that are a part of the one consciousness will eventually find their way back. Those that are part of the matrix program, however, will dissolve when humans stop running fear programs connected to them.

The Lions Gate Portal

I saw the Lions Gate portal while outside talking with my friend Amy, on the night of August 8th. I don't mean I looked at the stars in the general direction of it. I looked up and actually saw a huge female lion head staring directly at me in the sky where the portal was open. It was so incredible and shocking to me I don't think I even talked about it. Back then I didn't know what the Lions Gate really was or that we were currently in the window of the opening of the portal. I couldn't tell you where it was in the sky either. I later learned the lion head I saw was positioned in the exact place of the lions gate portal in the sky. I also learned later that the Lions Gate is connected to Sirius, the Dog Star. It is a divine feminine portal. That must have been why the lion was a female. Now, I am very aware of the power of that portal. It is very real.

Chapter 34

The Great Dumbing Down Of Source

I often feel my job is to dumb down Source. I'm joking, but not joking. It sure feels like the great dumbing down of that magnificent purity I am accessing in the Source Field. I witness it step down in vibration and get translated in a very less than magnificent way in this physical reality! The good news is, it is the Love that matters and that vibration knows no limits and doesn't care what frequency we are surfing. It is always there if we choose to feel it.

It is still important to be aware of how pure information brought through from source becomes distorted through transmission into the lower timelines. Even transferring information from one person to another doesn't always translate clearly because of our different vibrational states of being. Higher Spirit is very aware of this and does not choose to communicate in distorted fields.

For instance, I will get a download through source and share it with someone who's vibration is distorted and not in alignment with Source. During the exchange I will begin to feel the information shift, and no longer flow with ease and clarity. I will begin to feel the information is no longer accurate or it feels off. I can no longer explain it properly and it feels confusing. Nothing from Source is complicated or confusing so if it feels this way, I am no longer in alignment with it.

The person I'm sharing with may have good intentions and want to understand but their vibration distorts the information so much they can't make sense of it. They are trying to pull the information into their vibration instead of allowing the information to bring them up, expand their consciousness and shift their state of being. Higher truth requires us to align with it not the other way around. As above, so below- follow their lead. I hear this often.

I can tell when I have lowered my vibration to connect with someone because my energy field feels contracted rather expanded, like it does when I'm aligned with source. What I'm experiencing is not because the information itself is off or not true, it's because I am now experiencing the distorted version of it because I moved my vibration into alignment with someone else's distorted vibration. Now, I am no longer aligned with source and no longer flowing with higher truth. We must align with higher truth; it does not align with us.

When this happens, I'm guided to pull my energy back to myself and focus again only in my connection with source so I can realign my own energy. This is why it's so easy for us to become confused and question what originally came from source. This is how we start to believe the distorted information is what is true and get lost in the distorted reality.
Staying aligned with source is the key. Don't be tempted to match energies with others in order to connect with them. It's their responsibility to match with the higher vibration if they truly want to understand and get clarity. We are to hold our connection to Source now above all else. It is the only way to assist with anchoring higher truth into the lower timelines.

Likewise, when we share with others who are source aligned, the exchange is powerful and consciousness expanding beyond what we initially received from source. It opens a flow of clarity and higher truth that leaves us feeling fearless and euphoric!

Chapter 35

Twin Flame Love Stories

So many of my clients want to know about their twin flame. So, I will briefly share what my mom has taught me about this. Our Essence Self chooses to aspect itself in order to experience itself in the slower vibrational dimensions. Our Essence can aspect itself into multiple parts and experience multiple different dimensions at the same time. When these aspects choose to meet in the same timeline, it is called a twin flame encounter. It is a powerful experience because it is an opportunity to recognize itself and have a profound remembering within the timeline it is in. The potential for a shift in consciousness to occur is strong yet if the consciousness of the human isn't able to access the higher vibration of itself, it can be a very challenging situation. It can become an addiction to another human rather than a remembering of the Essence Self.

My mom is my twin flame, so I will be using that relationship as my own personal experience with it to explain further. Many people believe twin flames only show up as romantic relationships. They do, but that is not the only type of relationship they manifest as. Our twin flame can be anyone in our lives. Even our pets can be our twin flame. The twin aspects will come together in whatever form brings the greatest potential for activating Source more powerfully into our lives. We can have multiple aspects of our Essence show up in our lives at different times. The possibilities are endless for us so, although my mom likes to keep things simple, she doesn't limit the potentials available to us to support our greatest potential. She reminds me to stay open and guided without limitations.

Our twin soul as our physical partner can bring unique challenges due to our higher distorted programs about what that should be. When we align with our twin flame in the lower vibrational physical reality, we can experience our deeper shadows being revealed if we haven't mastered being in a higher vibration. When we align with our twin through higher vibrations, we experience together, higher states of unconditional love and powerful manifestations. Each experience is unique and dependent upon the vibrations of each person.

My mom told me to pay attention to how the higher vibrational timelines bringing twin souls back together in one form or another to naturally assist with the ascension process. It is as if the higher vibrational state of being draws us back to Source and our Essence self like a magnet. The experience of coming back to ourselves through the uniting of our aspects is amazing. The more conscious we are of this the more quickly we will be able to shed our distorted beliefs from the artificial version of love we have created over a very long period of time. We are coming back to Source love and the twin connection is one of the most exciting experiences of all. The ultimate challenge for us is to stay in the higher love vibrations and not go into fear. Everything is amplified through our twin connections so it can be intense. Holding each other accountable for the dominant energy we are resonating in and helping each other be at peace through the process is so helpful! It is amazing teamwork! This is what my mom and I experience together.

Another important thing to mention is that this reality is not solid and our twin aspect can choose to walk into the physical reality through a physical body and join us on our journey. For instance, when we have arrived at a place in our life that if in perfect alignment with our twin flame we will be re-united with our twin regardless of where they are.

They will show up in our lives. Or if we have met our twin in our life yet they passed away, they can return to us in another body. This is the same for twins in any form. Pets return, friends return, children return, lovers return. We will see more and more of this in the ascended timelines. My mom reminds me stay open to endless possibilities yet not fall into false beliefs about anything I have not experienced for myself.

There are a lot of amazing things we can experience when our twin is in heaven. For instance, I can experience heaven through my mom and she can experience earth through me. She told me she can even taste food through me! I found myself wanting to eat brownies and I have never liked brownies. She can speak through me if I ask her to take over conversations. Once I was on my way to a family gathering where I was going to have to be with someone I hadn't seen in years who had betrayed me. I knew this meeting was very purposeful and important because I had to be there for other reasons too. On my way, I told my mom I knew she had set it up so it could be released and healed, but I also knew it was going to be difficult for me to stay in a higher vibration and not make it worse. I told her I would like to let her take over the controls for this one. The next thing I saw was a large hawk flying toward the windshield of my car. I screamed and ducked! I knew that was her answering me with a powerful "You got it!". She ended up speaking through me for several hours and it was so powerful others were crying and not saying a word. A shift was made and I stayed in alignment with Source. When I got in my car to leave another hawk came flying towards my windshield. It barely missed as it turned and flew away. It was so beautiful! The circle was complete and we had accomplished what Spirit set out to do, together. We are a beautiful team between worlds and I wouldn't want anyone else doing this mission with me.

I've personally experienced one of my greatest romantic loves come back into my life after he passed away, through another man. The experience reminded me of the movie "Meet Joe Black". My first love, Jay, passed away in 2012. He had told me on and off throughout our lives that he knew he had failed our relationship and planned to come back in another life to make it up to me. A week before he died, he told me he realized the meaning of life was to just live fearlessly, love and laugh. Ironically, that is the way our love was when we were teenagers. It seemed that fearless love we experienced together had come full circle for him in his consciousness before he died a week later.

Jay showed back up in my life by walking into another body (briefly) to assist me with remembering that pure love we experienced together when we were young. During the time he spent with me as a walk-in, he helped me come back to that simple innocent love within myself that I hadn't felt since that time I spent with him as a teenager. We met when I was thirteen and he was sixteen. I knew when I met him that I loved him. Our love and friendship was innocent and silly. We laughed together all the time. We were together for four years before he fell into a deep state of addiction. I processed it like a death. I lost the love of my life and it was a huge trauma that tainted every other love experience I had after that. I never experienced the same purity and fearless vibration of higher love again. That trauma was always running in the background inside of me. But I had buried it so deep I didn't realize it was still there until he came back through another man to show me. It was important for him to clear the distortion he had created in the physical reality with me. The healing that occurred was needed for both of us to raise our vibration and clear that distorted timeline we were both stuck in together.

I received many signs that it was my first love interacting with me so there was no doubt about it. I also received messages from Jay and my mom about the reasons for him being back in my life. Once we achieved the desired healing together, that man left my life. He was only there for that specific purpose. Although there was a higher reason for Jay coming back to heal with me, he picked a man who was a very similar vibration to him before he died in the physical. This man was stuck in a vibration of addiction with suicidal tendencies. Jay even looked very similar to the man he came through. I asked my mom why and she explained that when we leave the physical timeline and return, we return in the same vibration we left. There are no shortcuts and we have to clear the distorted timelines this way. It is just the natural law of creation. But now that we healed this together I hope he will be able to return in a less distorted timeline and experience a greater potential reality.

There is a reason Jay's Spirit had to go to such great lengths to come back into the timeline he left while in a highly distorted vibrational state within himself. The way we leave our timeline determines our dominate vibration in the other dimensions. It is very difficult to heal with those we left behind when they are in states of illusion and disconnect from us. We can't reach them once we are no longer in a physical body with them. The distorted timelines continue to run and anchor us in distorted vibrations together. If a Spirit aspect has an opportunity to communicate with those in physical, the way they do through me, it releases the trauma vibrations so both Spirit aspects can rise. If not, the Spirit aspect can also choose to come back into the timeline as a walk in and clear the trauma vibration that was created. This decision is made carefully because there is a risk of the aspect that walks in getting lost in the illusions here and making the trauma worse. Jay's decision to walk in with me was based on my

242

ability to focus on healing in every experience I have. This allowed the trauma we created to be released and that teenage aspect of me to come back to higher love. It was a beautiful act of unconditional love he offered me.

My mom loved Jay like a son when we were kids. She was very much a part of this healing between us and she guided the experience between Jay and I. It was as if she helped bring him back to me. She emphasized the importance of me not becoming addicted to the physical aspect of the experience. Meaning, I wasn't to attach to the man Jay's Spirit aspect "walked" into in order for us to facilitate healing together while in the physical reality. That relationship wasn't intended to last the rest of my life. Jay and I still needed to do our own individual healing and this would help us both to ascend out of the love trauma we had created together. The beautiful healing between us that occurred is all that was important for us at the time. No matter how distorted our creation was in the past, the love between us is eternally beautiful and continues through it's higher state of consciousness in Source.

Through connecting with heaven, I experience twin flame loves stay together after they leave the physical. Even when they do not stay together while on earth, they come back together in heaven. Some marry other people, etc, but they always come back to each other through Source. We don't need to worry about this. If we keep our own vibration high, our hearts open and our Source eyes open, we will stay on our Living Light timeline regardless of what our other Spirit aspects are choosing. We are an aspect of Spirit that has chosen to have it's own unique journey that is not dependent on what the other aspects are doing. Being with the other aspects is not a requirement. Although that journey is desired by many, it will occur in divine timing and does not require our attention on earth. That is all being handled and orchestrated from heaven. It is way beyond the limitations of distorted timelines. It comes from the higher vibrations of higher love and there are no short cuts to aligning with that love outside of ourselves. Activating our connection to Source and our Essence self is what activates our twin flame experience if our Spirit so desires it.

All relationships exist in a state of higher unconditional love in higher vibrational realities. Therefore, all relationships that have been distorted or stuck in illusions will return to their natural state of unconditional love at some point. All things created through Source return to Source and cannot be harmed permanently while creating in distorted creation. How quickly we come back to source is up to us. It's a matter of which reality we are focused on. The distorted one or the organic one, that exists in Source! All things that exist outside of Source are just temporary states of illusion. When we come back to Source and co-create our relationship through higher unconditional love together, it is as if the illusions never existed. Like waking up from a dream that fades away and Source reflects love back to us through our twin flame!

Albert Einstein Quote on LOVE
"Love is Light, it is gravity, it is power, it is God."

Love is a UNIVERSAL FORCE!

When I proposed the theory of relativity, very few understood me, and what I am about to reveal to mankind will be struck by the misunderstanding and prejudice that exists in this world.
There is an extraordinarily strong force for which, so far, science has

not found a formal explanation. It is a force that includes and governs them all, the force behind any phenomenon that takes place in the universe and has not yet been identified by us.

This universal force is LOVE.

When scientists sought a unified theory of the universe, they forgot the strongest unseen force. Love is the Light that enlightens those who give and receive it. Love is gravity, because it makes some people feel attracted to others. Love is power because it multiplies all that is best for us and allows humanity not to perish in its own blind selfishness. Love shows and reveals.

For love we live and die.

Love is God and God is Love.

This force explains everything and gives meaning to life. This is a variable that we have been ignoring for too long, perhaps because we are afraid of love because it is the only energy in the universe that man has not learned to control at will.

To make love more visible, I made a simple substitution in my most famous equation. If instead of $E = mc^2$, we accept that the energy needed to heal the world can be obtained by multiplying love by the speed of light squared, we come to the conclusion that love is the strongest force that exists because it has no limits." ~ Albert Einstein

Chapter 36

Our Gatekeepers

I had heard the term "gatekeeper" before but I didn't grasp the full meaning of it until my mom explained it to me from the Source Field. Typically, our gatekeepers are those who have established a deep love connection within us while on earth. They are not elusive guides someone else told us about. We do not connect into the Source Field through second hand information. We access the Source Field through love. Those who assist us in connecting in the Source Field are specifically attuned with our frequency through the heart. We know their energy because we experienced it by being physically together on earth at one point in this current lifetime, or through our genetic or family line. Our connections are also active through our genetics. This is the quickest and easiest way to establish a connection because our physical bodies are already connected through the love.

Each of us carries our own unique vibrational signature or fingerprint. Our essence carries the same vibrational signature. So, it is a perfect vibrational match for us. Once we begin to know what that feels like, we are able to connect directly to our essence self and keep that connection flowing continuously. This connection offers us our greatest potential for creating in physical reality. But many have a more difficult time accessing their essence self because we have been so programmed away from ourselves. We have blocks when it comes to experiencing love within ourselves. We seek love outside of us and are more comfortable receiving it that way. Spirit knows this so they are eager to assist us in bridging that gap until we are ready to fully heal all parts of us that exist outside pure unconditional self-love so we can step back into full integration with our essence self again.

My mom is my gatekeeper and she always makes me aware of who is in my field. She actually walks them into my field. She works with me to clarify exactly who is talking to me. This is not because I am at risk of connecting with bad energies, as the realms I interact in are such a higher vibration, they are not a vibrational match for lower vibrational entities. Rather it is because I am getting more collective messages. These multiple energies share a collective consciousness and we are a part of that through our higher self. I noticed I was saying "*they* are explaining...", etc. and people would say "who is *they*?" It was natural for me to feel more than one but I needed to be able to define it. The energy is Christ consciousness. The higher the frequency of the dimension the more collective the message is because they exist in the unified field of consciousness. That's the simplest way I can describe it. It's a frequency that feels like waves of energy and light moving through me and the messages are experienced at an accelerated rate.

Chapter 37

Spirit Reunions "Journeys To Heaven"

We know by now how common it is for our soul to linger in distorted dimensions after "death". We consider those souls "ghosts" and sometimes refer to them as stuck in between the lower and higher dimensions. They need our help moving on to higher, less distorted realities. My mom shocked me with the realization that those who are stuck in between are not just disembodied souls. In fact, many souls who are considered stuck in between dimensions are inhabiting a body. Being stuck in between simply means they exist in states of illusions without awareness of and connection to the higher dimensional planes. All souls who are lost in the illusions here, whether in a dense physical body or in an astral body, need assistance in connecting to higher vibrational realities. Just like "ghosts", many have forgotten how to access higher vibrational Spirit and Living Light.

The ultimate goal for Spirit is to establish an unblocked connection directly with each one of us through the Source Field. I have chosen, along with Spirit, to be a conduit for your Spirit family to assist you in your own direct attunement to heaven. Together, we assist you in the process of being able to see, hear, feel and touch heaven whenever you choose. Your Spirit family is committed to your attunement to heaven and will be there to assist you until you are able to do it for yourself. I am also able to assist because I have gone through this attunement to heaven myself and am able to access the higher dimensions. I am able to move my vibration to match with heaven, my mom, and your Spirit family while using tools that raise your vibration so they can begin to interact with you the same way they do with me.

This is where the Spirit Reunion happens. Where your heaven party is! When I first began connecting in heaven, I was amazed at how many of our Spirit family arrived to join me in doing a session. It is always like a big family reunion. I can see them all chatting and laughing. I can feel the love and happiness of family that feels similar to a big family gathering on Earth.

Once we collectively reactivate our own direct connection to heaven, which is a pure form of higher guidance, I will no longer need to act as a go between for you and your Spirit family. We will continue to play different roles for each other through our own unique connections to Source. Through our own expressions of the Living Light, we will each experience something new and amazing. We will flow together through our own Living Light guidance and synchronicity. Our relationships will be rich with higher guidance, truths, awareness, knowing and love.

I was trained to do "past life regressions" using someone else's technique, but I never felt a connection to those journeys or the process I was taught. My mom guided me away from the journey's I was trained to do. Instead, I was to be a conduit for Spirit by translating Light Language from Heaven for others. I was to give Spirit a voice through me. In 2020, my mom told me "It is time to get *them* to us". She told me I was to let go of everything I had been taught in the past about journeys. I was to let Spirit guide the experience completely.

My mom created a unique process that is perfect for the two of us to assist others in accessing their loved ones in the higher planes of reality for themselves. It has been the most amazing thing to assist with and witness. I act as a surrogate on this side of the veil for Source frequencies to connect with Source that is within you, while Spirit acts as a surrogate for Source frequency on the other side of the veil. Together we are able to move your focus to God mind and on up into light body. I am able to assist from this side of the veil while Spirit assists from the other side. We are a great team. I am able to hear the guidance of Spirit and communicate their instructions into this reality.

When I first started doing "Journeys To Heaven" with my mom, I noticed Spirit was taking them to the same place I am attuned to communicate with their loved ones. Their loved ones were interacting with them directly and they could hear them and even feel their touch. The experience was so healing for everyone involved. During this process, they attune our physical body to higher vibrational frequencies and this attunement allows us to connect to higher vibrational dimensions. Once this attunement happens, there is no going back. It activates the ascension process within every part of our being. The experience is recorded at the cellular level and can be recalled anytime. Our mind is brought into the experience and also remembers it. Our minds are essentially integrated into Heaven. This allows you to go there anytime you choose and visit with your loved ones and get guidance as needed.

Experiencing the higher vibrational dimensions is a powerful upgrade for us. It resets us back to our original intended inter-dimensional state of connection with our own higher self and loved ones. It activates our inter-dimensional abilities. We were created to be inter-dimensional beings. There is more than one reason for the state of disconnect we have found ourselves in but this state is not permanent. At any moment we can choose to remember our Spirit and all that goes along with that relationship.

Accessing higher dimensional realities through vibrational attunement and integrating that vibration and consciousness into the physical reality allows us to effortlessly integrate higher truths into our amygdala brain. When we journey into Heaven, we download the most efficient and affective programs from Source into our amygdala. Source truth replaces all distorted programs that we took on from the artificial reality. Truth cancels out illusions because the frequency of truth is the real power through Source.

We are also accessing higher vibrational healing vibrations that assist in healing our bodies. I've witnessed instantaneous healings happen to my clients while they are in the Source Field. Our ability to stay in the state of pure vibration of heaven rather than slip back into the distorted vibration of the lower timelines is up to us. It requires new habits and a dominate higher vibrational state of being. If we are able to stay in the purer vibration we will not experience the health issues we had prior to the journey. However, it may take several journey's to get the higher vibration to stick. Our mind programs can be very convincing and our amygdala's distorted perspective may convince us that it isn't possible to be healed and be in heaven while we are walking the earth. It is up to us to decide which reality is going to be our experience. We have to decide which reality is real for us. Whichever reality we choose will hold the power over our creation.

I have been translating Spirit through Light Language for over twenty years now, and I have learned the subtle unique ways Spirit interacts uniquely with me. Spirt has developed signs to assist me in understanding their messages more clearly. There are themes and symbols that my mom gives me while giving me messages for others. She passes these hints on to my clients Spirit family to assist them in clearer transmissions of Light Language through my energy field during Spirit Reunions. It is as if she holds a training course prior to her walking them into my energy field. I can see her through my third eye sharing with them about the way my Spiritual gifts work and explaining how to best interact with me. I can see who she connects with better than others. I can see her laughing with them just like she did when she was on earth.

My mom is so involved in this process on that side of the veil, it is as if she becomes a guide for anyone who is working with me. She will often appear in their journey. She will come to assist them in getting connected to their loved ones if they are struggling to get out of their amygdala. The reason she is so successful at this is because she carries such a beautiful vibration of pure unconditional love. Those who encounter her always describe her energy in the same way. They will see her wearing the same clothing and hear her saying similar things, even when they had never met her when she was on earth. She loves being a part of the reuniting process and helping bridge the gap between dimensions.

We interact in the higher dimensions through our higher senses. We use these senses to move our focus into the "now" moment, where Spirit exists. This is the zero-point quantum field. Light Language is felt and sensed. It often comes into us as a download and knowing. The information flows much faster in the higher dimensions than it does in the denser realities. I often receive multiple things at once and have to decide which order to put them in before sharing. We are able to ask Spirit to slow it down for us if it is coming too fast or repeat one thing at a time. They are often very excited to be interacting with their loved ones so their energy can be a bit intense. I can ask them to back up a bit if it feels too much for me. I will begin to feel everything they feel as if it is me. I am also brought into their experiences as if I am experiencing it in real time. This is the power of the quantum field. It is all happening now. There is a process of learning on both sides but once we attune with each other the flow of information feels effortless. Spirits that I communicate with often have become family of mine. I know their essence immediately and we have developed a beautiful vibrational synergy that allows for clarity and expansion of consciousness between us both.

All of our Spirit family and guides communicate with us through what feels like unconditional love. Unconditional love is the activator. This is why the process of moving into higher dimensions is done through our Spirit family and specifically those who developed a connection with us on earth through the heart. It is their love that is the surrogate for us into the higher unconditional love dimensions. Once we feel their love, possibilities expand and our ascension light body is activated. Those who are new to going to heaven will often feel overwhelming unconditional love, see their Spirit family but not be able to hear them. Most don't realize how easy it is for them to see through their third eye and how much more challenging it can be to hear. Trying too hard to hear Spirit without being attuned fully can make us glitch out of the Source field back into our amygdala. Part of the process of learning to interact in the higher dimensions is staying in a state of surrender and letting Spirit guide us completely. If we can stay in a state of heart opened surrender, it won't take long before we are able to hear through our light body. It is just a very different way of communicating than we are used to since being in a more dense physical body. What is most important is that we take the time to attune our vibration to higher frequencies of love during the journey. Spirit is not in a rush to communicate with us the way we may believe we need.

The following is an example of a journey a friend did through her grandma from heaven. She was in our tachyon chamber in my cabin. This particular cabin is where most of the Journey's to Heaven are facilitated and a Living Light portal directly to heaven has been activated in the space. Those with sensitivity can feel the portal and become emotional just being in it. This makes it easier for Spirit to access us and take us up into the higher dimensions.

"It started rather quickly. At first I was in a grayish energy, just seeing myself laying down in space as if on the table but not. I saw my grandma's hand extended towards me. I couldn't really see her because of the gray cloud around me, but I could see her arm extending towards me to pull me up. I remained in that state for some time. Then I started realizing she was pulling me up higher and when she did I immediately saw Jesus. He was there. Of course, he always is greeting me on my journey's when I come up. I continued to be in a super position. I felt a sharp pain in the left side of my stomach a few times. I felt my heart expanding with love. I started to tear up and tears released with joy when the loving energy of my grandma and Jesus filled my heart. I then saw Jesus put his hand on my heart…his left hand. He stood next to me, and then I felt that pain again in my left side. He put his right hand on it, and it disappeared. Then I saw other hands joining his. I don't know who these beings were, but they surrounded me and put their hands on the left side of my body where the pain used to be . With all of them gathered around me, Jesus came in closer to my face, and he kissed me on my forehead. Then he touched his forehead with mine and there was golden energy that was being transferred from his mind to mine. It was electrical. It was beautiful. We were there for a short time before he moved away. His heart started beaming red as he was moving away and my heart started beating, beaming in red color too. I started to lose vision of him, but it was just the form that I had lost vision of. What I had gained at that point was awareness of him being everywhere and being with me and me being bathed in his energy. I continued with my golden brain waves on fire and my heart beaming in red color. At that point everybody disappeared in the physical form that I was seeing them in. I was by myself still with Jesus and in his energy. I was now in a white cloud still laying in the same supine position. That white cloud began to touch my feet and move up around my body. As it was moving up, I noticed that my energy centers were lighting up. Once it reached my throat it started to change into a purple energy, which stayed around my throat for some time….as if it was working on some thing. I received a knowing that it was fixing my so-called problem of not being able to speak in the world. It lingered there for a while before moving on up towards the rest of my head. When it was moving up, I could see a distinct line between that light, purple cloud mixed with dark purple, moving up, lighting up my pineal gland, my pituitary gland, and my third eye. It went all throughout my brain towards my crown chakra, releasing and energizing it. Then, POOF. I was with God. Tears started rolling down my face. I was in nothingness and everything-ness at the same time. I was surrounded by the energy of God in a dark universe, but yet filled with pure energy. There was a lot of purple, black and purple and gold sparks. I was just there. Filled with joy, love like there is no other. Like I feel from Jesus and my grandma, but I can't even explain it in words. I was there just delighting myself in God, feeling completely loved and safe and filled with everything I need. I was

told I was in the space of creation and encouraged to create whatever I desire. So I did. I started creating my future, regarding my daughters, my own health, and my own relationship. I saw it all, and it was beautiful. When I was satisfied with my creation, I stayed in that energy for a little bit longer, then I came back down. Amen."
Eliza

We are all returning back home to Source, but it turns out we don't have to die to do it! This is what is referred to as ascension. Our higher Earth timelines are merging with heaven. The bible tells us all about the path to ascension and I have found the Journey's To Heaven are a mirror of this. It is as if we are being prepared for something bigger that is coming.

 When we open to this experience, we activate this ascension process more powerfully within ourselves. It accelerates our Spiritual journey back to Source and we begin to understand what it means to be in the world but not of it. We begin to feel fearless and at peace again. We feel the power of love activate in the core of our being and we begin to simply know the truth again. We laugh, we cry, we breath deeper and relax. This is why it is the best kind of party. The only hangover is the feeling like we are still tethered to heaven.

Chapter 38

Quantum Technologies

We even have an ascension vehicle called a Merkabah. Who knew we had all these upgrades that came with our physical body? It's like believing we are driving a Pinto then realizing we are actually driving a Mercedes! Some have been able to see their Merkabah during journey's. I have seen mine surrounding my body during a journey into higher dimensions. It looked similar to a Merkabah as depicted in ancient art with all of the brilliant colors in the shape of a star around my body. I was sitting in a seat in the middle of it like I was driving a car!

Using quantum bio-feedback technology we are able to capture what this experience does to our aura or electromagnetic field. We take an aura photo before a journey or session and an after photo. The colors often change to the colors experienced in the Source Field and it is common to see light coming into the crown from Source, demonstrating that the connection has been activated and they are tethered to that realm even after returning their focus to their physical body.

I have attended several conferences with William Henry. The research he has put together regarding ascension is mind blowing. I can't say enough about how powerful that information has been in my own life for expanding my consciousness. One of the things that stands out the most is the ancient art he has shown depicting the rainbow light body or ascension body. This rainbow aura was painted around Jesus, Buddha, and many other ascended masters and it represents the human body existing in a state of ascension. When I starting photographing aura's after facilitating a Journey to Heaven, I witnessed the activation of the rainbow light body or ascension body in my clients. My mom told me the journey is an activation into the higher dimensional vibrations and once activated we are able to more easily access those ascended realities when we choose. We can now see this is truth through the change in our aura's.

Through quantum bio feedback we are also able to measure the frequency of the body. The before and after measurements are also profound. Many return from the "Journey to Heaven" measuring 963 hertz Solfeggio, which is the harmonic of Source connection. It is the harmonic my body naturally resonates at most of the time because I spend so much time walking between worlds. It is amazing to see people who have had no experience communicating with Spirit be able to Journey and have detailed interactions and conversations with their loved ones and continue to be in a higher vibration as a result.

Solfeggios* are the natural harmonic frequencies found in nature. We are always resonating with them through our natural state of being and this can be measured through quantum biofeedback technology. I discovered it through a friend who is using Genius Bio Feedback to read the vibration of the voice that accessed the quantum field to create a report that reads the Solfeggio frequency of the body. My body's vibration measured 963 hertz, the highest on the scale, and I was blown away by this. I would have expected this while I was translating Light Language from Source, but I wasn't. I was just in my average everyday state of being. That Solfeggio is in resonance with Source and the Christ Consciousness. I recall mom telling me that the more I connect with Source the more I will be anchored to it at all times. This was proof to me of what she told me, but I loved seeing it with my own eyes! Since this experience I purchased the Bio

Feedback so I could use it with my clients. I feel everyone should have access to their frequency and be able to monitor it often. It is so helpful in understanding where we are resonating and how we can master our vibration.

While using this technology during sessions, I began to see a pattern. When my clients arrived, I would measure their vibration and take a photo of their Aura or electromagnetic field around their body as well as their chakras. The colors of their most active chakras matched their Aura colors. Their vibration matched what they were going through in their life. After a session, this would all shift drastically. Their aura colors would change to the colors they experienced while in the Source Field on their Journey to Heaven and their vibration would shift to the highest, connected to Source solfeggio tone. There was no question they were moving into the Source Field during their journey.

Chapter 39

Source Solutions to Challenges

Every solution to any "problem" already exists in the Source Field. In fact, multiple solutions already exist. Everything we are experiencing has already been experienced and solved. We are just experiencing it through a different flavor of our energetic blueprint. This means as we access the already existing solution through Source "memory", we add our unique vibrations to its manifestation in our timeline. That energetic creation that came through us now exists in the Source Field for others, who are on a similar vibration as us, so they can more easily access that solution. This is how unity consciousness connects us.

 Our ability to access these solutions depends on our ability to align with them energetically. The more we expand our consciousness while intending to align with solutions, the more solutions we will receive. This means they come in stages or what feels to me like waves of energy. We may receive only one solution, but if we continue to stay open and aligned more will come.

When I am faced with a challenge, I take it into the Source Field immediately. Meaning I move my consciousness up into Heaven and allow my mind to experience solutions flowing into it from the Source Field. I will feel into each solution I align with and ask if this is the greatest potential solution for all involved. If not, I will expand further into the Source Field. I do this multiple times before I make a decision to act. It is a powerful process that takes practice to understand. I will speak the solution into my timeline to see how it "feels". Then I will wait to see what comes next. It is like layers of greater awareness flowing, just like the way I experience the information coming through during Spirit School. Our minds expand through layers of information. We only get the next layer as we are ready. After we have integrated and fully understand the layer we received. It is just the order of things being in a human avatar. Our artificial mind must integrate and learn the same way a child learns- one piece at a time. This is how we co-create reality through the Source Field.

We must expand our awareness through the field in order to access the highest solution for each unique situation in the new moment. They come in stages so keep seeking. You will finally access the highest solution as you continue to expand.

Chapter 40

The Spirit of Fear

My mom has shown me that fear is like a spell that carries a life-force of it's own IF we choose to give it life through us. I remember my Cranial Sacral therapist telling me that when she is releasing people, fear that is stuck in their body fights to survive like any other living thing. She has learned to speak to it like she would a terrified child. This was fascinating to me. It means fear is an entity that is thinking for itself and if we are filled with fear, we are being controlled by it's thoughts. It is like being under the Spirit of fear spell. The bible talks a lot about the Spirit of things. There is a Spirit for everything. A Spirit of perversion, the holy Spirit, the Spirit of Christ, the Spirit of fear. Maybe this is why I named all of my tiny houses with Spirit in the name. Tree Spirit, Native Spirit, Fairy Spirit. I love it when I do things without understanding why. I gave them the name Spirit so they would be alive. Since coming into this awareness, I decided I didn't want to give fear a Spirit.

I don't want to bring fear to life through me. I do not want to be susceptible to spells of any kind. This is easier said than done when we live in an artificial reality that runs on fear programs and fear spells. I've learned to not allow spells to work on me because I don't believe in them. They are not given power through me or made alive through me. Spells are dead energy because they don't come from Source. I prefer to let dead things stay dead.

The only reason anyone feels the need to cast spells is because they are not accessing their authentic power through Source. Again, it is an attempt to micromanage an artificial reality. I have had people try to spell cast me and it didn't work. It worked on others around me but not me. My knowing that if it doesn't come from Source it doesn't have power has been very beneficial in my reality. We can choose to manipulate energies all day long but the results will always be the same. Temporary and unpredictable. There are no shortcuts to creating our most positive experience. It can only be done through Source. But we can take as long as we need to finally figure this out.

Learning about who we really are and how we are creating our reality isn't always easy. Although I have been on this journey of accessing more and more information through my connection to Source, I still have moments where I feel I am disconnected and stuck outside of creating in alignment with my Spiritual path. I have far from perfected my vibration so this happens when I don't physically feel well; am letting myself feel fear and stress; or when something that I expected to turn out a certain way does not; just to name a few fear triggers of mine! Fun stuff!

This is a message I received from my mom explaining the process of moving out of the artificial timelines back into the organic timelines.

"You are in the ascension process. This is a timeline split. You are leaving the illusion and returning to the real. It is like trying to wake up from a nightmare that feels very powerful and real so you don't realize you are just dreaming. Your amygdala doesn't know the difference between the real and unreal.

The energies in the distorted timelines can feel very intense and real. It can feel as if you are being forced to face your deepest fears and love those parts of you back to source within you so you can be free and ascend out of the lower timelines. This can produce an experience of panic and anxiety.

This is your gift. The other side of this is where you meet your true empowered self again. You are being shown the door. You are leaving the fear timeline and parts of you are fighting to stay. They don't understand what is happening. They are trying to protect you from what they don't understand.

Be filled with gratitude for this process. You have asked for it and it is a gift from source. Source will carry you to the other side. This is like a powerful plant medicine journey back to yourself.

Use your power wisely. When you surrender and know you are safe always, no matter what, you will be able to talk your body into a state of peace when it is in fight or flight mode. But this takes practice and can be very difficult once your vibration has gotten too low.

Your amygdala is responding to the alarms in your body that are alerting it that something is imbalanced. That's it's job. As you become afraid of these alarms your vibration lowers and your body becomes more alarmed from the stress. This is the vicious cycle. Thank it for letting you know about the imbalance so you can stop the spiral. Your job is to feel into what is happening in your body and keep it calm while it works overtime to rebalance for you.

This is a team effort, a very sophisticated system within you that is either focused on healing through calm instruction from you or sounding alarms that create chaos and fear. You determine which occurs by your thoughts. You have the power to surrender and stay in the love vibrations or go into fear and lose your ability to be in charge of your experience.

Your mind can go into anxiety and you can observe it. It is not you. It is a trauma program running and it simply needs to be integrated back into love and source. It is more difficult to shift once you allow yourself to go deeper into the fear vibration. The key is to not go there at all.

Master being the observer of this part of you that's tempted into that energy because of past trauma. You are safe. Always. You must tell your mind this the same way you would a child that has fear. If a child is terrified of the boogeyman and you become terrified too, you can't help that child. You both become illogical. Your amygdala is your child. It senses something is wrong and it hasn't been taught how to handle it.

It has been in fight or flight for a long time. You are learning to stay in your power at all times throughout your physical experience. This is vital for you to master for your next steps on your journey. Your fear is not more powerful than you. It's time to integrate higher truth back into your fear programs so those parts of you no longer exist in states of illusion."

There is nothing to fight. We are choosing to take flight.

I learned from experiencing Cranial Sacral and Myofascial Release Therapy that these moments of fear easily get stuck in the cells of our body. Old fears can be held in our body from before birth. These memories of trauma remain until they can be released. I had no idea I was carrying around these trauma memories that were keeping my physical body locked into a constant state of flight or flight until I met Kathy Eason, my Cranial Sacral and Myofascial Release Therapist. She truly is a miracle worker through Source. The day I laid on her table and read the handwritten sign posted on her ceiling that reads:

Body, thank you for holding on to it for me,
Body, it is ok to let it go,
Body, it is ok if you don't understand it.

Just reading these simple but powerful words started the releasing process for me.

Regardless of where we are on our Spiritual path, we can find ourselves in a lower vibrational state of being. We can easily succumb to the heaviness of the illusional creation and forget that we are the ones creating our experience. This means we can start to the play victim role. When we go back down into the denser frequencies, we find ourselves co-creating on distorted timelines. This experience feels incredibly powerful. Depending on how long we stay there, it can be challenging to get our vibration back up so we can access our greater potential timeline experience.

While in surfing lower vibrations, it is difficult to get the clarity we need to move us out of the fear triggers that got us there in the first place. Spirit knows when we are in a state where they cannot easily connect with us so they will send someone who is in the physical reality they can connect with to assist. I am blessed to have several loved ones on this side of the veil who my mom can reach me through in my more challenging moments.

One of these "imaginal cells" is my friend Hamid. Hamid calls those of us that are creating from Source "imaginal cells" and I love his description! We are just that.

We were brought together through Source for many reasons, and one being the way our vibrations amplify each other. When we experience the vibration of those who are in vibrational resonance, it is a powerful experience. Hamid and I are an example of that! When I find my vibration is low, he can feel it even though we live in different countries. He and I will be drawn to each other precisely when our connection is needed.

One of the things that happens naturally is I can see myself clearly through his vibrational reflection of me. When our vibration gets low, we can't see anything clearly including ourselves. I can feel my higher vibrational self come back into resonance when we talk. It reminds of the way some healing tools work such as tuning forks or frequencies such as the one's created by Rife. When parts of our body have become immersed in a distorted vibration, and we expose that part of our body to it's optimal vibration through frequencies, that frequency calls it back naturally to its optimal vibration. My friend Hamid and I do this for each other effortlessly. This is one purpose of our Spirit family. They are like our tuning forks. Connecting with our frequency family is so important to our journey. We are meant to support each other vibrationally this way. It is very rare that humans do not find themselves in an ebb and flow vibrationally. We are here to offer our vibration through our love to assist when other's need a shot of higher vibration. Works every time!

Hamid is great at theatre improvisation. He has an ability to see and feel what people hide from themselves and others. He uses this ability to act out what he sees in us that we cannot see so that we can experience a clearer more empowered self. He can animate me and my creation in a higher vibrational way that eases me into clearing my fear that got me into a state of disconnect from source in the first place. His humor is his super power and I find myself laugh hysterically at the absurdity of my seriousness about the illusionary reality. I am able to get out of the quantum entanglement I am having with my fear trigger and step back into my authentic power through Source to create a better scenario.

Humor and unconditional love are in alignment with the medicinal frequencies that connect us into the Source Field. When we can activate those things within ourselves, we can gain the clarity we need in any situation to help us come back to center and peace.

One day, I had fallen off of my Living Light wagon, like Humpty Dumpty fell off the wall. I went tumbling down into a timeline filled with muck. I felt like the horse, "Artax", who was stuck in quicksand in the movie "Never Ending Story". No matter who tried to help me out of the muck, I still felt like I was in quicksand. I just couldn't feel my connection to Source. Without my connection, I felt like my life force was leaving me. The reason for this miserable energy I was experiencing was because I had trusted someone I had tried to help and they betrayed my trust and took without giving what was agreed to be exchanged. It was so upsetting to me because it was to be an exchange that would have helped my retreat to grow. I realized they lied and had taken advantage of me. My hope for humanity as a whole was challenged as I made my timeline spiral into the ego trap and abyss of victim consciousness.

Hamid reached out to me because, he could feel my less than happy state of being regardless of how much I think I'm hiding it from others. He proceeded to mirror this situation for me. I could feel the truth in his words and the role he was playing for me. The improv he did of my situation was hysterically funny.

He role played <u>Big Jennie</u> by putting his hands in the air saying (in his God voice):
"I am Big Jennie and I am connected to Source!
I have a Spiritual retreat for everyone to come to and use as they see fit.
I don't care about money or anything in this simulation! I am here to help humanity I don't need anything of this fake world. Take from me what you will!"

Then he quickly changed to <u>Little Jennie</u> holding his head in his hands and said
"I have to pay my bills and I have to eat. What am I going to do?"

Back to <u>Big Jennie:</u>
"I don't need to eat or pay any bills. I am living in the Source Field!".

<u>Little Jennie:</u>
"I know, I will build a barn where I can host bigger events and weddings, this will sustain my Spiritual retreat!"

Big Jennie:
"Ok I'll play along with 'Little Jennie' and hire someone to build this barn and then have him sabotage the build because she doesn't have the energy for all of that! She came here to help people see what I see, and know what I know, so they can create their greatest potential here! That will distract her from my higher path and purpose!"

Little Jennie:
"Oh NO! The barn build is sabotaged.
Now I will never be able to pay my bills or buy food!"

Big Jennie: "You will!"

Hamid's improv about my life was so hilarious and true, I couldn't stop laughing. The laughter was raising my vibration so quickly that I was able to get the clarity I needed to be back in alignment with the Source Field and relax knowing all was going to be ok. I had gotten so focused on what I thought was my only option that I couldn't see all of the potentials that were there and much more in alignment with what I was here to do with Spirit. This didn't mean I couldn't build a barn, it meant I needed to understand the higher purpose of it before it would be manifested. The barn wasn't what I believed it would be and the creation of it needed to be done through source not my amygdala. The energy of our creation is so important as it determines the experience of it. The barn will be a place for Spirit to express itself to others.

On a scale of 1- 10 and 10 being in a state of connection and joy, I went from a low 4 or 5, back up to my usually high 8 or 9. It is amazing what a relief it is when we come back to our laughter, unconditional love and joy within ourselves. It feels like that muck is going to suck me in for good and I have little energy to fight it. It feels so pointless to fight it. It's pure doom and gloom! The world is such a mess and there isn't a solution after all. I was wrong with all of my naive optimism. None of that love and light nonsense is truth. Do you see how the lower vibrational reality inverts the truth and tricks us into believing it? It always reminds me of the movie "The Never Ending Story". We all get lost in "the nothing" sometimes. I call it the upside down. The blood starts rushing to my head and I can't think my way out! It is funny once I get set right side up again but it isn't funny at all while it is happening.

Once we begin to see it clearly, we will know when it is happening and we will choose to get out quick. If we get knocked down and can't seem to pull ourselves out of the never-ending inverted story, contact your 'Hamid". If you don't have one, ask your gatekeeper to bring you one. Hamid's are an essential part of your earthly journey. Don't leave home (Source) without one!!

All distorted beliefs that we have taken on through distorted experience will have to come back into alignment with source in order to be cleared through higher truth. We clear our illusions by seeking the highest truth to replace distorted belief programs. We must be willing to let go of EVERYTHING we think we know.

There are many layers or levels of consciousness to choose from. We can accept the lower density truth if that is all we can access at this time. But I assure you no matter what you believe, there is so much more. I recommend reaching higher and intentionally expanding your consciousness more and more. There is always more to understand and experience about a particular subject.

Surrender humbly to source in order to pull all energetic aspects of yourself into that field. This is where true learning happens, outside of the programming. We are free to learn, to grow and to expand alongside Spirit and outside of distorted creation. Feeling this freedom is the best!

It is so important that we not attach to negative outcomes in order to prove we were right about the illusionary reality. Only attach to the positive outcome no matter what. It doesn't mean we weren't right about the lies we were told; it means we refused to co-create that distorted timeline and in the end, we aligned with the Living Light that healed all. <u>We are THAT powerful through our intention to flow with source!</u>

We all have our moments of feeling disconnected and stuck in our lower mind. The way my higher self-responds to that state of being is to allow those moments through observation and understanding. Then reach for my higher state of being in a more conscious connection to source. Once I'm back in the higher state of being, I'm fully aware that the other state of being is the illusion. It's not real. What is real always cancels out what is not real. It transmutes it through higher truth. It has no power in truth. Therefore, it is as if it never existed in the first place. Allow it to dissolve. It is not who we are and we don't need to hold on to it going forward. We don't need to dwell on mistakes we made while being in states of illusion. If we do then we keep the illusion alive and running on a distorted timeline. Cancel all distorted timelines through the field. They require our distorted creative energy to keep them alive. Don't feed it. Fully immerse back in the source field and shake it all off! Phew! Now have a good laugh.

My mom told me she would be the one who walks with me. No one else will be able to walk with me the way she does and I am to turn to her in the source field for my support, love and guidance. I have noticed that when deeper traumas come up within me, I have to ride it out and ask for it to be transmuted by higher truth and light. I reach for the higher answers for greater understanding. But I can't access it right away. I have to move through that lower vibration of my deeper fears and come out on the other side by raising my vibration before I can gain clarity. That's my process. I know it, but when I'm in that vibration it feels horrible. Like quicksand sucking me into a downward spiral.

During those times I try to tell my mind all is going to be ok. We just need to access clarity and it will come. But I am not my bigger self in those moments. I'm experiencing reality from my trauma self. I am very aware of it and know it is my illusion. That doesn't make the feeling any less intense. It's my own private hell. I have to continue to transmute within me. But I also realize I exist in a greater state of accountability because of my greater awareness. I can't get away with being in my smaller self for long or my life will manifest hell on earth! The more conscious we become the more powerful we become. I can't continue to entertain those illusionary parts of me. Yet I can't deny them either. I get out as quick as I can and raise my vibration back into the source field and then look at that fear while accessing higher truth. I am then able to see it for what it is with love and understanding.

Once we come back to connection with the source field in a more conscious way, we are at another level of experiencing physical creation. We become a conduit for the light and the light does its thing through us. We are now along for the entire ride! This includes encountering others who are given a choice to come back into their connection as well. It can be a challenging thing to be doing when sometimes we experience the ugly side of them that just won't let go of the stronghold, they have on them. Other times we witness the most beautiful and amazing transformations. For me, being the observer without attachment to any of it is the key.

Each time I do this I rise higher and expand more. That's really all we are doing here is expanding and with each expansion the entire collective expands. This is why we are here. My mom shows me how every time a soul steps out of its illusions and chooses its God self, all creation breaths, expands and dances with us.

The solution to all of your challenges is already out there, dancing in the energy of love, waiting for you to quiet your mind and allow your heart to simply feel it.

Below is a channeling that exists in the now quantum field moment for you to experience if you desire to assist with clearing old programming and trauma.

"Spirit is excited to be welcomed into your energy field today to offer their high vibration of love and light and share their perspective about your experience with old programming and trauma! Let's get a view from their eyes!

As I moved my focus into the source field with you, I witnessed the light interact uniquely with you. You carry a different vibrational pattern within your soul and the light attuned itself to a harmonious vibration unique for you. As we know linear time does not exist the way we understand it, you were here in this moment all along. This understanding enables your connection to be made with source and a shift to be made within your individual field. Your trauma pattern is also unique and the Living Light knows precisely how to dissolve and reset these patterns within your crystalline and cellular being.

I see the most beautiful colors and energy spinning like a vortex around your auric field. Attuning and activating your source field trinity of your heart, your third eye and your source mind. While doing this, I am witnessing the Living Light communicating with your trauma. Helping it understand the higher truth and reasons for the experience. The truth from Source shall set you free! Your parasympathetic nervous system in your physical body is now activated. The trauma response existing within your programmed mind is calm and at ease. Your body no longer feels like it must be on guard, in protection mode, because it knows you are safe. You are no longer in a state of fight or flight. This vibration of Source unconditional love flowing through you allows a beautiful heart opening and is a relief! This shift lets the light in to dance within your energy field more and more as your vibration expands and increases. The colors are more vibrant now and I can see the light sparkle like glitter. It is so beautiful. There is celebrating and laughter echoing throughout the Source field.

Within this space, outside of linear time, you are free from all trauma and programs. You are free to experience your creation in the physical reality through your divine essence self, connected to all that simply is. It is the most beautiful feeling of unconditional love, feel it wrapping around you like a comfy, warm blanket.

You are safe and free to remember who you really are and where you came from. You are pure, creative, source energy playing in a physical realty. What would you like to co-create next within this connection and vibration? What do you want to experience while witnessing your creation through the eyes of source? Your new source perspective is like opening a new gift in every new now moment. A gift full of new clarity and understanding. There were so many things you couldn't see or understand when viewing the world through old programs and trauma. You can now see the world through the eyes of Spirit/ Source. Everything is new.

It all makes sense now. There is a reason you have experienced everything that has led you to this moment and it was all helpful in assisting you with a greater and deeper understanding of love. But the trauma is not who you truly are. The love is.

The trauma is over. The old programs are no longer needed. You are free to take what is real from your experience and leave what was not true behind. You are free to flow with Source in every moment of your life. It's as if the trauma experience was just a blip in linear time that was a fleeting experience to help bring you back to this connection and remembering. Dance with this Living Light often! Feel the peace and love flowing through you without limitations. What colors do you see? What is the light teaching you about the true nature of your Spirit? There is so much to learn and understand! It's so exciting! This is what you came to share with the world!
Thank you for being a part of this beautiful exchange! It is a powerful integration of trauma and activation through the Source Field. Remember to come back to this place whenever you need a reset! Spirit is always eager to meet you here!"

Chapter 41

Walking Between Worlds
Mastering the Inter-Dimensional Experience

Translating Light Language from The Source Field

Heaven exists inside of me and I am connected to all things. I co-create through the Source Living Light in every moment. Everything we experience here is intended to be mastered through our connection in the Source Field and then translated into our physical reality. We offer our unique creation which flows through us from Source to be used to help others do the same. Bringing all distorted creation back into alignment with higher truth is the medicine. Every experience of disconnect from Source and distorted reality I experienced from childhood which I experienced as trauma, from the victim consciousness, the narcissistic societal programming, my mom's traumatic death, distorted relationships with others due to my distorted relationship with myself, etc. These experiences can awaken our Spiritual gifts once we align with Source. I, along with Spirit, now assist others with states of victim consciousness, narcissistic abuse, grief, and traumas in all forms. I wouldn't be able to assist with these states of distortion without my own direct experience with it. This is a common theme for those of us who have chosen to offer a path to higher truth. We walked through our own self-created hell and found the door out so we could also help walk others out. Those that come to me are brought by Spirit. We carry keys for each other and those I have a key for are predestined to show up and vice versa. This is why I don't worry about promoting to others what I can do. I let Spirit align us perfectly in divine timing. The purest vibrations of healing and love are two things that can only be experienced through the Source Field. When we are not accessing the Source Field, we are only experiencing distorted versions of healing and love. This is why my mom's main teachings were how to be and stay in the Source Field at all times. All else flows beautifully from there. It is the natural order of all physical creation.

The more time I spent keeping my focus to the higher dimensions, the more I understood that things look completely different from the higher dimensions than they do from my amygdala brain. Her death from the perspective of my 3D brain, looked and felt like a hospital murder. Her death from 5D heaven looked like a divine plan guided by her higher Spirit. This is not Spiritual by passing, it is understanding the difference between the various vibrational realities. How can this be? I know what I experienced. The hospital did horrible things to her. She didn't have health insurance. It was not only that they allowed her to suffer and die, but they seemed to hurry the process along. I recall her telling me never to take her to a hospital because she wouldn't come back out. She was very aware of the corruption of this reality. But she was traveling when she blacked out and an ambulance was called. I had no control over her trip to the hospital but she was right, she was taken to a hospital and didn't come back out.

Which part of this story is true? Do I have to pick one to attach to and believe is the real one? Or are their two completely different vibrational experiences happening at the same time on two different timelines? Once we understand that our experience is dictated by our vibration and the timeline we are matched with, we will be able to be more intentional about our experiences. If we choose to see everything through the eyes of Source, we will no longer be programming our amygdala with trauma that comes from a lower timeline reality.

Many of us know someone who has mastered this. Someone who experienced the exact same thing we did. It was traumatic for us but it was the opposite for them. They didn't experience the trauma that we did. It is as if they are immune to distorted experiences. I was always so fascinated by these people. I was always drawn to them. I noticed that when I was with them, I didn't experience the distortion either. It was easier for me to stay above it all and just enjoy the experience no matter how crazy things got. It wasn't that we didn't experience distorted creation around us, but we were able to create the outcome through Source. This typically involved a lot of laughter and light heartedness, and not taking ourselves or life too seriously. But it was even more than that. It was Source connection. My mom was one of those people.

I didn't understand it back then, but now I know I was allowing them to *surrogate** me into higher vibrational states of being through their higher vibration. It was easy for me to be fluid in my vibration because I was open and willing to allow the experience.

Do not confuse this with Spiritual bypassing. Spiritual by-passing is a state of denial about the reality we see on the 3D timeline. We do this when we know the reality is distorted but we don't know how to access Source in order to know what is actually the higher truth. When we are in a state of denial, we are not viewing the reality from the source field. We have memories of the source field so we try to apply them to the 3D reality but it is still based in distortion because we are not fully experiencing and co-creating our reality from the accessing the highest truth through the Source Field. I call this Source speculating rather than Source streaming!

It is important to be aware of how pure information brought through from source becomes distorted through transmission into the lower timelines. Even transferring information from one person to another doesn't always translate clearly because of our different vibrational states of being. Higher Spirit is very aware of this and does not choose to communicate in distorted fields.

For instance, I will get a download through source and share it with someone who's vibration is distorted and not in alignment with source. During the exchange I will begin to feel the information shift, and no longer flow with ease and clarity. I will begin to feel the information is no longer accurate or it feels off. I can no longer explain it properly and it feels confusing. Nothing from Source is complicated or confusing so if it feels this way, I am no longer in alignment with it. I can feel my energy field contract rather than expand during this exchange and I can feel cut off from streaming Source.

The person I'm sharing with may have good intentions and want to understand but their vibration distorts the information so much they can't make sense of it. They are trying to pull the information into their vibration instead of allowing the information to bring them up, expand their consciousness and shift their state of being. Higher truth requires us to align with it- not the other way around. As above so, below- follow their lead. I hear this often.

I can always tell when I have lowered my vibration to connect with someone because my energy field feels contracted rather expanded like it does when I'm aligned with source. What I'm experiencing is not because the information itself is off or not true, it's because I am now experiencing the distorted version of it because I moved my vibration into alignment with someone else's distorted vibration. I am now no longer aligned with Source and no longer flowing with higher truth. We have to remember that we must align with higher truth, it does not align with us. It is a great reminder for me to pull my energy back to myself and focus again only in my connection with Source so I can realign my own energy. We don't want to continue conversations that are distorted and not streaming higher truth from Source.

It is easy for us to become confused and question what originally came from Source. This is how we start to believe the distorted information is what is true and get lost in the distorted reality. Staying aligned with source is the key. Don't be tempted to match energies with others in order to connect with them. It's their responsibility to match with the higher vibration if they truly want to understand and get clarity. We are to hold our connection to Source now above all else. It's the only way to assist with anchoring higher truth into the lower timelines. Likewise, when we share with others who are source aligned, the exchange is powerful and consciousness expanding beyond what we initially received from source. It opens a flow of clarity and higher truth that leaves us feeling fearless and euphoric!

Chapter 42

Lighting the Way for Others

Many Spirits chose to aspect themselves to come into the simulation to try to pull other Spirit aspects out that got lost in the illusions. This is done by channeling source into the artificial timeline through us. Yes, it really is just aspects of ourselves from the perspective of the higher dimensions. But the aspects that exist in creation as we step down into lower density gives us the beautiful experience of creating through unique individuality. Not everyone in the lower timelines desires to come up out of it nor is this a requirement for their journey. We must approach their journey without judgement and honor their free will as Spirit does. Spirit does not interfere with the choices of others yet offers their higher vibration of love to assist with them increasing their vibration if they so wish.

One of our greatest challenges in being in the illusion of separation is feeling helpless when we see those we love suffering. We want to help them so much that we are willing to compromise our own vibrational state of being to do so. We feel this is required in order for us to connect with them. This is another misconception of the inverted reality. In the old timeline experience, the denser energy was dominant. It was challenging to be able to hold the higher vibration and when we did, we felt alone and disconnected from those unable to connect in the higher energy. The dominant vibration felt so powerful it seemed impossible to operate in a different vibration without causing more problems.

We tend to automatically adjust our frequency to make a clearer connection. For instance, when we are around someone who has a slower vibration than ours, we will slow our frequency down so we can communicate clearly with them. If we don't, it is very difficult for them to hear us. We all communicate through vibration. Even when we are using words, the words carry vibration that is translated by the receiver's vibration. If their vibration is too far off from ours, the connection becomes distorted. Like a radio station that can't pick up the station clearly so it is glitchy with static. Where we come from in Source, we adjust our vibrations naturally in order to truly connect with each other. This creates a beautiful exchange between Spirits. But in the linear timelines, the vibrations are much slower and therefore it is not the same flow as it is in source. In effect what we are doing is natural and beautiful in Source but in linear can be too distorted between vibrations that are not in alignment.

It is also the same when those of us focused in the linear timelines are communicating with Spirit. Spirit exists in much higher vibrations than us. Their timelines are a dominantly higher frequency which makes it easy for them to stay in a higher vibrational state of being. Whereas our dominate timeline here is much lower so it can feel like a challenge to hold a higher vibrational state of being at all times when we feel like we are being sucked into a dominantly lower vibration constantly.

This is where the practice comes in. Because we were allowing our dominate vibration to be dictated by the collective timeline, we developed habits connected to this. Habits that need to be corrected in order to master staying on our higher timeline no matter what is happening on the dominant lower timelines of which there are many. Once we become aware of this and set our intention to choose our own vibration and not lower it for any reason, our entire reality shifts.

My mom was a good example of this. She was able to access higher vibrational dimensions so she was able to discern the real from the fiction. But none of her family or friends were able to join her there. Thus, she seemed crazy to those who could only see from their limited view in the lower timelines. She tried to help lift us up but it seemed impossible. We were trying to understand with our linear mind rather than connect with her through the unconditional love of source. Her state of being was triggering a myriad of inverted belief programs in others. I recall her calling me from a payphone while on a trip with family to Tennessee. A woman she was with couldn't understand her ability to communicate in higher dimensions and told her it was the devil. My mom's state of vibration had triggered fear programs in this woman to the point where she started screaming at my mom. My mom told me I might need to come to Tennessee to pick her up because she didn't know if she could get back in the car and finish the trip with her. My mom always understood these reactions from others and never condemned them for it. She managed to offer them love to help them calm down so they could continue in peace.

She learned not to talk to everyone about her abilities or what she knew from her communication with my grandma. Although she didn't have the words at the time, she told me she saw them as scared children unable to control their programmed fear responses and she had empathy for that. She never responded with the same energy that was coming at her. She responded with a higher vibration to offset the lower. It is the natural way of defusing the artificial reality. Laugher is a vibrational match to higher love. Laughing at the absurdity of the inverted artificial fear programs gives us an opportunity to raise our vibration quickly out of the lower experience.

She used this tool all the time. She helped people "lighten up" as she would say and laugh. She did this so beautifully and still does.

Just as my mom would not lower her frequency to connect with me when I was in lower vibrational states of being, we cannot affectively assist others in lower vibrations by lowering our vibration. Spirit understands how to use their energy in a way that doesn't compromise their own state of being in order to make a connection.

We are much more effective in helping others when we are holding a faster frequency space. It offers them a higher vibration to choose to come into alignment with rather than us going into slower frequencies to try to connect better with them. It feels natural for us to lower our vibration because it is the only way we can communicate. If we stay in a higher vibration and they are in a lower one we cannot hear each other as easily. It is the same with Spirit. This is the reason most of us are not able to interact with Spirit. They understand this discrepancy but they also understand that if they come down into our frequency resonance, we are going to distort the information. The messages becomes distorted as they step down in vibration.

Trying to jump into lower frequencies with the intention to and save those who are disconnected from Source is a risk for us because we can easily find it difficult to access higher clarity. Higher Spirit doesn't go into lower vibrations to connect with us because it doesn't serve them or us. They hold their higher vibration and offer it to us when we are ready to rise and connect with them. There are those who insist on being trapped in that lower denser vibration and desire to pull others into it with them. They don't always do it consciously; it is a very inverted way of being that is a result of being immersed in a state of disconnect from Source's Living Light. Without their Source connection they are seeking energy through others who are Source connected. They are seeking Source through others instead of themselves.

My role is to assist the souls to come back into Source while staying in their physical body. Spirit from higher dimensions assist in their raising their vibration and I assist in this dimension. This activates the inter dimensional DNA and allows the physical body to adapt to being in more and more Living Light. It activates the inter-dimensionality of the physical body. I have been assisting as a medium for many years and I act as a surrogate vortex to allow others to experience higher dimensions through me. Now we (souls) are collectively ready for the next level. We are being called back into the source field without experiencing the physical death. This is the ascension. We walk in source while in the physical body. The higher essence Spirit becomes one with its physical manifestation. All things inverted get flipped right side up. This is the only way to clear the distorted timelines and gain back control of our own programming. We now are programming our own artificial brain through the source field rather than the distorted artificial reality. The artificial cannot exist with the organic. We are choosing one or the other now. It is my feeling all SOULS are now coming back to source-as it was intended.

It is my understanding from my communication with Spirit that all SOULS are now making their way back to source, as it was intended. Some are shifting their vibration slower than others. But even those who seem to be deeply immersed in the lower density timelines will be rising into a higher vibration, even though it might not be as high as we would like to see, it is still a shift for them.

It is important for us to understand how to properly assist those who are in deeper states of illusion. We cannot help others until we have established our own foundation of being in higher vibrational states. Otherwise, the illusions can overpower us and we can become confused and attacked by entities that love to manipulate us from the shadow dimensions.

Through my communication with Spirit, I now understand why some get so deeply lost here that they can't feel Source enough to shift out of their deep states of illusion. My mom explained that Spirit is very aware of the deep level of trauma humans have been subjected to in the lower timelines. Severely abused and traumatized humans, in some cases, would rather betray their own hearts by doing things that are not positive for them, but makes them feel temporarily safe and powerful, rather than face and heal the horrible (typically from childhood) traumas they endured. This fear and pain are buried so deep they can't even reach in there while maintaining a sense of sanity. It makes them feel like they have no control and the dark is so powerful that it will destroy them. It's like being only a hologram of the true self. This is why their behaviors make no logical sense, they exist in a state of damage control. They are stuck in states of terror and their inner child is stuck in a trauma loop.

Imagine that facing your buried trauma is actually more terrifying than letting a dark entity take you over. Most know these entities well; they were passed down to them in their families. They believe they saved their lives. That's how deep the distortion goes.

Spirit is gladly here to assist in illumination. They are happy to offer you a better choice and they can see beyond what our eyes can see. They know what energies are operating behind the scenes making us believe their thought projections are our own. Spirit isn't afraid of getting close to you and loving you even when you allow these shadow energies to use your physical vessel. Spirit isn't afraid of projections or dark spells. They won't work on Spirit or those who are streaming Living Light from Source. But no one can do this for anyone else. We all have to choose to stream Living Light from Source for ourselves because we are very split between our higher and lower minds. No matter how confusing it might seem to be for us, the Living Light always has the upper hand, the power, the grace we need to shift out of the shadows.

My mom is my eyes and ears for the unseen realms and she creates my divine appointments. I have had people schedule with me and my mom has told me she was not allowing the session. Once my mom woke me in the morning to tell me I didn't need to do a session for the woman coming that day because it wasn't her, it was an entity in her coming. I told her she would need to handle that since I had already scheduled her. The woman called at the time of her appointment to tell me she was on my road but couldn't come up my driveway and was turning around. This is how powerful Spirit is to override the lower vibrations in our reality. These energies have no power when Source gets involved but that doesn't mean they will be cleared within the person. Regardless of what they choose, it will be cleared from your reality.

Many of us are here to assist in clearing these entities from our family lines and we have no fear about it because the Source is with us. We have an army of protection around us in the higher vibrations. We aren't going to be drawn into dark games and we are no longer creating distorted realities with those who need us to in order to stay in the illusions they have created. The more we allow Living Light to flow through us the more illumination of these distorted vibrations will occur. It simply cannot continue in the Living Light frequencies.

Many are experiencing negative entity influences and we are to unite in the Living Light together in order to amplify the higher vibrations. These entities love to isolate us and play on our good hearts and encourage us not to speak "negatively". They do not want us to expose them because they have no power in transparency. They only have power when they can hide in the shadows and manipulate without being seen. We don't need to jump into their dark creation and get drawn into their drama but we do need to acknowledge their presence and courageously speak the truth. We simply blast it with the higher truth. Distorted creation cannot exist in higher truth.

Dark entities think they own humans. If they have been attached to one since childhood, they don't want us assisting that person. They will fight to keep us from loving them. They need them trapped in a state of separation not trusting anyone. They will create as much conflict as possible and they can be very vicious to anyone they feel is a threat to their controlled state. Love them anyway. Love is the medicine. Meaning, we must stay in a higher vibration of unconditional love no matter what. Do not jump into the fear or conflict being created or we will find ourselves co-creating reality with lower entities. It is ok to distance ourself from the person we love and still interact with them in the higher dimensions to promote healing.

It may feel like your heart is breaking for those you love who are trapped in these dark cycles. Especially when kids are involved. Don't go into that energy for long as it co-creates more distortion. Stand in the higher truth and knowing of what is real and not real.

These are the talks my mom and I have through the veil regarding those who wish to try and "take me down" for trying to help save them. She keeps me from allowing myself to become their scapegoat by only offering Living Light and not playing along in their distorted creation. Rest assured, according to Spirit, we will all be ok in the "end". They will, at some point in their journey, decide to step out of their delusional state of separation.

Assisting others is best done while accessing source field guidance to prevent falling back into a distorted interaction. Remember distortion exists in the fight or flight part of the mind. Conversations that are done through that energy do not contribute to accessing expanded states of awareness. The lighter and more relaxed the interaction, the more our energy flows with source for higher clarity. Thus, the more your energy fields will connect and flow naturally through our higher heart star-gate portal to source. May the source with with you.

Chapter 43

Tools To Assist Us in
Activating Our Living Light Timeline

We now have access to a variety of tools we can use to assist us in experiencing Source frequencies. The more we ascend into higher frequencies the more frequency tools will reveal themselves to us. These tools are being created into our reality at a rapid rate now. There is no limit to what we can harness from Source into our physical reality.

Frequency tools are intentioned based, higher intelligence. They are organic Source Living Light frequencies. They are not a part of the artificial timeline. This is why they were not offered to us through that reality. They offer us higher frequency energies to use however we choose. They work with us similar to the way higher Spirit does. Spirit can offer us their healing vibrations through our energy field but we have to choose to allow it heal us. We can only heal ourselves, no one or nothing outside of us can do that for us. We are always the master of our own experience and creation.

They offer us their energy to assist us in increasing our vibratory rate but they cannot create for us. They assist us in getting our vibration up higher so we can become clearer on what we desire to create and experience. If we are not clear on what we intend to create, we will not experience the highest benefit from frequency tools. The more conscious we are in our creation the more powerful the experience. It may take practice for us to understand how to allow different frequencies to be a surrogate for us into the Source Field. They offer us a beautiful opportunity to expand our consciousness and activate the parts of us that exist in Source frequency at all times, but have not yet been accessed within us. Some call this our God Spark. The God Spark within us is Source Living Light and is a part of all that simply is. Activating it through higher vibrations is beneficial.

These frequency tools are only needed to help us align with Source, where all things come back into alignment with their most optimal vibration. For instance, every part of our body vibrates at a unique optimal frequency. When we become ill, it means there is a distorted vibration affecting that part of our body. It is vibrating out of alignment with its optimal frequency. When the optimal frequency is offered, it calls it back into alignment and healing occurs.

Vibrational Realignment Light and Frequency Bed

One of my favorite experiences regarding vibrational healing tools was when I met a man named Steve Tawbush. He was brought to me through a friend for a session. I knew nothing about him and he sat in front of me waiting for me to give him messages from Heaven. The first thing my mom said to me was "We are going to need your vibration much higher for this communication." I shared what she told me and asked for extra time for this process. I could feel my vibration rising as my body shifted into higher states of vibration. I became aware of a man in my field. I could feel his vibration was very high and he felt like a Spiritual teacher. He said he is a master of frequency and vibration and that he had left a legacy for Steve. Steve was the one he chose to receive his life's work. He hoped Steve would continue to use it to assist others. I had no idea what this was about and I could tell that Steve was completely shocked by this message. Steve started to share with me about who this man was and how he knew him. His name is Sherm and he had developed a vibrational realignment light and frequency bed that he had used to assist people in overcoming a multitude of physical distortions. Steve had been a client of his and had experienced miracles through his work. But since Sherm's passing, it seemed his work had died with him. No one knew what to do with the information nor how to access the information through his computer. Through our continued communication with Sherm and the help of others who Sherm helped bring to us, we were able to gain access to the files and recreate the "med" bed that Sherm had built.

These beds have been created for several other centers and continue to assist people in calling distorted frequencies in their body back to their frequency of optimal health. Sherm is very happy his project continues and he has let us know that he continues to learn himself. He offers more knowledge to us as he receives it. This is just one of many examples of how Spirit works with us so that we all grow together into our greater potential co-creation.

Tachyon Chamber

I was invited by a friend to go experience a tachyon chamber in Virginia. I had never before heard of Tachyon's or a Tachyon Chamber. I was told a man had recently had three sessions and his brain tumor shrunk in half after experiencing it. That's all I needed to know. We loaded up and headed to Virginia. I didn't have time to even research it. I love experiencing things without being told anything. I had no preset ideas other than it was clearly able to have a healing effect on brain tumors!

When we arrived the next morning, we weren't able to find the doctor's office. Our GPS kept telling us we were there but we saw nothing to indicate that was true. We walked up and down the street and passed the office several times before contacting him to explain that we couldn't locate his office. He stepped outside and there it was! Right in front of us the whole time. It was as if his office was invisible!

When I saw the Tachyon Chamber it looked like nothing I had imagined. I thought it would be some complicated contraption I was to be cocooned within. Instead, it was a metal pyramid with a mattress under it to lay upon. There were several tachyonized crystals in the room. I climbed under the pyramid and laid down. I laid there focused on my intention, waiting to have a miraculous experience although a part of me was skeptical. I began to feel light dancing through my body. I had goosebumps all over! I have felt this before but never this intensely. It was as if the light was activating my cells and they were dancing with joy! I couldn't lay still. I felt like every part of my body was in motion. I didn't know whether to laugh or cry to release the pent-up distortion in my body! I felt so much joy!

Communication with my mom was much easier and clearer for me in the chamber. She explained to me that the Living Light she had taught me about was being channeled into my body through the chamber. It was streaming down into the chamber. I was enjoying my blissed-out state in this Living Light bath when I was told my time was up. I got out and could barely walk. I tried to sit and missed my chair and almost fell down. It was hilarious!

My friend didn't have the same experience I did, initially. She came out and was disappointed that she didn't feel much. My mom explained that my experience was more intense because I have been attuning to the Living Light for several years. The Light was able to get in much easier. The next time she got in the chamber she had a beautiful experience. After our sessions we were in such a high vibration we felt like we were loopy. We laughed about how the doctor must be invisible because his vibration is so high being in that chamber all day every day.

He and I were talking and I mentioned this to him. He looked at me with excitement and said he does feel invisible. As an example, he said he will go to the bank and the person behind him will walk right past him and the teller will look at them as if he isn't there. This reminded me of the part in the book "The Celestine Prophecy" by James Redfield, where the main character, Will, had raised his vibration so high that the bad guys who were after him came up on him in the forest and ran right past him because they couldn't see him.

I recalled my mom telling me back in December of 2018, after being in Spirit School with her for just over a year, that at some point my vibration would be so high that my physical body would become much less dense. She explained that at some point, if I continue to work with the Living Light, I would appear to be transparent to those who can see into the higher vibrational dimensions. In other words, some would only see me through their own dense vibration but others would have a wider range of vibrational sight.

We laughed so much during the time we spent with him. The vibration was so high and beautiful it felt like heaven on earth. I left knowing I had to have a Tachyon Chamber at my sanctuary. "According to documentation in the field of quantum physics-tachyons are sub-atomic particles that travel faster than the speed of light and beyond [linear] time, unlike electrons, neutrons & protons. Because tachyons are the highest frequency particles that can be combined with physical matter, nothing negative can co-exist with

them. As a result, when combined with human tissue & electrical systems, any diseased aged or damaged cells are entrained with an extremely high frequency of tachyon particles and thus restored to their optimum state of health. It is documented that not even damaging electro-magnetic radiation (EMF) from things like cell towers & WIFI can even exist with tachyons around."
AdaTourtsakis – Author of Sedona Quantum Consciousness Tachyon Healing Blog

This explanation is right in alignment with what my mom taught me about the power of the Living Light and how distorted frequencies cannot exist in the presence of Living Light. My direct experience with Living Light and Tachyons confirmed this to be true. Again, these frequencies are intentioned based. They exist in a state of Super Position waiting for us to direct them with our intention.

Ever since I experienced the Tachyon Chamber, I have felt like I am on a higher timeline. I have heard other people saying they feel this way as well after their experience.   I am sure a big shift occurred in that chamber. I feel the chamber assisted me with this collective bump up. So many amazing experiences have occurred since then. I am in a state of joy and gratitude effortlessly. This energy has continued to build within me.

After I returned home, I began having higher Spirit interactions in ways I had not had before experiencing the tachyon energy. It was amazing for me in the realm of Spirit and expanding consciousness. One night, I woke at 5am and was reading to try to go back to sleep. My partner, at the time, was asleep next to me. Suddenly his higher self appeared through the veil and kissed me. He was glowing in beautiful white and blue light and he kept his lips on mine as that light filled my being. It was like nothing I have ever experienced before. I was fully conscious and awake.

I was doing sessions for people the rest of the day and the information that flowed through was also next level. Many of us are shifting into higher vibrational states of being and accessing higher timelines. The Tachyon Chamber accelerated this change for me. These shifts are subtle for some and not so subtle for others. However, the feeling is the same. It's easier to be at peace and connected to source frequencies. We are coming out of the lower timelines back to our more natural resonate higher self frequency with less effort.

My mom reminded me that the pyramid shaped centrum part of our brain is a Tachyon Chamber. It harnesses Light the same way a Tachyon Chamber does, but of course with much more efficiently. Spending time in a Tachyon Chamber activates the one within our own body. All things that exist outside of us also exist inside of us. Everything we need to be inter-dimensional and aligned is within us. We are walking, vibrational healing, Tachyon Chambers! Mind blown! Once we understand how to activate and use our physical avatars property, the tools we have created outside of us for healing, will no longer be necessary.

These activations through vibrational healing tools are all part of the timeline split. They are assisting us in coming back to Source and remembering how to heal ourselves. There are many artificial timelines that exist in states of distorted frequencies that create illness within our physical bodies. These cannot exist in the same space as the higher, organic, healed timeline.

This is the timeline split. The artificial timelines (there are many) cannot exist in the same space as the higher organic timeline. Where we are connecting depends on our own vibrational state of being. The artificial timelines are holograms (some call them simulations) that we have agreed to co-create together. They are not real. They are the dream. We have to understand this or we are continuously playing along and co-creating in the illusions. This does not mean we do not assist others, but can only assist those who are able to access the Source and make the leap. We can offer our connection to Source that flows through us and those that choose to feel it in their hearts are those who are ready. It's always a heart opening experience for us.

Our higher selves are more easily able to interact with us from Source. We will soon be interacting with our own higher selves as well as those around us as the norm. We will be integrating that part of us back into our creation here. We are accessing more and more Living Light and our bodies are acclimating to it. It's so exciting. We now have a Tachyon Chamber of our own and receive the most amazing testimonials from our guests who experience it.

Chapter 44

Co-Creating through Living Light
(Heaven on Earth)

Ascended Spirits are dedicated to assisting us with our Spiritual remembering. We are all a part of the one consciousness in the highest, vibrational dimensions and therefore our individual creations affect each other. Those who exist in the higher vibrations have gone ahead of us and are happy to offer their love and support to us as we continue on our Spiritual journey in the lower density physical reality. They have been here before and understand how challenging this dense reality can be. It is easy for us to get locked into our amygdala trauma loops and forget everything we know from our connection to Source. Source doesn't exist in that place so it is easy to fall into states of amnesia again.

As we train ourselves to recognize what is occurring and why, we become the observer rather than the victim. We are able to make a choice to feel the unconditional love of Source again. This simple choice is what moves our vibration up and out of the distorted trauma frequency so we can get the guidance we need to transmute those energies we are still carrying. This allows us to master our own creation and choose to only co-create our experience through Source. When we command our own creation to be in alignment with the co-creation of Source, so it is. From that point forward we no longer need to question whether the creation we are experiencing is for our greater Spiritual awakening as it always will be. Our role is to recognize what the purpose of the experience is and connect the dots that lead to our greatest potential in it.

My mom is often reminding me that my experience is determined by my focus. If I am focused on co-creating through Source Living Light, then that is what will be manifested. It is like the saying "keep your eye on the ball" if you want to hit it. We must keep our eye or focus on what we want to experience rather than what we don't want to experience. If I am distracted by being focused on the artificial distorted reality I will begin co-creating in distortion. Any time we have an emotional response to distorted creation we are now co-creating in that distortion. This does not promote Spiritual bypassing. Meaning, Spirit always encourages us to have awareness of what is being created in the distorted reality so we can set our intention to bring Living Light into it through us. Having a positive emotional response to it is key. We can observe it and declare that we will only create Living Light into it. Choose to have an emotional response to what it looks and feels like to see the Living Light transforming a situation into a Source miracle. It is amazing to feel the power of Source inspiration move through us just by visualizing and feeling it. That's the sweet spot of creation in which we want to stay, in order to achieve our greatest potential together.

The following is a channeled healing to assist you in activating your Spiritual Contract you made before coming to the earth. This message exists in the quantum field in this now moment so you can experience the activation anytime you desire to experience it.
"We come to you now so we may begin aligning with you and your desire to access the higher truth about your Spiritual contract. Contracts, as we perceive them in the realm of Spirit, are sacred agreements made with your higher self. The YOU that exists within your physical self is an aspect of your higher self that incarnated into this earth timeline to fulfill this sacred contract. While in this dense

vibration, it is common to forget the details of your sacred plan. We would like to help you remember.

During our healing session, we will be sending you frequencies of healing that include downloads of source light that carries your higher self memories. We, along with your higher self exist in the Living Light of the source field. When you open your heart to feel our love for you, you will begin to attune your vibration to us and this field.

It is most beneficial for all of us to meet in a vibration of love. As you set your intention to receive this higher knowing, spend as much time as you need to feel our love encompass your energy field and entire body. Feel the warmth of the Living Light permeate every cell of your body and every part of your being. This is how the information can be transmitted to you. Feeling our love is the key. It raises your vibration and allows you to access higher truth. We begin to align our frequencies and we can hear each other without distorted frequencies interfering.

We remind you that in order to do this, you must surrender all you believe you know about who you are and your present life path. We will be offering you another option to consider for your Spiritual journey, or we will be clarifying the Spiritual journey you are on already.

Our sacred Spiritual contracts are created through our desire to be of service to all things natural meaning to nature and all things in it, within the physical reality. Spirit comes here to create from its essence or higher self, and to channel itself into a physical reality that affects the reality through the Living Light in which it exists. When we *come back to our connection with the Living Light and choose to embody it, we become a vessel for it to create through us.*

The reality you incarnated into can be challenging because of the illusions of separation from source. Source is where we come from and to where we return. If we embody it, we never experience separation from it. We can choose to return to this embodiment at any time and it is in that state of being all things needed for us to honor our sacred Spiritual contract are fulfilled.

We view these sacred contracts as amazing and fun! They were created with the intention that you live your most beautiful life. You knew when you created it that it was not only possible, but guaranteed if you choose it. Your sacred contract is simply you sharing who you really are, your essence self, with the world. It is impossible for you to not know your essence self when you choose to know it, to remember it. There is nothing more powerful and this is your sacred contract.

There is nothing in the physical reality that can keep you from this. You, as well as your contract, were created in the source field and hold within it the Spiritual gifts you have developed since the inception of your Spirit. During your journey through eternity, you have chosen to master certain abilities and those abilities are always alive inside of you. Many have dismissed them, ignored them, or been afraid to use them. But we are here to encourage you to use them in some way every day.

We recommend, before activating this healing, you ask yourself what is your greatest heart's desire? What makes your heart sing? What moments of your life did you feel one with source? What happened to bring you that knowing? These are your clues about your Spiritual gifts and what you are here to share with others.

Everyone has Spiritual gifts. They are all unique and that is purposeful. When you choose to use your gifts in every moment, it creates a vibration that becomes a beautiful song. We can hear your song! Others will be so captivated by your song that they will begin to hear their own Spirit song within themselves. When everyone chooses to create their Spirit song and play it to the world, all will harmonize together and it becomes a beautiful orchestra. It is one song. We love hearing your songs and we play our songs along with you! Soon, all of creation is singing and dancing together in the most beautiful resonance of the source field.

When we witness you using your Spiritual gifts, we see miracles unfold. Regardless of what challenges you may encounter on your journey; your gifts can be used to transform it into a miracle. You did not create a sacred contract believing you would exist in a perfect world. You created your contract to encourage you to create a perfect outcome to every imperfect situation. The perfection flows through you and your gifts.

Let's dance and sing our Spirit songs back into alignment with the source field of the most pure and beautiful love.
Thank you for allowing us to share this higher truth with you and for playing your beautiful sacred song along with us!
Let's dance!"

Chapter 45

Fulfilling Our Contract

The realization that my mom, through her connection to her higher essence self, literally chose to birth me, then "die" early in her life, in order to save me from the illusions I was creating in a distorted reality, is overwhelming for me to accept at times. It is a constant reminder for me that I do not want her decision to do this unbelievably beautiful thing out of her powerful love for me, to have been made in vain. I want, with every part of my being, to join her in higher love and fulfill our agreement to help as many others as possible while I'm still in this physical reality. Because I choose to only co-create miracles through Living Light with her, I insist on absolute truth to guide my journey. My deepest passion, to assist others, the same way she assisted me, comes from this awareness and desire within me. I know what is possible for us because of what I have experienced through her love. I also know how deeply immersed in illusions I was, and that anyone at any time can choose to come back to alignment within their Source connection.

One morning she woke me early to tell me that if I ever decide to go back into my ego, it will kick me off of my Spiritual path with her and there is nothing she can do about it. She will not be able to assist me because she won't be able to reach me. I don't recall my mom ever being so serious with me about something. She imprinted me with the importance of this wisdom and it is always in the back of my mind as I continue to assist others the way she has assisted me.

She also reminds me that ultimately it is a decision each person makes and I cannot have attachment to their choice. They simply offer a connection to Source love through their love. We want everyone to feel what it feels like. The unconditional love, the joy, the peace. I am witnessing more and more who are choosing to raise their vibrations and be a channel for Source love themselves. It is beautiful to witness them choose Source love over fear in their own lives. My mom wouldn't have chosen a path that wasn't possible. She wouldn't have embarked on this amazing journey with me if it were going to be a waste of our time.

There are also those to whom I have offered a better choice. They haven't made that choice and instead have chosen to try to pull me down into the fear and density with them to confirm they are right and in control. It reminds me of the scene in the movie "What Dreams May Come" with Robin Williams, where his wife puts herself in her own created hell and he goes in to try and help her wake up and see her own creation. It was thought to not be possible by everyone around him but he knew their love was the more powerful force and he chose that over fear. We all have access to that powerful Source love. We were born of it and return to it. It is within us and if given the power it will transform every situation into its greatest potential creation right before our eyes. Even though I know this, it is my responsibility to stay in my own vibrational lane, the same way Spirit does, and not get tangled up in anyone else's distorted creation. I can only continue to be in Source love and offer that vibration to them when they decide they want to be in it too. Spirit does not interfere with free will choices.

What I am sharing next applies to everyone. Not just those of us who are focused on being in Source love. It is a guide given to me by my mom for being true to our own hearts in every moment and turning our focus away from distorted creation back to Source for guidance. We cannot continue looking to a distorted reality to bring us clarity.

We don't let anyone tell us what we should or shouldn't be doing in our life other than Spirit. It's our own unique, individual path and journey and no one else knows more about that than ourselves and your Spirit family. We must always follow our own heart voice. Half the lesson is just standing in the truth, as we feel it in our heart, along with Spirit, without fear. Learning as we go along and perfecting our Source connected experiences makes this journey a profound and beautiful experience.

Our experiences and truth can trigger others who are perceiving life only through their fear programs. When we are triggering peoples' old, fear programmed beliefs they will project their fears onto us. They will want us to stop doing the things that trigger them. That is about the inverted, distorted creation of micromanaging the external reality instead of managing the inner reality through the Source Field.

I've walked this path for a while and I do not take unsolicited advice from anyone regarding my own journey. I know my own path because Spirit shows it to me daily. When we start waking up through being in the Source Field, it ignites a fire that comes from our Spirit. That fire can't be put out. Those who are telling us to stop following our fire and conform to the distorted reality, haven't awakened to their own fire within. Many people are like the walking dead, playing damage control with their fear programs.

One of the most important things my mom told me is this world was created from many distorted energies. "When you are not connected to your own heart and soul you are not creating from the Living Light.

You are creating in distortion and separation. Fear. This separates you from the Source Field and me. Learn to recognize the distortions in the inverted reality and then discern the truth in it through the Source Field. Focus only on the truth. Stand in that always and share it fearlessly. Learn to see your own distortions and fear programs for what they are and bring it all back to the truth and Living Light within yourself. We are here to help each other remember the truth and stop creating in distortion and fear. Do that in whatever way your heart guides you. That's the only advice anyone should ever give you. Many came here for this purpose. Don't let anyone tell you what you should or shouldn't be doing with your life. Do what your Spirit nudges you to do. That's what ultimately makes you feel happy and alive. " Easy peasy! Thanks Mom!

The organic reality is fluid and conscious, therefore it is always waiting for us to get clear on what we choose to experience. What do you want to create? I hear my mom say this to me often. She needs for me to get clear so she can co-create it with me. The more we unite our creative focus the faster and more powerful things manifest for us in the physical reality.

If we do not see our creation show up as we expected, it is so important that we not attach to negative outcomes in order to prove we were right about the illusionary reality. Only attach to the positive outcome no matter what our mind conjures from past experience or what the external reality looks like.

It doesn't mean we weren't right about the lies we experienced in the artificial reality, it means we refused to co-create that distorted experience and in the end, we aligned with the Living Light that healed all by overriding the illusions through higher truth. <u>We are THAT powerful through our intention to flow with source!</u>

Every challenge we face has already been faced and a solution was created through source. It is never the exact same as what occurred before because it is a new creation through us, but the solution that exists will adjust itself to fit our exact situation and create the greatest potential from it. Focus on Source bringing the solution and it will. Focus on the guidance of source and you will receive it. Focus on Source love and you will feel it. Focus on Source vibrations and your own vibration will rise. Focus on being shown the next thing you need to remember for your own unique journey and you will see it. It really is all a matter of focus and allowing. It is already there waiting for you to turn your awareness to it and surrender. We are all learning how to be in this physical reality while focused on Source. Don't be distracted by all of the illusions calling for your attention. Become the real within the unreal.

Below is a channeled healing for you to access through your quantum field connection in this now moment if you desire to experience it.

"As you move into alignment with the new earth timeline experience, we are eager to share with you what we see through our "eyes", our vision of the opportunities that await you! There are higher vibrational experiences available for you to co-create with us, if you choose to align your vibration with them.

As you desire more and more alignment with the source field, the source field also desires to align with you. It is from this desire that a purer knowing of higher clarity and truth is activated within your higher heart field and higher mind. It is through your higher heart star-gate that the point of creation flows. It is here in this quantum zero-point moment that you can feel the beautiful simplicity of your Spiritual path and purpose. Where you come back to the understanding of what you have known all along. It is through this zero-point portal to "heaven" you remember you exist in this field always, in a state of pure love for all things natural. That when you are creating in this field, you are feeling the miracles of every moment. You are shown the simple truth in every new experience so you understand what your Spirit's purest desire is in being and creating there now.

Linear time is no longer as real as it once was. Your deepest desires are being accessed much easier and faster than ever before. Focusing on your greatest potential reality will allow it to unfold almost effortlessly. There will be lots of laughter, excitement and joy which will perpetuate more and more of these beautiful experiences.

It is most important now to clarify what you feel your greatest creation looks and feels like. Feel the love and purity of your Spirit coming through to guide your vision. Healing becomes instantaneous as you flow in states of peace and happiness! This is all not only possible it is here for you now! It is more real than the artificial reality you have been playing along in. The artificial reality exists outside of this source flow of creative energy. We are either experiencing one or the other in every moment. We recommend choosing the source field experience.

When all things in the artificial reality are stripped away what is left? Who are you? What do you now want to create on your blank canvas? The more real the source field experience becomes the less real the artificial reality is. Step through the doorway into the field. 2022 is a year of integrating source field on earth and expressing ourselves through our Spirit. It is our purest point of creation. Allow it to blow your mind.

You can choose to become a living beacon of Source field energy, streaming through you into a highly distorted collective reality. You are no longer the doer; the doing is being done through you. You become more of an observer, offering a clearer perspective assisting others to heal. We offer you our visions in every new moment, showing you that you have a choice to create on a higher octave with us. Allow us to show you how to flow with vibrations that promote healing everywhere you go. Imagine we are giving you a pair of glasses that allow you to see through our eyes. Anytime you are not feeling connected in the field, just ask and we will gladly offer you the glasses so you can see higher truths clearly again. Happy creating in this magnificent new earth timeline!"

Through our eyes,

Chapter 46

Nature

Nature itself exists in the organic reality, which exists within the Source Field. It is as if an artificial reality was overlaid on top of the organic reality. Nature is a channel of Source. Animals, trees, water, plants, stones, etc. speak light language through telepathy. It is only humans who have immersed themselves in the artificial reality to the degree that they can no longer interact with nature through light language. They have disconnected from nature itself, which means they are disconnected from their own true nature. This is why nature is a beautiful surrogate for us into the Source Field. Anything that is streaming Source can be a surrogate for others. Spirit will often suggest for people to go sit in nature to assist them in feeling Spirit with them. This is because the earth has a frequency that exists in a higher frequency that helps bring our frequency back into its natural state of alignment with Source. It is all here for us to use at any time.

We have two trees on our property we have witnessed what appears to be them communicating with each other. We tied a rope to each tree and the rope will vibrate very quickly when there is communication. It stops when they are no longer communicating. We have considered the wind but it happens when there is no wind. It's unpredictable. There are other trees we have done this with but the vibration doesn't happen.

There was a time when humans were highly in tune with nature as they existed within it. They had heightened instincts, a sixth sense, and were using Light Language to be in telepathic communication with the consciousness of nature. Humans and animals communicated through Light Language. Even the plant kingdom communicates through Light Language. Native American's were able to communicate with plants and animals. Nature was considered, consulted, honored, and loved in every moment. It was a beautiful dance that humanity and nature did together. Animals did not feel threatened by humans. Fear was not a part of the experience. Nature knows no fear. Fear exists only in the artificial reality. One of the most beautiful stories I have read explaining this was in the book, "Rolling Thunder" by John Pope. I highly recommend that book. The natives were nature alchemists. They would work in harmony with nature to co-create what was needed for the greater good of all.

When we return to our divine selves in connection to nature, we realize we no longer need anything artificial to survive. We activate our natural state of connection to all things natural including each other. True relationships are understood. Our telepathy through Light Language is remembered and activated within our physical avatars. I'm not suggesting we no longer use things that have been created in the artificial world such as cell phones, television, etc. I am suggesting we don't need a dependence on them for survival. Our avatars are connected to the earth grid which is a built in communication system. Our meridian system within our body is also a communication system. It was created by Source and it exists in much higher states of consciousness than anything created artificially. The artificial web means entanglement. Source web means connected. We have a choice to be entangled or connected.

Plants, trees, and animals are here to help us remember who we really are. They are an amazing part of our physical journey. They are tethered to Source and exist in higher states of unconditional love naturally. They are always willing to offer their higher vibration to us when we need a boost. Spirit often recommends my clients connect in nature in order to hear Spirit. There is a reason for this. It activates the centrum part of our brain and calms the amygdala fight or flight mode.

When I allowed plant medicine to show me nature through its own eyes, I experienced Light Language communication with the trees. I could see the most beautiful sacred geometry essence of trees and feel their Spirits. They are alive in ways I had no real concept of prior to this experience. I felt their powerful presence and I realized they have been there all along assisting me in my Spiritual journey back to Source. I walked by a big, very, old tree and I immediately wanted to give it a hug. I moved back realizing I needed to ask it permission and not just invade its space. It felt rude to do so. I said "Can I hug you?" I heard a clear "yes" in my mind. I felt so much love pouring out of that tree into me and I could feel the love coming from my heart to blend with its beautiful energy. It was one of my favorite experiences ever.

Animals are much more advanced Spiritually than most humans love even after they have left their physical bodies. It is such a perfect exchange for us to have with them when we understand their higher Spiritual role in our journey. Because they have stayed connected to Source and light language, they can teach us a lot if we allow them to. When we stop seeing them as less than us and start tuning in, we will feel the unconditional love we have forgotten. Animals play a larger role with us as Spirit guides. They continue to incarnate with us as an anchor of unconditional love in a very distorted timeline of distorted versions of love. They will often come through when I am communicating with Source for my clients and let them know they are a part of their Spiritual journey back to love even after they have left their physical bodies. It's such a perfect exchange for us to have with them when we understand their higher Spiritual role in our journey.

Earth has a magnetic Field just like we do and we exist within its field. As the Earth raises its vibration, our vibration rises as well and it heals us.

I will share a message that came through Spirit for a healing session regarding this topic. This message exists in quantum time, which means the healing offered through its Source vibration is available in each new now moment for those who wish to experience it.

"Ah yes, let's talk about Earth grids, also known as Ley Lines, Dream Lines, Dragon Lines, Meridians, or other names depending on where you reside on Earth.

Grid Lines are the source communication centers or life force centers of Earth. Like a telephone line direct from source. They amplify the frequency of the planet. Earth also has a chakra system connected to its grid. You may have already discovered that your physical body is a mirror of your Mother Earth. The nature of how things work electrically within you is also the way things work electrically on your planet. In other words, you have electrical communication grids within you that are the same as Earth's electrical communication grids. Understanding their purpose and how they work efficiently is valuable!

We are not going to go into all of the exciting details about the grid systems in this message but we will be working with each of you individually during the healing session to communicate what will benefit you most to understand in addition to what we share here. It is our intention to bring clarity for you to better comprehend the grids and how you can attune your own grid with the Earth grids to assist with ascension.

Grids, in your body and on Earth, carry information from the Living Light, or Source Light. They are inter-dimensional energy centers that assist the earth and humanity by providing a continuous connection to the Source Field. They carry the spark of source light consciousness or life force in the physical reality. If these grids get blocked, it decreases the life force flow. This causes illness and disconnect from source.

The grids are inside of us and outside of us so when we connect to them within, we also connect to them on earth. There is no separation in the source field. As we explained before, Living Light energy is intentioned based. It is helpful to set intention to come back into alignment with source grids.   To work with these grids to heal your body and the earth is a powerful action to take. It also brings you into the experience of being at one with all things natural in your world.

Grids are not able to be artificially created. So those who have desired to control the world have only been successful at suppressing and manipulating the energy grids for their own benefit. They could not have hidden so many truths from humanity if the grids were flowing properly in their highest vibration. They cannot reproduce their own grids to use for their own agenda. This is why they have their buildings on the points where the Earth grids intersect. This is where highest truth of Living Light is released into our world and downloaded through the entire grid system of the planet and our bodies. It is a source communication system. They have been hiding this information from humanity for a very long time. Once you begin *connecting with the grid again, it will reveal truths to you as you are ready to receive them. All you do is simply connect with it. It will then activate your own grid system and assist you in healing yourself and the earth.*

Grids carry source light information and exist in multiple layers of frequency and consciousness. As with all Living Light streams, you will get what you are ready for when you connect to it. The grid you were experiencing in the past is not the same grid you will experience in your new awareness. There are grids that are fully suppressed and being used to control on the old timelines. Those same grids in the ascended timelines are being used for the greater good of all.

Which grid are you experiencing? It's important to know. If you are connecting with the slower frequency grid there is a reason. Choosing to clear and heal all distortion in your reality and adjusting your frequency to align with the higher vibrational grid is recommended. The more humans that align with the higher grids the more amplified their energy will be and the more it will allow the Living Light to get through and saturate your world with its healing. It will out power the slower vibrational grid and more easily and naturally attune others to the higher frequency.

Many are witnessing the old carbon-based reality becoming crystalline again. After all it was just a "carbon" copy of source you were playing in. This is happening within your body and on Earth and it is directly related to the grids. They are returning to their crystalline form where higher vibrational information can be transmitted to humanity and your world again. You are ready! You are coming home! Becoming a "grid worker" encompasses all of this and much more.

We are eager to meet you in the source field to assist you with integrating these concepts that have been offered to you. Be open to receiving this information into your being so you will understand how to access the Living Light communication through the grids and assist with its natural flow through you and the planet.

Thank you for the opportunity to share this important knowledge. We are amplifying the, joy, healing and laughter echoing through the grids!"

Chapter 47

Sacred Experiences

I know that as distorted as things get in our physical lifetimes, we all end up coming back to ourselves. It is true that this is just a blip in eternity and we always get an opportunity for a do over. This knowing used to bother me though. I wasn't sure just what about it didn't sit well with me, but I know when I feel this that I am not accessing the highest truth on the topic. This is my sign that I need to focus more in the Source Field for clarity.

Here is what Source explained to me when I asked this:
Yes, it is true, but there is more to it. There is always more. Because you are able to connect with a higher level of consciousness, higher consciousness is calling you to connect with it.

Source is experienced through our Centrum (Source) mind. Every moment we experience carries within it layers and layers of consciousness. When we are not focused in the moment with Source, we are seeing and experiencing reality through the programed linear brain. This limits our ability to see through the eyes of Source. There is so much we miss, so very much- miracles, beauty, joy, bliss, fun, laughter, connection, and unconditional love. These things can only be experienced through Source. We are only experiencing the artificial version of these things because it is only through being in the focused moment that we can access what it truly is from the perspective of Source. Our linear brain cannot be in the moment. It exists in artificial time where it perceives reality from past experience only. This is the same way artificial intelligence exists and learns. When we come back into alignment with Source, we can see the expanded consciousness view of the experience, but we can't experience it. We can see the potential that existed in that moment and that we missed it. We can recreate it again but it is still never the same as that particular moment.

For instance, it is the time together and the memories and connection we miss or regret. We do have eternity for a do over even though it is never exactly the same. There will never be another you, your children, your pets, your spouse, parents, or loved ones. These unique creations are so beautifully manifested and sacred through the eyes of Source. When we come to source, it can be difficult to face. We can get so lost and disconnected that we miss the moments spent in love. We do grieve the loss of the potential we had to simply offer higher unconditional love to our co-creation. Imagine the miracles that we would have witnessed. If we can imagine it we can create it. Imagine the healing and the joy we could have co-created through Source. I experience this knowing all the time through my communication with those who have left this physical reality as I sit in between this world and the next. Death has brought them back to the love and the moments and I assist in the healing of these huge wounds as a result of their disconnect with themselves and their loved ones.

We are all given the opportunity to choose to live through Source or through illusions. Therefore, I honor those choices as Spirit does. I am at peace regardless of what others choose because I know that no matter how big the messes, we have made here, we do not have anything more powerful than love and we cannot destroy that love which simply is. Thank God! This gives me so much peace and lets me surrender and let go of what I cannot control. I can give it over to Source Love, knowing it is safe and sound until all things are called back into alignment with it. Knowing we can choose to do this at any time is exciting and allows us to enjoy the journey no matter what.

Chapter 48

Higher Truth is not Subjective

Truth is a frequency that is chosen, felt, known and walked in. It is lived out loud. It speaks, it feels, it knows, it is free. It is alive! Thus, it is a relationship just like any other. Only it isn't distorted as are many of our lower frequency relationships. It is our most important connection and relationship and we all have access to it.

Follow where higher truths lead...

Let's imagine that higher truth is what some call Source, Creator, or God. – Allah, Buddha etc. Some have an image of a man up in heaven. When people speak outside of alignment with higher truth (God) -he knows! Yet, it still doesn't tell us to not express those things. It wants to hear it all! It doesn't take it personally that we do not know it well enough to speak for it. It sees it as an opportunity to show us what it really is so we can advance our consciousness to our next level of deeper understanding.

Now, let's imagine that you exist in a state of subjective truth. If someone speaks about you in a way that is not in alignment with the truth about you or your life as you see or experience it, you might be upset about it, try to correct it by stating what is true from your own perception. Giving our truth a voice through sharing how we feel is our way of having a deep talk with truth and getting feedback. It is like talking to your best friend. We always get powerful feedback full of love and understanding. Do it out loud when you are alone or with people who love you. Or if you are brave, post it on Facebook. It doesn't matter how you get it outside of you. Truth will echo back to you regardless.

Truth never asks us to suppress and hide. Suppressing and hiding or being afraid to share our feelings contributes to blocked energy. It is self-abuse. Collectively we were taught to suppress and be nice and kind. We were not to confront lies when we encountered it. We were taught to doubt what we knew inside to be true. This is how a distorted reality got bigger and bigger then traumatized us and confused us. It has ultimately disconnected us from our knowing and our connection to higher truth.

Higher truth simply is and cannot be lost. It can only be hidden until we choose to find it. It exists in higher frequencies outside of lower frequency distorted creation, and knows it is the ultimate state of empowerment. It is where we have come from and to where we will return.

Nothing should come before our connection to truth. Not kindness, rules, lies, manipulation, deceit, fear, nothing in the illusionary reality in general.

Let truth flow through you. Even if it is not fully in alignment with the highest truth in that moment. If we truly seek higher truth above all else, it will align and clarify itself for you. It is a natural and a beautiful process of growing expanding and learning. This is a lost art!
The truth doesn't care about anything other than helping us and everyone else get to our highest point of clarity! The fastest way is to allow the energy to connect and flow freely outside of us! Humans being afraid of expressions of thoughts and feelings are living out their own fears and trauma. They need to reconnect to higher truth so

they will stop trying to suppress others. Nothing is personal! It's all just distorted creation choosing to come back into alignment with truth.

If I can see it, feel it, or experience it, I can share it. I honor all of these things in me and I know I am in a process of becoming clearer and clearer in every moment. I know my intentions are to access higher truth and clarity and I always do. It is always ok. This is a natural process that all of us should be allowed to go through in their own way. It's all perfectly ok.

We must allow ourselves to observe everything here and not react to it. Everything has been distorted by design. Once we understand this it now becomes a matter of being focused on not believing in everything we experience here and not accepting it all as truth, but always reaching for highest truth for clarity. We can immediately ask higher truth to show us what we can't yet see. Then pay attention! This process takes courage and it helps others step out of their self-imposed states of suppression and confusion. It creates empowerment through freedom and higher truth.

There are energies here that do not want us to live and express out loud because it knows this gives us the access to absolute truth and power because absolute truth is the ultimate power. If you are choosing to lock into the distorted reality here through fear and control, know that energy is not of absolute truth. It is what has gotten us into this mess of deceit and manipulation of truth. Deceit holds the energy here on Earth in the state of very distorted vibrations. It has created weak humans who can't handle hearing other peoples' expressions and perceptions because they take it as truth when in actuality -it is not. Or they know it will lead to their own exposure because they are living in deceit themselves.

Transparency is the way out of this house of distorted mirrors in which we find ourselves. We must learn to access higher truth and let it show us what it is. Then boldly speak the truth over lies…always.

Spirit always honors and supports this when it's done through our hearts' desire to know higher truth and assist others. This is the ultimate state of being in service. I am in service to higher truth always.

Lastly, do not be afraid of other people's perceptions. It is theirs not yours. Unless you are self-abusing or afraid to be transparent in your own journey, then you must clarify any and all distorted energy within your own self through higher truth. It can't be managed long term through suppressing the thoughts and perceptions of others because then it becomes inverted thinking on your part. Even if they don't see or connect to the higher truth activated within you, it doesn't matter. You already have established your connection with higher truth and you will know exactly what you need to know in every new, now moment to stay in that alignment.

There is always another level of higher truth to access, as it is endless! But there is a point where we can access the source field and download our next level quickly. Higher truth comes from the source field and cannot be experienced in the inverted reality. We can however, stream line the process by reprogramming our minds through source.

We have to learn to only speak higher truth! My mom will whisper to me when something I say is not in alignment with higher truth. She simply says "that's not true". She will give me the higher truth to speak and cancel that out. I realized every negative thought is a lie. Negative thought forms do not exist in higher dimensions. They can't be there. We are moving into higher dimensions. We can't take lies with us. Truth is so powerful. It dissolves all distorted reality!

We must decide once and for all to only speak the truth!
We have been conned into speaking lies into reality and co-creating in deception. Lies create trauma and fear because we come from higher truth and deceitful creation makes no sense to us at our core. Truth heals us and sets us free! We must learn to recognize truth when we hear it verses lies. Every time we hear a lie spoken; we are to speak higher truth over it. Higher truth cancels out lies. Anything the artificial reality does, Source can do better!

My truest love is higher truth:

Lies disempower	**Truth Empowers**
Lies contract	**Truth Expands**
Lies create fear	**Truth creates courage**
Lies invert reality	**Truth flips reality right side up**
Lies are poison	**Truth creates medicine**
Lies uninspire	**Truth creates inspiration**

Lies drain our life force energy	**Truth creates stamina**
Lies enslave	**Truth sets us free**
Lies create confusion	**Truth creates clarity**
Lies create doubt	**Truth creates knowing**
Lies are destructive	**Truth is creative**

It is so easy to know the difference when we pay attention!

My truest and deepest love is higher truth, which is Source, Holy Spirit, Spirit family, us, you, and me. When we know this, our actions are in alignment with higher truth. We are creating reality through higher truth. We are experiencing the love, power, beauty, joy, freedom, and excitement of the manifestation of it in all things, in every moment…every single moment. It is like being on a ride that is full of the most amazing things we have ever seen or felt. This is what higher truth has to offer us. Why would we fear that? Why would we choose anything other than that? Because we simply forgot! It is time to remember and insist upon the higher truth experience in every moment. Then take off your seatbelt for this ride!

Chapter 49

Cities of Living Light

Where two or more are gathered in Source Love

Source consciousness is constantly in a state of expansion. Energy expands and contracts, but in general, consciousness does not contract. Once it expands it does not return to its prior, more limited state. It can choose to stay at the same state for a period of "time" in order for it to experience specific things, but it doesn't go backwards. All of Source creation is conscious. How does this apply to Cities of Living Light? They are conscious cities. They exist in higher vibrational timelines that exist in alignment with the Source Field. They are in vibrational alignment with the Living Light timeline and the higher vibration of nature. The land itself exists in the higher timelines.

They are essentially in the world but not of it. Once we understand how to exist in this state ourselves and come together through this connection in communities, it becomes a collective Source Field experience. It is constantly expanding in consciousness because humans are designed to grow and learn from each other. It is the natural design of relationships.

The glue that holds these communities together is Source's unconditional love. Without this love, these communities will not thrive. It is essential that everyone access their higher hearts and be able to experience Source guidance. In years past, many communities had been established and they became more like cults than heart centered communities or cities of Light. *Cults** are communities where people are peer pressured into group thinking rather than individual direct Source connection. This is because those leading were not connected to Source love themselves. Therefore, the co-creation was distorted. It is impossible to co-create our greatest potential here together without Source being involved.

I created my sanctuary by acting on blind faith and Source guidance. I surrendered to Spirit and was building according to my mom's blueprints from the Source Field. I am doing what my mom told me she could not do when she was alive but could do through me from the other side.

I didn't build with a large amount of money; I built with love and Spirit. Money flowed as needed but many things came in different forms through Source. The creation is in service to Spirit and humanity, not money. Money is just a form of energy exchange. It is part of the illusion and artificial reality and has a lot of fear programs attached to it. Like everything else, money flows when needed. We have been programmed with lack when it comes to money which in turn, allows our creativity to be controlled through money. The sooner we understand we do not need money to create through Source, we will be free to create whatever we desire.

These cities of Living Light are communities created and guided through Source. They exist in higher vibrational realities and are assisting in the collective awakening. They exist in a "Heaven on Earth" frequency and are merging with Heaven. We are free to co-create through Source without the programs of lack or fear. We can return to our true authentic selves in harmony and connection with nature. We will be guided once again by Spirit and experience a greater potential reality because of it. It is exciting to know that in our lifetime we will witness the greater potential of humans walking with Spirit.

The communities we are creating together are all encompassing. We are assisting each other in all areas of life. One of my favorite things to assist with is our return to heaven. Humanity became so afraid of death that we disconnected from the death process. We are coming back to Source therefore we can assist each other in our return to Source. This is such a beautiful and sacred process and experience. When we learn to Journey To Heaven, we can walk our loved ones up to heaven. We can actually go with them to ensure they arrive. We become a part of a team, assisting higher Spirit while in the physical reality. This is one of the reasons why we are being urged to learn to journey with our loved ones in heaven as well as our loved ones in the physical. There are endless possibilities for us through this reactivation of our multi-dimensional selves.

We are moving our focus back into the Source Field together! It is GO time! We are being called back out of the artificial reality to the organic where we value the living creation over the dead creation.

Chapter 50

Activating our Spirit Gifts

Our Spirit gifts are the things we developed while in Source before we were born into the physical reality. These gifts were carried into our physical body from that aspect of our higher self that came into our avatars. These gifts exist inside of us, waiting to be unwrapped, used, and shared during our journey here. Spirit gifts are magical. They are not of the artificial world. They are not subject to linear time. They are not bound by the constructs of the artificial, distorted creation. They are free flowing and expanding through each new opportunity we choose to share with others. They are a living, breathing conscious aspect of the Living Light consciousness that connect us to our higher self and Source. When we are using our gifts we are flowing with our Spirit.

Many of us forgot our Spiritual gifts along the way and have to come back to them. This remembering is such an amazing experience. Although it can be a bit awkward for our family and friends to see us stepping into something new, they will adjust, I promise! Even the story of Jesus's life details how his Spiritual gifts were not as easily accepted by those who knew him before he activated them in his life. This is a natural process for us and we have to be brave and step into it with confidence. This is the only way to continue to develop and master what we have come to this reality to share. It is the legacy we intended to leave behind.

Our Spiritual gifts exist through Source Love. This means when we are using them, we are connecting to Source Love and it is strengthening our ability to walk in our connection to that love. Using our gifts is the most beautiful thing we contribute to the world. We cannot use our Spiritual gifts without Source Love pouring through us and healing our mind, body and soul. It is our service to humanity and ourselves. To be in service is to be in Source. If we want to strengthen our connection to Source, we strengthen our action in service to others. That is the quickest way to BE with Source. Do you notice when you do a kind deed or act in love with others it opens your heart and raises your vibrations instantly? That's by design. We are being urged towards more of that all of the time. Walking in that state of being is the most powerful and affective way to activate Source into the lower distorted timelines.

Many often struggle to maintain their connection to Source Love while in the lower vibrations. Spirit often advises them to start with activating their gifts of Spirit. When I communicate with Spirit for others, they are often focused on helping them know what their gifts are and how they can use them. It is so beautiful for me to witness how this changes their lives and assists them in mastering with walking in alignment with Source Love. This is when the journey here becomes a much more beautiful and fun experience.

Activating and sharing our Spiritual gifts within our communities is beneficial for everyone. We are all unique and able to offer the unique vibration of Source to others as it flows through us. This is why there is never any competition between us. We are never sharing the exact same modality as another. That would be impossible due to our own unique energetic dance with Source. Source will never flow through another vessel the way it does yours. No one is more Spiritual than another. We are either streaming source or we aren't and if we are, the result is always powerful healing.

The idea that our gifts are limited to a specific training we receive from the constructs of the 3D reality is a belief that will be dissolving as we ascend into states of being in resonance with the higher timelines. We only need to be "certified" through Source. Spirit will be offering what is needed through us in each new now moment. Our 3D trainings served us well before we were streaming our essence self through Source. All things in the old timeline were necessary to compensate for our disconnect from Source. I call it substitutes for Source!

Of course, we will always benefit from learning from each other and this will continue. Spirit is also always learning from it's experience and connection to others. This is a beautiful endless part of the way consciousness expands itself.   How do we activate our Spiritual gifts? Through Source of course!

I could hear Spirit talking to me when I was young in my dreams. I couldn't see them in detail, but I could see them as a blurry image and clearly hear their voice. I was told that I am a healer and I came to help others heal. I was told this was much needed and I should be doing it. Of course I wanted to help others heal. I did not like seeing anyone suffer.

One day a friend of mine had a migraine. I remembered the dream and decided to see if what I was told about being a healer is true. I had no training on how to heal, everything I did came natural to me. I got quiet and started pulling Living Light into my crown and witnessed it move through every cell of my body. It was amazing to me how I could see what looked like liquid sparkling light coming into my head. I was tangible to me. I could touch it. I then watched it go out of my body through my hands into my friends head. I saw the light healing his migraine and at that same moment I saw light flashing in my minds eye like a bright white strobe light. I was so bright and fast it was blinding me! I somehow new it was done, that he has been healed.

He woke up shortly after and I didn't mention what I had done. He told me his migraine was not only completely gone, but that he had no after shocks from the unbearable pain. Those shocks typically lasted for days. I was so excited. I told him what I had done. He was shocked. This started me on my journey of healing others. I have many stories I can share about this same thing happening over and over. At the time, I didn't realize I was working with Living Light the same way my mom has taught me to.

I recall a Journey To Heaven I took along with a friend. We were taken to a temple where Jesus was standing welcoming us. I walked up to him and he poured liquid light into my mouth. I felt it activate my light body and I felt the bliss and healing it carried within it. He told me I could "drink" it anytime. It is through this liquid light that I experience healing. We all experience it differently but this is connected to my unique Spirit gifts.

There are so many amazing things that come from us choosing to embody what our Spirit came here to do. We just have to have the courage to do it. Become it. We don't have to manipulate reality or others to do it. We don't have to struggle to do it. It is much more powerful than anything in the physical reality. It comes from Source so it trumps everything in the artificial reality. When we become monetarily wealthy by doing something other than through offering our gifts from Source, it is empty, dead energy. We do not find happiness in it. When we do our Spirit thing, you know that thing, we are fulfilled by it authentically. We are taken care of in every way. We are blessed for it in more ways than we can imagine.

We have all heard the term "sell my soul". This is what happens when we focus on the artificial reality instead of Source for our wealth. We are guided to stay in higher states of accountability and integrity when we are using our Spirit gifts. We can't compromise them for anything in the material reality. We can't manipulate them for false power. They can be taken from us by Spirit. This isn't a threat, it is just awareness of how sacred this is. We are entrusted to use our gifts through Source not manipulate them through the artificial reality.

The power of Source, the organic, the alive, is what has the power to heal the distorted timelines. Once we feel this energy activated within us we have no desire to trade that in for dead energy. When we connect with source, we know what source is and what it is not. We don't need to play in anything else for any reason. I work for Source and that is the source of my abundance.

I remember knowing I was going to help a lot of people. I had that fire in my belly from the time I was born. Then I got lost in the illusions here and was trying to find my way back. I started a life coaching program. But I was not yet connected back to source, and it did not go anywhere. I had to push it and sell it. That was not who I was. Then I experienced Source through plant medicine and integrated my brain and mind and was set on my Spirit path. I didn't have to push or sell anything. Ready or not, Spirit brought the people who also needed to know what Spirit was teaching me. I felt strong resistance because I had to face my fears in order to activate my gifts. It was no joke, I knew it came with a whole lot of responsibility and I wasn't sure if I was ready for that. But all I had to do was stay in my heart and my mom walked me through step by step.

When I see people struggling and pushing and selling, I recommend just being in alignment with the Source Field. That's where we step out of all illusions and allow Spirit to guide our journey. There are no short cuts to this and no amount of money makes up for the dead energy we are creating through illusion. There is nothing wrong with desiring to reach as many people as possible and receiving energy in exchange for the energy we give, in whatever form that shows up for us. I often say "Source gives me my paycheck". Which means I am always in flow with abundance through Source and that intelligence knows exactly what I need. But selling Spirituality is an oxymoron because it locks us into the lack program. It limits Source and healing. The belief that money, created by the artificial timelines, is required to create reality is not true.

There is a divine flow that comes with being in flow with Source and being guided every moment. When we surrender to Spirit and do our Spirit "work", we are naturally living in the organic timeline not the artificial one. We are in the power of Source and synchronicity. We are in the world but not of it. Source is doing through us; we are just the vessel. I recall a sermon from church when I attended with a friend where the preacher said "In order to experience God we must do God's will". That is how I see the experience of using our Spirit gifts.

There is nothing in the artificial world we need beyond seeing Source create through us. There is nothing the artificial world could give us in return that would compare to what we receive from Source in return. We experience the feelings of being in heaven while on earth. Our state of being glows with Source Living Light and we exist in states of joy and peace. We are free, light, happy. We just need to pay attention to what is next. Are you ready?

Chapter 51
The Art of Surfing the Source Field
Welcome Back to Source!

Let's Get This Party Started!

Without Source Love there would be nothingness. Source is alive. Anything not streaming the aliveness of Source is essentially dead energy. Nothing can exist without Source Love. Source Love is our only true and pure life-force. We come from Source Love and we return to Source Love. Because we are also alive! We are Living Light energy that wishes to express itself and create through us. That is all. That is all, yet it is ALL there truly is. Living Light calls all distorted creation back to its higher essence to be aligned with Source perfection. It heals all things that have been distorted, including our physical vessel. The only way for us to truly heal ourselves is through the Living Light of Source. We are in command of our creation and experience at all times through our connection to Source Love. Nothing can over power or control us outside of Source. Living Light is an intelligence that exists in quantum superposition waiting for us to tell it what we want to co-create with it! When we do this consciously instead of unconsciously, we are now in charge of our own creation! This is the art of surfing the waves of Living Light in the Source field flowing into every part of our being. We are always in flow with Source creation, all we have to do is attune to that part of ourselves. That part of us does the heavy lifting so we can be in the artificial reality through a state of ease, joy and excitement. Watching what we perceive as "miracles" unfolding constantly.

We are fully capable of having our greatest potential experience in this reality through our connection to Source Love. When we choose to be Source centered rather than self-centered! Although many of us have disconnected from this love within us, many are seeking it and that is all that is required for this higher love to be activated within us, to assist us in finding our way back to Source Love. Source is always here with us, but remember in order to be actively co-creating through it, we must feel that love. I often hear my mom say "just feel my love". This is enough for us to be carried into Source in that moment. We can do the same for others by loving them and seeing them through the eyes of Source. In doing so, we are assisting with every aspect of Source returning back to itself.

We are being called back to Source because we have realized that to be outside of our connection to Source is to be disconnected from unconditional love and who we really are. We suffer in distorted creation and it creates imbalances that lead to illness or disease. We don't have to suffer any longer. Suffering is not required for us. In fact, it was never intended for us.

Since my mom and have become "ONE" through our connection in the Source Field, my life has become a blend of her energy and mine. I notice myself loving the things she loved. For instance, she loved to fly and travel, and always dreamed of going to Europe. I was always terrified of heights and flying. I never left the States! But I now joyfully fly all over the world with her and we have so much fun. I never liked chocolate, but we enjoy eating chocolate together now in Europe. It really becomes a beautiful blending of our Spirits desires and imagination. This is a true twin Spirit experience! When I reflect back on this book and her telling me over twenty years ago she was going to write it with me from the other side, it is so surreal to me that it has now been creating into our reality for others to experience. There is nothing we cannot create together through Spirit. This book was not only created through the dance of our Spirits in Source, but it was put on paper while flying together to our favorite high vibrational places on earth. Those vibrations are a part of this as well. I realize if she were still on earth with me in her physical body, we would not be having these incredible adventures together. We would have been together and loving each other, but we would not have activated our higher Spirit connection in this big of a way. She chose this path over the physical path and I understand why. We are in agreement about all of it now because the larger mission in service to Spirit has been realized as a result. I am filled with gratitude and laughter. She and I a couple of silly goofballs most days!

It is my deepest desire that I will be able to share this level of Spirit connection with my own children and loved ones when I leave my physical body behind. This book serves as my guidance manual for them to remember how to find me through the Source love they carry in their hearts during their darkest moments of disconnect from their own Source love. I want the same for you and your loved ones and it is one of my greatest blessings to witness these connections being made through me all of the time. One day we will all return to our connection to Source and I can only imagine how absolutely magical this world will be when that happens. This is what happens we when come back together through Source love. Our creation becomes amplified and it is much easier to experience our deepest heart's desire when we create together. I am sitting here right now eating popcorn and chocolate on my flight home from magical Portugal. Thanks Mom (and many others she brought into my life)!

Below is a channeled healing that can be accessed in this now moment if you desire to experience it. Together let's activate self-ascension in order to expand our consciousness.

"We come together again in gratitude to meet you in the Source Field for healing and clarity.

Through this healing you will receive exactly what is most important for you to receive for your next step on your Spiritual journey. We ask that you stay open to whatever comes to you and make note. There will be more because there is always more. Feel the excitement of what is to come!

Notice how the time we spent together in the Source Field naturally expands your consciousness. It is almost effortless. You receive clarity and understanding you did not have before, even if it is just another piece to your puzzle, and this allows you to access higher states of clarity and peace within yourself. We celebrate this with you!

You are ready for another level of understanding to build on this clarity you have received. Although our messages may sound redundant, they contain within them your next level of conscious understanding. Our worlds flow in a little different way to activate different parts of knowing within you. All you need to do is be open to that activation and experience. We are now focusing our intention with you to gain clarity about how to activate individual states of ascension and expanded states of consciousness. We will also clarify our understanding of "oneness".

Let's start with Oneness! It is "one" of our favorite topics to discuss. The source field exists in a state of oneness at all times. It simply is, "one" consciousness. Meaning all things are connected within it. It is impossible to separate anything because separation is an illusion. Illusions do not exist in the source field. That is impossible. Yet we can all choose to experience a reality that exists outside of the Source Field. But eventually all things created through Source, come back to Source.

There are parts of you that remain in the Source Field at all times. They cannot join you in the illusion of separation, just like the parts of you that exist in states of separation cannot join you in the source field. This feels like we are speaking of two different people, and in a sense we are. You can call forth the part of you that exists in one the Source Field to teach you at any time.

These different parts of you exist in different vibrational states of creation. Different worlds or dimensions. How is this possible? You are one person in one body! Because consciousness is omnipotent. It is not bound by space and time or to a physical body. It exists at all times in the source field and does not experience illusions of separation from the Source Field, or the oneness. Only parts of your physical being can play in the realm of illusions of separation. And it is not the biggest part of you, although it may seem to be. That's just another part of the illusion.

We encourage you to notice, in each now moment, which part you is having the experience. Is it the part of you that believes and feels you are separate from the world, Source, or others? Or is it the part of you that knows all things are connected and there is only love? This awareness is what expands your consciousness.

Our conscious awareness expands and contracts according to which part of us we are focused on. It is only a matter of attention and focus. If the Source Field exists within you at all times then it is simply a matter of turning your attention to it. You don't have to seek it, find it or discover it. You simply choose to be there. Focusing there to allow it to permeate all parts of your being. So you can simply feel it again.

Humanity is awakening from the illusions of separation. This is what ascension is. Bringing all parts of you that exist in states of separation back into vibrational alignment with the Source Field so they may realize the higher truth. Everyone and everything is one consciousness experiencing itself through multiple aspects. The quickest way to do this is through love. Allow yourself to feel the highest and purest vibration of love you are able to in that moment. The way a child would. Now you are in the Field.

Just because you are experiencing states of separation that feel very real to you doesn't mean the oneness doesn't exist. It just means you are not focused there. Just because you cannot see or feel someone in another room next to you doesn't mean they are not there and having their own experience. The Source field is the only "place" that is a constant. It exists with or without your awareness. But when you choose to turn your attention there and become aware of it, you will remember it is who you are. Your true essence exists there. You are one with it. You are one with all things at all times.

Experiencing this oneness activates your ascension naturally. Ascension means to rise. Your heart, mind, soul is rising in vibration so you can access higher states of clarity and knowing in the Field. The more time you spend in the Source Field the more your consciousness will naturally expand and you will rise. Just like the more time you spend in the illusion of separation the more your consciousness will contract and find yourself in states of confusion. So it is a simple way to know which you are experiencing in each moment. Do you feel your heart, mind and soul expand or do you feel it contract? Love expands our consciousness, fear contracts it. The Source Field is love; the illusions are created from fear.

Remember we must all let go of our fear and move our being into the Source Field experience with our hearts and minds wide open, ready to receive and know what we did not know before. If we think we already know, we will not be open to receiving something new. We come into the source field with our hearts open. We return to the purity and innocence of a child, through a field of unconditional love. It is through this energy we are able to learn and expand our consciousness. It is this new understanding that changes our physical reality. It is through this higher vibration that all distorted creation returns to it purer form. Suffering is no longer a part of our experience. This is the choice we are all making now. We can continue co-creating distorted reality that creates suffering and fear or we can choose to co-create through Source. We will be witnessing more and more people choosing Source over the artificial reality. We will witness the artificial reality dissolve through higher truth streaming into the reality through us. This is the solution to all of the messes we have co-created in the artificial timelines. The cleanup is well underway.

The Source Field is an intelligence that you are one with. You are it. It knows exactly how to speak with you and teach you for your next lesson. It is only through the Source field that we can experience expanded states of consciousness and ascension. We access the field *through the purity of our hearts and our love. From there you will understand which creation is of Source and which is of illusions. Lesson number one! Let's go!*

Feel the peace and knowing wash over you! This is the Source Field! Let's meet here to play in the oneness until you are able to integrate this oneness into all parts of you, your creation and experience! This is how you clear all illusions in your reality. Through keeping your focus in the Source Field at all times. Seeing the illusions for what they truly are. False. It is time to understand the truth through the eyes of Source, exposing the illusions for what they truly are. They are a false reality."

It is time for us to come back to knowing these truths through the eyes of the Spirit. This is the party and we can create this party into our physical reality. Spirit is ready to assist us in doing just that. Our Spirit party if full of laughter and joy just like it is in heaven. Our party on earth echoes throughout heaven and the love between us and our loved ones in heaven coming together in this happiness is the most beautiful experience we can have and feel while on earth.

Because of Source Love, we are remembering!
Because of Source Love, we are alive!
Because of Source Love, we are always safe!
Because of Source Love, we are free!
Because of Source Love, we are never lost!
Because of Source Love, we are in unity!
Because of Source Love, we are walking between dimensional worlds!

Because of Source Love, we are creating our greatest, desired experience!
Because of Source Love, we are healed!
Because of Source Love, we are remembering everything we have forgotten!
Because of Source Love, we are connecting to all things from Source!
Because of Source Love, we experiencing Source in everything!
Because of Source Love, we are loving!
Because of Source Love, we are laughing!
Because of Source Love, we are choosing!
Because of Source Love, we are feeling!
Because of Source Love, we are knowing!
Because of Source Love, we are expanding our consciousness!
Because of Source Love, we are experiencing greater potential creations!
Because of Source Love, we are just being!
Because of Source Love, all things are simple!

WELCOME BACK TO SOURCE LOVE
LET'S GET THIS PARTY STARTED!

We love you!!

This book would not be complete without a movie list! My mom love using movies to teach others about Source Love. Here is her list. I've also added my favorites! Please feel free to share movies with me that you experienced a connection to Source Love while watching! I'd love to watch them!

What Dreams May Come
Made In Heaven
Molly
Michael
Braveheart
Thunder Heart
Phenomenon
Ground Hog Day
Drop Dead Fred
Powder
The Never Ending Story
Mary Poppins
Patch Adams
Defending Your Life
The Shack
Arrival
I Can Only Imagine
The Nines
What The Bleep Do We Know
Lucy
The Ultimate Gift
Avatar
Harry Potter
Tomorrowland
Heaven Is For Real

The Last Mimzy
The Family Man
The Bridge to Terabithia
The Notebook
Frequency
The Ghost Whisperer
The Truman Show

Made in United States
Troutdale, OR
10/27/2024

24176624R00193